Dictionary
of
Culinary Terms

Hippocrene is NUMBER ONE in
International Cookbooks

Africa and Oceania
Best of Regional African Cooking
Egyptian Cooking
Good Food from Australia
Traditional South African
  Cookery

Asia and Near East
Best of Goan Cooking
Best of Kashmiri Cooking
The Joy of Chinese Cooking
The Art of South Indian
  Cooking
The Art of Persian Cooking
The Art of Israeli Cooking
The Art of Turkish Cooking

Mediterranean
Best of Greek Cuisine
Taste of Malta
A Spanish Family Cookbook

Western Europe
Art of Dutch Cooking
Best of Austrian Cuisine
A Belgian Cookbook
Celtic Cookbook
English Royal Cookbook
The Swiss Cookbook
Traditional Recipes from Old
  England
The Art of Irish Cooking
Traditional Food from Scotland
Traditional Food from Wales

Scandinavia
Best of Scandinavian Cooking
The Best of Finnish Cooking
The Best of Smorgasbord
  Cooking
Good Food from Sweden

Central Europe
Best of Albanian Cooking
All Along the Danube
Bavarian Cooking
Traditional Bulgarian Cooking
The Best of Czech Cooking
The Art of Hungarian Cooking
Lithuanian Cooking
Polish Heritage Cookery
The Best of Polish Cooking
Old Warsaw Cookbook
Old Polish Traditions
Taste of Romania

Eastern Europe
The Cuisine of Armenia
The Best of Russian Cooking
The Best of Ukrainian Cuisine

Americas
Cooking the Caribbean Way
Mayan Cooking
The Honey Cookbook
The Art of Brazilian Cookery
The Art of South American
  Cookery

Dictionary
of
Culinary Terms

by
Ellen Shannon

HIPPOCRENE BOOKS
New York

First Printing
1962 by A.S. Barnes and Company, Inc.

This edition
© 1998 by Hippocrene Books, Inc.

For information, address:
HIPPOCRENE BOOKS
171 Madison Avenue
New York, NY 10016

ISBN 0-7818-0692-5

Printed in the United States of America.

Key to Abbreviations

AF.	AFRICA
ANGLO-IND.	ANGLO-INDIAN
ARAB.	ARABIA
AUS.	AUSTRIA
BELG.	BELGIUM
CAN.	CANADA
CHIN.	CHINA
CZECH.	CZECHOSLOVAKIA
DEN.	DENMARK
ENG.	ENGLAND
EUR.	EUROPE
FR.	FRANCE
FR. CAN.	FRENCH CANADIAN
GER.	GERMANY
GR.	GREECE
HAW.	HAWAII
HOL.	HOLLAND (THE NETHERLANDS)
HUNG.	HUNGARY
IND.	INDIA
IR.	IRELAND
IT.	ITALY
JAP.	JAPAN
JEW.	JEWISH
MEX.	MEXICO
N. AF.	NORTH AFRICA
PAN.	PANAMA
POL.	POLAND
POLY.	POLYNESIA
PORT.	PORTUGAL
RUS.	RUSSIA
S. AF.	SOUTH AFRICA
SCAN.	SCANDINAVIA
SCOT.	SCOTLAND

S. Am.	South America
Sp.	Spain
Swed.	Sweden
Switz.	Switzerland
Turk.	Turkey
Un. of S. Af.	Union of South Africa
U.S.	United States
U.S., New Eng.	United States, New England
East.	Eastern
North.	Northern
South.	Southern
West.	Western

Dictionary
of
Culinary Terms

Abalone
A large, single-valved mollusk native to California waters. It is served as steak, in chowder, etc., and has now become so popular that it cannot be bought fresh outside the state. Fresh abalone must be tenderized for use as steaks.

Abats (Fr.)
The head, heart, liver, kidneys, etc., of any animal. Also spelled *abatis* and *abattis*.

Abbrustolito (It.)
Toasted.

Abernethy Biscuit (Scot.)
A small, plump cooky made with very little liquid and caraway seed flavoring, developed, according to one account, by a Dr. Abernethy, or according to another, in the town of Abernethy, in the last century.

Abertam Cheese
A hard central European cheese made from goat's milk.

Absinthe (Fr.)
A strong unsweetened liquor containing oil of wormwood, usually diluted for drinking, and so toxic, in addition to being supposedly an aphrodisiac, that it is now outlawed in many countries.

Acacia (Fr.)
A shrub whose pink or white flowers are used by French chefs in the making of certain fritters.

Ac'cent
A trade name for monosodium glutamate, now referred to in so many recipes that MSG is little known by any other name.

Achaja (Gr.)
A sweet table wine.

Acid Drop (Eng.)
A candy made with sugar, tartaric acid, vinegar, and lemon, and rolled into drop, or bite-size, form.

Acini Di Pepe (It.)
Tiny rounds and squares of pasta. Literally translated, the name means "pepper kernels," and they are so called because of their shape.

Acorn
The seed of the oak tree; used to make ersatz, or substitute, coffee and in the curing of Westphalian ham.

Acorn Squash
A winter squash having a dark green, vertically ribbed rind often streaked with yellow, and yellow, sometimes pulpy meat. It is round or oval and anywhere from two to six inches in

diameter. Acorn squash are either baked in their skins or peeled and baked in a casserole.

Acrid
Having a sour, sharp, burned, or bitter taste or smell.

Adam's Ale (Eng.)
A whimsical name for water in some older recipes, as, for example, "Adam's ale pancakes."

Ade
A name, generally used as a suffix, for any drink composed primarily of fruit juice or flavoring, sugar, and water.

Adobo (Philippines)
Chicken, pork, etc., marinated with garlic, vinegar, and seasoning, and then usually fried. A national dish.

Advocaat (Hol.)
A Dutch liqueur made with brandy and egg yolks.

Aerated Water
Distilled water to which purified air has been added to improve the taste; also, though less correctly, water which has been charged with carbon dioxide.

Affogato (pl. affogati; It.)
Steamed.

Africaine, À L' (Fr.)
In the African manner; used, for example, in referring to dishes with horseradish, chicken, or rice as an ingredient.

After-Dinner Coffee
Coffee, preferably made from very dark-roasted beans, and served after dinner, often in demitasse cups without cream or sugar.

Agar-Agar
A gelatin obtained from seaweed, used in desserts, soups, etc. It is pearly white, semi-transparent, tasteless, and odorless. Also called Japanese gelatin.

Agaric
A kind of mushroom used extensively in cooking.

Agave
Any of several large Mexican and Central American plants having sharp, fleshy leaves; various species are used in making mescal, pulque, and tequila. Also called aloe, maguey, and century plant.

Age
As a verb, to tenderize meat, especially beef and sometimes lamb and mutton, and to improve the flavor of meat, cheese, wine, etc., by allowing them to rest and ripen, often in a cooled storage area, before use, sometimes for a few weeks, sometimes for many months.

Agemono (Jap.)
That method of frying in which the food is not given a batter coating as it is in tempura frying.

Agnelotto (pl. Agnelotti; It.)
Ravioli dumplings stuffed with minced meat or some other filling.

Agnes Sorel (Fr.)
The mistress of Charles VII, after whom various dishes are named, for

example, a rich cream soup made with chicken and mushrooms.

Aguardiente (Sp.)
A liquor similar but inferior to brandy, distilled from molasses or wine in Spain and South America.

Aiguillette (Fr.)
A very thin slice, especially from the breast of chicken or turkey.

Aileron (Fr.)
The wing; for example, of a chicken.

Aioli Sauce (Fr.)
See PROVENCE BUTTER.

Ajinomoto (Jap.)
Monosodium glutamate, a tasteless white powder which heightens the flavor of foods it is used with. First used in the Orient.

Akala Berry (Haw.)
A raspberry-like fruit, sometimes as much as two inches in diameter, shading from purple to orange in color, quite sweet in flavor, and very juicy.

Akee
A tropical fruit popular in the Caribbean area as an accompaniment to salt fish, especially in the breakfast dish "salt cod and akee." The avocado is a suitable substitute. Also called akee apple.

A La (Fr.)
Literally, "after the manner of," a term used in the naming of a great many French sauces and garnishes generally followed by the name of a person, place, or ingredient. It also often indicates a method of preparation, in which case the phrase is à la mode de.

Al, Alla (It.)
The Italian equivalent of the French à la; see preceding entry.

Alaska Crab
An alternate name for the king crab, which see.

Albacore
A tuna, or one of several smaller but related fish.

Albert (Fr.)
The name given to a rich butter and horseradish sauce.

Albondiga (Mex.)
A meat ball.

Albufera Sauce (Fr.)
See IVORY SAUCE.

Aleatico (It.)
A red table wine made from the black Tuscan grape of the same name.

Alecost
See COSTMARY.

Alemtejo Cheese (Port.)
A soft, round cheese made from sheep's milk, curdled with the flowers of a native thistle.

Alewife
A food fish common along the Atlantic coast of the United States, related to the herring and cooked in the same ways, or used as sardines.

Alimentary Paste
See ITALIAN PASTE and PASTE.

Allegretti Cake
A cake with a bitter chocolate icing.

Allemande (Fr.)
Prepared "in the German manner." Allemande sauce, for example, is a thickened velouté.

Alligator Pear
A more imaginative name for the avocado.

All-Purpose Flour
A mixture of hard and soft wheat flours usable in almost all recipes except those for the most delicate cakes.

Allspice
The dried and ground berries of the West Indian pimento tree with a flavor resembling that of a blend of spices, especially cloves, cinnamon, and nutmeg.

All-Spice
An infrequently used term, not to be confused with the preceding entry, which refers to a mixture of bay, thyme, coriander, cloves, cinnamon, nutmeg, ginger, mace, pepper, and cayenne.

Allumette (Fr.)
A match-like strip; used to refer to a food so cut.

Aloe
An alternate, though incorrect, name for the agave, which see.

Aloo (Ind.)
The word for potato in Hindustani; thus any aloo curry is a curry dish having potatoes as a main or chief ingredient.

Alpina (It.)
A delicious, fiery, golden-yellow Italian liqueur generally served in minute quantities.

Altar Bread
Bread prepared for the Eucharist, usually, and always correctly, without salt.

Alum
A salt of a double sulphate, aluminum and potassium, with a very astringent effect and consisting of cloudy white, rather glossy crystals usually under one-half inch in size. Alum is sometimes used to make pickles crisp.

Amandine (Fr.)
Containing or garnished with almonds.

Ambrosia
A fruit dessert containing shredded coconut.

American Cheese
A name frequently used for a very mild Cheddar.

Ammonia
See HARTSHORN.

Amourettes (Fr.)
Marrow from the spine of a calf or sheep.

Anadama Bread
A yeast-raised bread unique for having corn meal and molasses among its ingredients.

Anchovy

A slender, herring-like, salt-water fish, about six inches long. When used in paste, essence, butter, or as fillets, anchovies have a sharp, distinctive, salty flavor and a reddish-brown color.

Anchovy Pear

The russet-colored, egg-shaped fruit of a West Indian tree, eaten pickled like the mango, whose taste it resembles.

Andalouse (Fr.)

In the manner of Andalusia, in Spain; generally used to describe a dish containing tomatoes, for example, *sauce andalouse,* a mayonnaise to which tomato purée has been added.

Angel Food Cake

A white sponge cake distinguished by its use of eight to a dozen stiffly beaten egg whites and by the shape of the pan in which it is baked, one having high sides and a center tube, now chiefly associated with this cake. Cake flour is an essential ingredient and particular care must be taken during baking, as the cake falls very easily. It is usually served un-iced.

Angelica

1. An herb with a sweet aroma and an exotic appearance, whose root is often crystallized for use as a decoration for cakes and cookies. The leaves are used in an herb tea, the seeds for flavoring, and the oil in perfumes.
2. A white wine originated in California; also, a liqueur.

Angels on Horseback

Oysters wrapped in strips of bacon or ham and broiled. Also called devils on horseback and pigs in blankets.

Anglaise, A L' (Fr.)

Prepared in the English fashion, usually meaning in a plain manner.

Angostura

1. The trade name of a widely known bitters, which see.
2. An aromatic and rather bitter oil from the bark of a South American tree, which, however, is not used as an ingredient in the above.

Animal Fat

Any fat derived from an animal, such as butter, lard, or suet. See also FAT and SHORTENING.

Anise

An herb belonging to the carrot family, anise has been put to culinary use for many centuries. The light green, lacy leaves are used in salads, in white sauce, and with shellfish, while the small, oval, greenish-grey to brown seeds lend a sweet, licorice flavor to the same dishes as well as to appetizers, cheese, meat, cookies, and cakes.

Aniseed

The seed of the anise.

Anisette (Fr.)

A liqueur either colorless or tinted green, containing anise and thus having a licorice flavor.

Anjou Pear

A large, almost oval pear with a sweet, rich, juicy flesh. Its skin is green to russet, and it is one of the best winter varieties.

Anna Potatoes
Layers of sliced potatoes baked in a casserole.

Annatto
A yellowish-red dye, used to color cheese and to add color to butter. It is obtained from the fruit of a tropical tree of the same name.

Antipasto (It.)
Literally "before the meal," i.e., the first course of an Italian dinner, consisting of hors d'oeuvres such as salami, anchovies and pickled relishes.

Apéritif (Fr.)
An alcoholic drink taken before a meal to stimulate the appetite and digestion.

Apician
Dainty or expensive cookery; from Apicius, the name of a Roman gourmand.

Apollinaris
An unflavored effervescent European mineral water used at meals by those who do not take wine.

Appetizer
Any tidbit of food, such as a canapé or hors d'oeuvre, eaten before or at the beginning of a meal to whet the appetite.

Applejack
A liquor distilled in the United States from fermented cider.

Apple Pan Dowdy (U.S., New Eng.)
Sliced apples topped with a thick biscuit dough crust and baked.

Apple Par (Eng.)
A sweet dessert made of apples and sugar with lemon, boiled till stiff and poured into a mould. It is often served with almonds and whipped cream.

Apple Snow
A dessert consisting of applesauce and stiffly beaten egg whites and flavored with vanilla and lemon.

Aquavit (Swed.)
A dry, clear, white liquor distilled from potatoes or grain and flavored with caraway. It is served either before or during a meal.

Arabique (Fr.)
In the Arabian fashion; gracefully or tasetefully prepared for serving.

Arancini (It.)
Sicilian meat and rice balls.

Arkansas Apple
An apple for cooking or for baking whole and in season from November through May. Also called the Mammoth Black Twig.

Arlésienne (Fr.)
In the manner of Arles; usually fried in oil, accompanied with tomatoes, onions and eggplant.

Armagnac (Fr.)
A dry, aromatic brandy. Also called "The Brandy of Lafayette," similar to Cognac although generally considered less fine.

Armoricaine (Fr.)
In the manner of, or typical of, Brittany, the old Roman name for that

peninsula being Armorica, or "seaside." Not to be confused with "Americaine," in the American manner.

Aromatic
Having aroma; hence, any herb or other seasoning used to give an aroma in cooking, as for example, sage, basil, rosemary, cinnamon, ginger, vanilla or juniper berries.

Arrostito (pl. *arrostiti; lt.*)
Roasted.

Arrowroot
The starch made by grinding the root of a Central American plant. It is easily digested, clear and almost tasteless when cooked and is thus an excellent thickening agent for cooked fruits, puddings and sauces. Arrowroot biscuits, a children's favorite, are also made with it.

Arroz Con Pollo (Sp., Mex.)
A famous dish; chicken with rice.

Artichoke, French, Globe or Italian
The true artichoke is a green, cone-shaped, fist-sized flower head of a thistle-like plant, with an edible bottom or heart and large, pointed scales with edible bases. It is generally boiled and served hot or cold with melted butter or mayonnaise.

Artichoke, Japanese
A perennial plant whose white, underground rhizomes are valued for their sweetish flavor which resembles that of the globe artichoke when they are boiled or fried. Also called Chinese artichoke, crosne, and stachys.

Artichoke, Jerusalem
The gnarled, tuberous root of a wild sunflower with a flavor of the globe artichoke, used in the same way as a potato.

Asado (S. Am.)
Lamb roasted on a spit—a very popular dish, especially in Argentina.

Ash Berry
The rowanberry, which see.

Ash Bread (U.S., South.)
An old-fashioned cornbread which was usually wrapped in cabbage leaves and then baked in the ashes of an open fire.

Aspic
A jellied dish, made with the broth obtained from long cooking of meat, poultry, or, sometimes, fish, or some other form of gelatin. The word is said to originate from spike (French *spic*) lavender jelly, and was originally a dessert with that flavoring.

Assam Tea
An India black tea with a hard leaf which brews a strong, pungent, colorful liquid.

Asti Spumante (lt.)
An Italian sparkling wine, somewhat like champagne.

Astrachan Apple
A red variety, good for eating raw, and also one of the few which are excellent for jelly.

Athole Cake (Scot.)
An unusually sweet muffin made with

corn meal, grated lemon peel, candied peel, and quite a lot of butter.

Attereau (pl. *atteraux;* Fr.)
A small piece of meat cooked on a skewer.

Au, Aux (Fr.)
The contractions of *à le* and *à les,* respectively, found in such expressions as *au beurre* (with or in butter); *aux fines herbes* (containing chopped herbs); or *pot au feu* (literally, "pot on the fire").

Aubergine (Fr.)
The eggplant.

Aubergiste, A L' (Fr.)
Literally, "in the style of the innkeeper." The specialty of the house.

Aurore (Fr.)
1. Having a rosy or golden-yellow color; *sauce aurore,* for example, is one containing tomato purée.
2. High, or domed, in shape.

Aurum (It.)
An orange liqueur with a delicate flavor.

Autrichienne, A L' (Fr.)
In the Austrian style; a dish containing or garnished with paprika, caraway, sausage or stuffed cabbage.

Avocado
A tropical or subtropical fruit having either a shiny, smooth, dark-green skin or a rough skin of purple-black. It is the size of a large fist and somewhat pear-shaped. The tender, melting pulp is creamy white to pale green and contains a single large, central seed. Also called alligator pear.

Baba (Fr.)
A yeast-raised cake containing dried fruits and usually flavored with rum or brandy.

Babka (Pol.)
A cake shaped like a full skirt, and similar to the Russian koulich. Babka is Polish for "old woman."

Babotje (Un. of S. Af.)
A meat loaf made with bread, milk, almonds and curry powder, and usually with a light custard poured over the top and cooked after the meat itself is done. A few orange or lemon leaves are also sometimes included.

Baby Beef
A young beef animal usually weighing between 400 and 500 pounds.

Bacalao (Sp.)
Salt cod with a hot or savory sauce.

Backhuhn (Aus.)
A young chicken, halved or quartered, and fried.

Bacon
The cured back and sides of the pig in which a good mixture of fat and lean is desirable.

Bael
The aromatic, orange-like fruit of a thorny tree native to India, from which preserves and jam are made. Also called Bengal quince.

Bagel (Jew.)
The New York Times has described the bagel as "an unsweetened doughnut with rigor mortis." This ring-

shaped roll is traditionally made by hand from wheat flour and water, dropped into nearly boiling water, and then baked, a process which gives it its tough, chewy texture. Usual accompaniments are lox and cream cheese.

Bagration (Fr.)
1. A cream soup.
2. A salad, almost a meal in itself, of macaroni, chopped hard-boiled eggs, tongue, etc.

Bahamian Mustard
A hot, sweet mustard, light brown in color, and very distinctive in taste.

Bain-Marie (Fr.)
The French double boiler or water bath, consisting of a large pan which holds the water and in which are set several smaller pans containing the food to be cooked. It is used for slow cooking, for steaming, and for keeping preparations warm without drying them out.

Bake
To cook with dry, indirect heat, generally in an oven.

Baked Alaska
An impressive dessert made of ice cream, usually on a cake base, covered with meringue and put briefly into a hot oven to brown.

Baked Eggs
Eggs broken into a pan as for frying, but cooked in an oven instead of over a fire.

Baking Ammonia
See HARTSHORN.

Baking Powder
An inorganic leavening agent consisting of bicarbonate of soda combined with cream of tartar or calcium acid phosphate or else with sodium aluminum phosphate. The first (tartrate) type reacts rapidly and almost completely when liquid is added to the dry ingredients at room temperature, releasing a gas which then expands during baking. The other (phosphate or double-acting) type reacts partially at room temperature and partially during baking.

Baking Soda
Bicarbonate of soda. An inorganic leavening agent which, when combined with an acid, releases carbon dioxide gas, thus causing a batter or dough to rise.

Baklava (Gr.)
A rich pastry made of layers of paper-thin pastry filled with a butter and nut mixture and covered with syrup.

Baldwin Apple
A deep red winter variety grown in both East and West, in season November through April. Although it may be baked, it is best for general cooking.

Ballottine (Fr.)
Birds, such as quail or chicken, stuffed with a forcemeat of poultry, ham or game.

Balm
An herb, related to mint, also called lemon balm because of its aroma, having broad, rounded, very dark green leaves and clusters of pale yellow flowers. It is native to Switzerland and

southern France, but can be grown in any temperate climate, and is used wherever a lemon flavoring is appropriate. Such names as fragrant balm, bee balm, and red balm refer not to balm but to red bergamot or Oswego tea.

Bamboo Shoots
A staple in Oriental diet, consisting of the saplings of a tree-sized tropical grass. They are usually diced.

Banbury Cake (Eng.)
A flat round of puff paste, generally not more than three inches across, filled with currants, candied peel, spices and honey, and traditionally given two diagonal cuts across the top before baking. First mentioned in literature by Ben Jonson around 1608, Banbury Cakes appear to have become really popular in the mid-eighteenth century.

Banbury Cheese (Eng.)
A soft cheese, usually small and round, and of rich consistency.

B and B
An after-dinner cordial made of equal parts of Benedictine and brandy.

Bang (Eng.)
A spiced cider-and-ale drink made with a little gin or whisky and served warm.

Bannock (Scot.)
A large, round, flattened cake, originally unleavened, made of flour or oatmeal, sometimes with the addition of almonds, butter and candied peel.

Baobab
The large, downy, edible fruit of a low, thick-trunked tree native to Africa but also grown in Florida. The interior is like that of the grapefruit.

Bap (Scot.)
A floury-coated breakfast roll, flat, white, and rather soft.

Bara-Brith (Wales)
The national bun loaf, made with yeast, raisins, peel, and spices, and baked in a loaf tin.

Barbecue or Bar-B-Q
To cook food, especially meat, with direct heat over coals or in a broiler, often basting with a hot sauce. The term is derived from the French "barbe a queue," "head to tail," which implies the cooking of a whole animal.

Barberry
A red berry, the fruit of a European shrub, which now grows in New England. It is excellent for jelly and jam as it has a tart, pleasant flavor. A Japanese variety has no culinary use.

Bar Cooky
Any cooky made of a dough which has been spread in a pan, baked, and cut into rectangles, or rolled and so cut before baking.

Bard (Fr.)
To cover with thin slices of fat meat; or one of the slices. Roasts and braised meats are sometimes prepared in this way. See LARD.

Barinbreac (Ir.)
A cake made with caraway seed, but-

termilk, and, often, currants. In olden days, it was served with ale on February 1, the Feast of St. Bridget. Also barn break and barm brack.

Bar-le-Duc (Fr.)
A very fine jelly in which whole red or white currants are suspended. It is said to have originated at Bar-le-Duc, France, in the fourteenth century.

Barley
A cereal grain resembling wheat, from which the malt used in making beer and distilled liquors is frequently made and which is also used, especially in Scotland, as an ingredient in soups.

Barley Sugar (Eng.)
A brittle candy of sugar, lemon or orange juice, and cream of tartar, cooked to a delicate golden color and then pulled and twisted into long strips. Once barley water was an ingredient.

Barm
Yeast formed on fermenting liquors.

Barmbrack (Ir.)
See BARINBREAC.

Barn Break (Ir.)
See BARINBREAC.

Baron of Beef
The whole sirloin from both sides of the animal, corresponding to the saddle of mutton and weighing from forty to eighty pounds.

Barquette (Fr.)
A small, boat-shaped pastry shell used for garnishing.

Barracuda
Primarily a game fish, weighing from twelve to fifteen pounds, one Pacific coast variety is sometimes eaten. It has a fat meat and is best smoked. Also called sea pike.

Barsez (Pol.)
Beet soup, comparable to the Russian borsch. Also spelled *barsch*.

Bartlett Pear
The leading American pear, large, golden, with a juicy, aromatic, melting meat.

Basil
An herb belonging to the mint family, native to the Near East, but now grown around the globe. The flavor is strongly aromatic, suggesting a blend of licorice, pepper, and cloves. Many Italian dishes are flavored with basil.

Bass
Any of numerous spiny-finned fresh- or salt-water food or game fish, many of which have fine, plump meat.

Baste
To drip or pour pan drippings, water, or some other sauce over meat while it is cooking.

Batavian Endive
Also called escarole. See ENDIVE.

Bath Bun (Eng.)
A sweet, yeast-raised bun containing raisins and candied peel, with coarse sugar and sugar-coated caraway seeds sprinkled over it.

Bath Chaps (Eng.)
The lower part of the pig's head, cured and smoked like bacon; so called for Bath, England, where its use originated.

Bath Oliver Biscuit (Eng.)
A thin, sugarless cooky originated by Dr. William Oliver, for his patients in the eighteenth century, and manufactured ever since. The original recipe is still a secret, but stout was supposedly one of its ingredients.

Bath Polony (Eng.)
A bologna sausage, very small and delicate, with a thin layer of fat under the scarlet skin.

Baton-Royal (Fr.)
A pastry shell, filled with a salpicon of chicken and game.

Batter
A mixture of dry and liquid ingredients beaten together and thin enough to pour.

Batterbread (U.S., South.)
A spoon bread.

Battercake
A pancake.

Bavarian Cream
A cooked custard made with gelatin and whipped cream and chilled in a mould.

Bay Leaf
The aromatic leaf of an evergreen tree native to the Mediterranean region. The elliptical, tapering leaves are smooth and waxy, from one to three inches in length, and just under an inch in width. They are used in many vegetable and meat dishes for their strong, pungent flavor.

Bay Salt (Eng.)
A very coarse, unrefined salt obtained through the evaporation of sea water.

Beach Plum
A sour plum common on the seashores of New England and southward, and good only for making jams and jellies.

Bean Feast (Eng.)
Originally, the Twelfth-night meal for which a cake containing a bean was baked; whoever found it in his slice became "Bean King." The term is now often applied to the meal served at any large gathering.

Bean Sprout
The two- to three-inch-long, pale, translucent new shoot of an Oriental bean, either the calorie-rich soya or the less nourishing mung, much used in Oriental dishes. The flavor is exceedingly bland, but in combination with other vegetables helps impart an "Oriental aroma."

Béarnaise Sauce (Fr.)
A variant of hollandaise sauce flavored with green herbs.

Beat
To turn ingredients over and over briskly in order to blend or make the mixture lighter. By hand, the motion is a quick, repetitive, firm "down-up-over-and-down" movement of spoon or fork. The Dover beater or an electric beater makes the job much easier.

Beaten Biscuit
Traditionally a small, round, fine-grained, very hard biscuit, made in the South, especially in that part along the Atlantic coast called the Eastern Shore, from a stiff dough without leavening, which is beaten with a woden mallet for an hour or more.

Beauharnais (Fr.)
A garnish for tournedos, etc., named after Napoleon's first wife, Josephine Beauharnais, and consisting of stuffed mushrooms and sliced artichoke hearts cooked in oil.

Béchamel Sauce (Fr.)
A basic white sauce made like velouté but distinguished from it in that cream or milk is largely or entirely used in place of stock.

Bee Balm
A name sometimes given to balm, though incorrectly; bee balm is actually the red bergamot or Oswego tea.

Beef Tea
A kind of beef broth.

Beestings (Eng.)
The first milk given by a cow after calving.

Beeswing
The fine, light sediment that often forms in old bottled port wine. Since it does not cling to the bottle some may come out in the pouring, but this does not affect the taste.

Beetroot
The English term for beet.

Belgian Endive
Also called French endive or witloof chicory. See ENDIVE.

Bellflower
See RAMPION.

Bell Pepper
The common sweet pepper of the market, so called from its shape. It is used while still green or after ripening, when it turns bright red. It is very mild, always, in taste and may be eaten either raw or cooked.

Bel Paese (It.)
A semi-soft, mild-flavored cheese.

Beluga Caviar
The largest-roed of all caviar, and also considered by many as the finest.

Ben Davis Apple
A red apple grown in the West and used only for cooking; in season from November to May.

Bene or Benné
Sesame seed.

Benedict, A La (Fr.)
A poached egg on a toasted English muffin, topped with a thin slice of ham, and covered with hollandaise sauce.

Bénédictine (Fr.)
A sweet, aromatic herb-flavored liqueur, one of the oldest and finest, originated in the sixteenth century, and still made by Benedictine monks in France.

Benzoate of Soda
A food preservative, used in relishes or pickles.

Bercy Butter (Fr.)
A sauce containing butter, white wine, shallots, and herbs. Served with grilled beef.

Bercy Sauce (Fr.)
A sauce made with a fish velouté base, white wine, lemon juice, parsley, and shallots; for poached fish.

Bergamot
A member of the mint family native to the western hemisphere. It grows from two to three feet tall, has soft, cotton-like foliage, clusters of red or purple flowers and a lemon-like scent. The leaves are most used in tea and in cool drinks. A tea made from bergamot is said to have been drunk by the Massachusetts Bay colonists while they were boycotting British shipments.

Bermuda Onion
A large, flattened, yellow-skinned onion, fairly mild in flavor.

Betel Nut
The nutmeg-sized seed of an East Indian palm tree, which is chewed for its pungent taste.

Betty
A baked dessert made of layers of apple or some other fruit, buttered crumbs, and sugar.

Beurre Noir (Fr.)
Black butter, which see.

Bhurta (Ind.)
A mash containing onion, green chilis and lemon juice and a choice of meat, fish, vegetables and seasonings.

Bibb Lettuce
A small-headed, very tender lettuce, also called limestone lettuce.

Bibleleaf
See COSTMARY.

Bicarbonate of Soda
See BAKING SODA.

Biffin (Eng.)
A deep red cooking apple; the name, derived from "beefings," refers to its color.

Bigarade Sauce (Fr.)
A brown sauce made with oranges, caramelized sugar, and usually served with duck. *Bigarade* is the French word for bitter orange.

Bigos (Pol.)
A stew of cooked meats, sauerkraut, wine, mushrooms, onions and various other ingredients; traditional and very popular in Poland. It keeps for some time and is better with each reheating.

Bilberry (Eng.)
The European whortleberry, is a small, round, dark blue fruit of a low shrub.

Binder
Any ingredient, for example eggs, starch, cream or butter, or a combination of any of these, added to a mixture to bind the ingredients together

and to give body and an even consistency.

Bing Cherry
The familiar, large, and very dark red, sweet cherry.

Bird's-Nest Pudding
A mixture of apples, sour cream, and beaten egg white baked in a casserole, spread with melted butter, sprinkled with sugar, and served with heavy cream.

Birds'-Nest Soup (Chin.)
A soup made from the gelatinous substance lining the nests of certain Oriental swifts.

Biriani (Ind.)
A dish resembling a pilau and a curry combined, in that it contains rice, and the meat, poultry, eggs, or vegetables used in a curry. Also spelled *briani.*

Biscotte (Fr.)
A type of dry rusk.

Biscuit
1. (U.S.) A type of raised bread, especially one made with baking powder or soda and baked in a small round cake.
2. (Eng.) A simple cooky.

Biscuit Tortoni (It.)
A mousse flavored with sherry and almonds, chilled in individual paper cases, and sprinkled with sherry-soaked macaroon crumbs.

Bisk (Eng.)
An ancient dish (no longer prepared) made of wild and domestic birds mixed together with an aphrodisiacal accompaniment.

Bismarck
A jelly- or jam-filled roll made of rich dough and fried like a doughnut in deep fat.

Bismarck Herring
Fillet and roe of herring pickled in white wine, vinegar, and seasonings, and served as an hors d'oeuvre.

Bisque (Fr.)
A thick, rich cream soup made from shellfish or, sometimes, game.

Bitki (Rus.)
A poultry dish containing the meat of the hazel hen or some other game bird, browned, and with a sauce made by stewing the bones with seasoning and then adding sour cream poured over the pieces. Also meat patties. See following entry.

Bitochke (Rus.)
A meat ball or patty. Also spelled *bitoke.*

Bitter Almond
An almond, distinguished from the familiar sweet variety by its bitter taste; grown as a source of oil and of flavoring, but not itself much used in cooking.

Bitter Orange
An orange whose bitter, aromatic rind is much used in preserves and whose tart, juicy pulp is used in cooking and in bigarade sauce. Also called Seville orange.

Bitters

Any of various liquors used in mixed drinks and in some food preparations, and made from a variety of substances: bitter herbs, orange rind, myrrh, quinine, juniper, and cloves, to mention only a few. It is often as much as forty per cent alcoholic.

Black Bean

A dried bean, blackish and of modified kidney shape, used most commonly in a soup flavored with lemon.

Black Bottom Pie

A chiffon pie having a dark chocolate-flavored bottom layer topped with a rum-flavored custard and whipped cream.

Black Bread

See PUMPERNICKEL and SCHWARZ BROT.

Black Butter

Butter heated until it browns and begins to smoke. Also called brown butter and nut-brown butter.

Black Drum

One of the drumfish—a type so named for its musical drumming—which may grow to great size but which is generally eaten when around eight to twenty inches long.

Black-Eyed Pea

See COWPEA.

Black Haw

A bluish-black, sweet fruit, about half an inch long, having a single, usually flat seed, and growing on a shrub of the honeysuckle family common east of the Mississippi.

Black Jack (Eng.)

Burnt sugar boiled with water and used as a coloring for soups, sauces, and certain liquors.

Black Pudding

1. A crumbly sausage pudding made with pig's blood, suet, and oatmeal. Also called blood pudding.
2. In Ireland, a steamed suet pudding made with currants, candied peel, spices, etc. Elsewhere, a steamed pudding made with molasses and without currants.

Black Strap

A very strong, somewhat bitter molasses from the third boiling of sugar cane, in which the sugar is burned to a very dark caramel.

Black Sugar

See SPANISH JUICE.

Black Tea

A tea fermented before firing as contrasted to the green or unfermented variety.

Blanch

To cover a food with boiling water for a few minutes to whiten or to make removal of the skin easier.

Blancmange (Fr.)

A flavored milk and cornstarch dessert, usually with a fruit or sweet flavoring added. It is white and opaque and is generally set in a mould. Correctly, though not usually, this dessert contains almonds or almond flavoring.

Bland

Very, very mild.

Blanquette (Fr.)
Any food which has a white color, generally a meat dish prepared with white stock; for example, a stew of veal in cream sauce.

Bleeny (Rus.)
See BLINI.

Blend
To combine two or more ingredients until each loses its individual identity and the whole becomes smooth in texture and uniform in color and flavor.

Blenny
A general name for numerous salt-water fish, such as the gunnel, which are often scaleless.

Bleu, Au (Fr.)
Briefly boiled in a court-bouillon; especially a method of preparing freshly caught trout.

Bleu Cheese (Fr.)
See BLUE CHEESE.

Blini (Rus.)
A small, fluffy pancake made with yeast and buckwheat flour and often served with cheese or caviar.

Blintz (Jew.)
A delicate, filled pancake much resembling the crêpe of France. After being fried lightly on one side it is topped with filling, most often cheese, rolled up and either fried or baked till brown.

Bloater (Eng.)
A large herring which has been salted, smoked, and partially dried. Generally served fried or grilled.

Blood Orange
A variety of orange with a ruby-colored juice and pulp, and often a rose-tinged rind, grown in Europe and in California.

Blood Pudding
See BLACK PUDDING.

Blowfish
Any fish which can inflate itself until it is almost round. Only the meat around the spine is eaten, as the rest of the fish is comprised of the inflatable belly.

Blue Cheese
A cheese of the Roquefort type, made in France, the United States and Denmark. (i.e., one which is creamy or white, crumbly, blue-veined, and pungent in flavor.)

Blue Crab
The common Atlantic coast crab. Its meat is excellent in salads, cocktails, and various hot dishes. See SOFT-SHELLED CRAB.

Blue Dorset Cheese
See BLUE VINNY.

Bluefish
A food and game fish of the Atlantic and Gulf coasts, blue above and silver below and generally eaten when weighing from three to six pounds. Its meat is plump and delicate in flavor.

Bluegill
A small fresh-water pan fish with opalescent blue gills.

Blue Hyssop
See HYSSOP.

Blue John
A colloquial name for skim milk.

Blue Point Oyster
Strictly speaking, an especially fine oyster from a specific section of Long Island waters, but often used to designate any good-sized oyster from the Atlantic or Gulf coast.

Blue Vinny Cheese (Eng.)
A blue-veined cheese, whence the name, the best grade of which resembles Stilton. Also called Blue Dorset after the English county in which it originated.

Boar's Head (Eng.)
Traditionally, a royal Christmas dish, which was carried in, much decorated, on a gold or silver platter to the feast. The elaborate cooking process involved stuffing the head of a male pig with forcemeat, boiling, glazing, and, usually, browning in an oven.

Bobotee (Un. of S. Af.)
See BABOTJE.

Bock Beer
A sweet, heavy dark beer with a high alcoholic content, made, usually in spring, by a process said to have originated in Germany in the thirteenth century.

Body
A term used to designate strength and excellence of flavor in tea, wine, and other beverages.

Bohea Tea
A black tea, i.e., one fermented before firing. Originally, the name of a fine Chinese tea, it now designates an inferior grade.

Bohemian Sauce (Fr.)
A béchamel with egg yolks, oil, tarragon vinegar, and mustard.

Boil
To cook in a covering liquid (water, fat, etc.) which has been heated to the bubbling, or boiling, point.

Boiled Coffee
Ground coffee in water brought to boiling point and simmered together till a suitable taste is achieved.

Boiled Icing
A white or tinted icing made of sugar and water boiled together and added slowly to stiffly beaten egg whites. The mixture is then further beaten until it is light, smooth and spreadable.

Boiler
A chicken fit for stewing, usually one year or more old and weighing at least three, but often six or more pounds.

Bollito (pl. *bolliti*; It.)
Boiled.

Bologna (It.)
A mildly seasoned sausage, generally made of finely ground veal and pork, compressed to a fairly soft or flexible consistency, and enclosed in a casing which must be removed before the sausage is eaten.

Bolt
To sift out chaff or hard grains from flour.

Bombay Duck
No duck at all, but a small fish

caught in Indian waters, dried, and used as a relish with curried dishes.

Bombe (Fr.)
A dessert made by lining a spherical mould with one or more layers of ice cream, ice, or custard, filling the cavity with ice cream or a mousse, generally of a contrasting flavor, and freezing the whole for several hours.

Bonbon (Fr.)
Any piece of candy or confection, especially one having a center or coating of fondant.

Bondepige Med Slør (Den.)
A dessert made of layers of stewed apple pulp and grated rye bread, with sugar and butter. The whole is topped with grated chocolate and whipped cream. Literally, "peasant girl with veil."

Bonito
The striped tunny, or any of several kinds of large mackerel-like fish common in the Pacific.

Bonne Femme (Fr.)
Literally, "housewife"; applied as an adjective to several dishes prepared in a variety of ways.

Bonnefoy Sauce (Fr.)
A velouté sauce containing white Bordeaux wine, herbs (especially tarragon), and seasonings, and served with white meat or grilled fish. Also called white bordelaise.

Bonnet Pepper
A very mild tropical red pepper, the source of paprika.

Bonny Clabber
An old-fashioned summer dessert, consisting of slightly soured and thickened milk, set on ice for a few hours, and served with sugar and nutmeg. Yogurt served in this way is probably the closest modern equivalent.

Borage
An herb growing some two feet tall with large, somewhat coarse and prickly, oval leaves and drooping clusters of star-shaped, sky-blue blossoms, native to Asia Minor and the Mediterranean area. The foliage, when young, is sometimes used in Europe as a cooked green, but more commonly to flavor iced drinks, in salads, or with vegetables. Candied borage flowers are used also as a cake decoration.

Bordelaise Sauce (Fr.)
A brown sauce containing red wine and seasoned with herbs and lemon juice, served primarily with steak.

Borecole
Another name for kale.

Borrachito (Mex.)
A rich cooky whose name means "little drunkard," from the fact that wine is the only liquid it contains.

Borsch (Rus.)
A highly seasoned beet soup made with stock and containing a variety of vegetables. Also spelled borscht.

Boston Baked Beans
New England, and especially Boston, is traditionally considered the "home" of beans, usually of the small pea

bean variety, baked long and slowly in a deep pot with pork, molasses, mustard and onion as seasonings.

Boston Brown Bread
A dark, sweet, quick bread containing molasses and often raisins and nuts, and characteristically steamed in a cylindrical mould. With baked beans, this formed a usual Saturday meal.

Boston Cream Pie
A two-layer sponge cake filled with a creamy custard and sprinkled with confectioner's sugar.

Boston Lettuce
A variety with crisp, tender leaves in a loosely packed head and of a somewhat darker green than iceberg lettuce. Also called butter lettuce and salad bowl lettuce.

Bottom Round Roast
See ROUND ROAST.

Bouchée (Fr.)
A very small tart or cream puff shell, filled with a cream, lemon, lobster, or chicken salad, depending on its use.

Boudin (Fr.)
A meat, poultry, fish, or game pudding made in the form of a sausage; especially a black pudding.

Bouillabaisse (Fr.)
A chowder made of several kinds of salt-water fish and shellfish and characteristically seasoned with saffron. A dish typical of Marseille.

Bouillon (Fr.)
A clear meat soup, stronger in flavor than consommé, usually made from beef stock. Commercially it is available in cans or in concentrated cube form, one cube making one cup of bouillon.

Boulette (Fr.)
A small forcemeat ball, used as a garnish.

Bouquet Garni (Fr.)
A bunch of aromatic herbs, usually including parsley, thyme, and bay, and generally enclosed in a cheesecloth bag, used to flavor soups, stews, sauces, etc.

Bourgeoise, À La (Fr.)
In simple or family style.

Bourguignonne, À La (Fr.)
1. A beef stew with spices and seasonings in red Burgundy wine.
2. A red wine sauce for snails.

Bouride (Fr.)
A strongly garlic-flavored fish soup, similar to *bouillabaisse* but containing no saffron.

Bowfin
A North American species, also called the mudfish, which is said to burrow in mud during periods of drought. It is not particularly good eating unless smoked or very skillfully prepared, and even then may be displeasing.

Boxty on the Pan (Ir.)
A potato pancake made of raw and boiled potatoes, flour, and buttermilk. Boxty dumplings and boxty bread are made with much the same ingredients but are cooked differently.

Boysenberry
A recently developed hybrid resembling, though larger than, the raspberry and having a pleasingly tart taste.

Braciole (It.)
A small square of meat rolled up with a filling of chopped onions, herbs, ham, etc., browned, and cooked in a sauce.

Braise
To cook by first browning in a little fat, then to continue by adding a little liquid, covering the pan and simmering over low heat till tender. Meats and certain vegetables are prepared in this way.

Brambleberry (Eng.)
The blackberry.

Bran
The ground husk of any cereal grain.

Brandade (Fr.)
A dish consisting of shredded fish, especially salt cod, in a sauce.

Brander (Scot.)
A grill or griddle. Anything grilled is said to "brandered."

Brandy Snap (Eng.)
An extremely thin ginger cooky which is rolled around a stick when not quite fully baked, returned to the oven and then, when done, filled with brandy-flavored whipped cream.

Brassica
The Latin word for cabbage applied to vegetables such as broccoli, Brussels sprouts, cauliflower, and kale, as members of the cabbage "family."

Bratwurst (Ger.)
A small pork sausage made of finely chopped lean pork trimmings and spices, and usually sold in small links. It must be cooked prior to eating.

Braunschweiger (Ger.)
A liver sausage, i.e., a seasoned liver paste packed into a casing. Usually ready-to-eat.

Brawn (Eng.)
Pickled or potted cuts of pork, especially from the head and feet, cooked, cooled in a mould, and usually eaten cold.

Bread
Used as a verb, to roll a food such as a cutlet or slices of meat, eggplant, etc., in bread crumbs, usually after dipping in beaten egg.

Bread-and-Butter Pickles
Unpeeled cucumber slices, sometimes with onions and shredded green pepper, marinated in salt water and then boiled briefly with brown sugar, vinegar, celery seed, and spices.

Bread Flour
A flour made from hard wheat, rich in gluten, which makes the bread elastic enough to expand in baking.

Breadfruit
The round fruit, about the size of a man's head, of a tropical tree, which when prepared and roasted is eaten like bread.

Bread Pudding
Any pudding which has bread crumbs or slices as one of its ingredients.

Bread Soup
Panada, which see.

Bread Stick
Special dough drawn out into pieces about three-quarters of an inch in diameter and from eight to ten inches long, and baked. Generally eaten with Italian foods.

Breakfast
The first meal of the day, although through usage it has come to be applied only to the morning meal.

Breakfast Steak
A small Spencer steak.

Bream
A yellowish fish, varieties of which are found in both fresh and salt water, used as a food fish in Europe.

Brew
To steep or let stand in hot water to extract essence or flavor.

Briani
See BIRIANI.

Brick Cheese
A cheese with a strong sweetish flavor, elastic texture, and many small round holes or eyes; originated in the United States.

Brick Ice Cream
Ice cream packed into a rectangular form, originally the size of a building brick, but now of any size.

Bride's Cake
A white cake to which citron or candied fruit may be added. Now usually synonymous with "wedding cake,"

i.e., an elaborate, tiered cake, served at a wedding reception. Formerly, however, the bride's and groom's cakes were separate.

Brie Cheese (Fr.)
A disk-shaped, creamy-yellow soft cheese with a mild, rich flavor but a strong aroma, and an edible russet-brown crust. It is properly eaten with fruit or crackers at the end of a meal.

Brine
A solution of rock salt, saltpetre, brown sugar and water, in which meats are preserved by soaking.

Brinjal Curry (Ind.)
Any curry containing eggplant.

Brioche (Fr.)
1. A feathery yeast roll of unsweetened dough, popular for continental breakfasts.
2. In America, the term is often applied to the well-known sweet roll with jam or jelly filling, frosting, etc.

Brisket
A cut taken from the lower part of the front section of the beef, just below the chuck. It requires long, slow cooking to be tender, and is thus boiled rather than roasted. Corned beef is generally from this cut.

Brisling
The finest smoked Norwegian sardine, noted for its tender and delicate texture and mellowness.

Brittle
A candy made of melted sugar which has been cooked to the hard crack stage, and usually containing nuts.

Broad Bean (Eng.)
A variety resembling the lima bean in shape, but having a rounder pod and a more globular bean. When young, the entire pod is eaten; when more mature, the beans must be shelled.

Brochette, En (Fr.)
Broiled on a skewer.

Broil
To cook food by exposing it to direct flame, generally located above, as in the arrangement known as a broiler.

Broiler
1. See preceding entry.
2. A chicken two to three and a half months old and weighing one to three pounds; the smallest cooking chickens, especially suitable for splitting and broiling.

Bromose
A meat substitute popular with vegetarians at the close of the century. Bromose was a ready-to-eat product made of cooked nutmeats and predigested cereals put up in jars and in tablets resembling caramels.

Brose (Scot.)
Generally a mixture of oatmeal and water to which meat, cabbage, etc. may be added.

Broth
A clear, thin soup, generally made of meat or fish stock.

Brown Betty
See BETTY.

Brown Rice
Rice with the hull and some, but not much, of the bran or covering of the endosperm removed. Also called Patna rice.

Brown Sauce
A basic or "mother" sauce consisting of butter and flour, meat stock, and seasonings; distinguished from the basic white sauces, velouté and béchamel, in that the butter and flour are first browned together.

Brown Stock
Also called *estouffade* and *fonds brun;* see STOCK.

Brown Sugar
Granulated sugar containing some molasses, i.e., the syrup which remains after the process of refining from sugar cane. It may be either pale golden or deep golden brown in color.

Brûlé (Fr.)
Literally "burnt"; usually referring to caramelized sugar and also to *crème brûlé,* which see.

Brunch
A colloquial term for the meal combining breakfast and luncheon, with dishes appropriate for either, and generally served between 10 a.m. and 1 p.m.

Brunoise (Fr.)
The process of cutting vegetables into small cubes, rounds, etc. and cooking in stock to prepare them for addition to a clear soup.

Brunswick Stew (U.S., South.)
A stew of squirrel meat, lima beans,

corn, tomatoes, and okra. Rabbit, chicken, etc. are substituted for squirrel when the latter is not available.

Brush
To cover the surface lightly with a liquid, such as melted butter, or with a dry substance such as flour.

Brussels Biscuit
An alternate name for rusk or zwieback.

Bubble-and-Squeak (Eng.)
Fried cakes of chopped cabbage and mashed potatoes. This old recipe originally added minced salt beef and derives its name from the sound it made in cooking.

Buckwheat Flour
Flour made from the triangular seed of the cereal plant buckwheat. By itself it is very pungent but blends pleasantly with other flour. Very popular in Europe, it is used in the United States primarily in buckwheat pancakes.

Buffalo Berry
A wild member of the blackberry family growing in the northern and western United States and in Canada. It is round and smooth in appearance, tart in taste, and red in color, and was used in early days for the making of jams and jellies.

Buffalofish
Any of several Midwestern fish belonging to the sucker family; it is also called "rooter" because of its manner of getting food. The flesh is best smoked but can also be baked or filleted.

Bulghour Wheat
Cracked wheat, a traditional accompaniment to Middle Eastern dishes, especially to shish kebab. Cooked and eaten much like rice, it is nutritionally rich, delicious in flavor and of an attractive golden brown color. Also variously spelled Bulgur, Boulghour or Burghul.

Bulk
The portion of the diet which is also called "roughage" and which has a high cellulose content. In itself it is indigestible but it aids in proper action of the alimentary tract.

Bulk Ice Cream
Ice cream packed in a bucket, or cylindrical form, as distinguished from brick ice cream.

Bullace (Eng.)
A plum related to the sloe and damson, and used for jams and jellies.

Bull's Eye
An old-fashioned peppermint candy, striped in black and white.

Bully Beef
Canned corned beef.

Bun
1. A generally round or oval, rather flattened, unsweetened roll or small sweetened cake.
2. In Scotland, a rich spice cake, or sometimes, a loaf of bread.

Buñuelo (S. Am.)
1. A fritter of rice, grated cheese, milk, etc., fried in deep fat until puffed and golden brown; popular in Nicaragua.

2. In Mexico, a pancake made of a rich dough, fried, and served with syrup.

Burbot
The fresh-water relative of the cod, found in northern lakes and fine eating when prepared like either cod or haddock.

Burdock
A coarse, leafy plant known chiefly as a barnyard weed, whose flowers were once used to make burdock wine.

Burdwan (Ind.)
A dish of curried poultry, meat, or game.

Burghul Wheat
See BULGHOUR WHEAT.

Burgoo
1. (U.S., South.) A soup or stew, thick and filling, made with pork, salt pork, veal, beef, lamb, chicken and as many as nine vegetables. Also called Kentucky burgoo.
2. (Eng.) A seaman's name for oatmeal porridge.

Burgundy
Either a red or a white wine; correctly, any of several made in the Burgundy region of France and named for particular towns in that area. General usage, however, recognizes "Burgundy" as a red wine, usually somewhat heavy and best suited for serving with red meat or game. A quiet Burgundy is served at room temperature; a sparkling Burgundy is chilled.

Burnet
A lacy-leaved herb with rose-colored or white flowers and a taste resembling that of the cucumber. It is grown in the southern United States but is not widely used elsewhere though it is pleasant with vegetables, in salads, or in certain soups.

Burning-Bush
See GAS-PLANT.

Burnt Sugar
Sugar which has been melted slowly over an open flame until it is brown in color, a process also known as caramelizing and which is used to make the sugar suitable for coloring, as well as sweetening various candies, cakes, sauces, and liqueurs.

Burnt Sugar Cake
A cake containing burnt sugar, as described in the preceding entry. It is usually baked in layers.

Burro, Al (It.)
Buttered.

Butt End of Ham
The top and thicker portion of the ham of a pig.

Butter Bean
A lima bean, either small and rich-meated or large and plump, but dryer textured. Local usage determines which type is referred to.

Butter Cake
The general name for cakes other than sponge, chiffon, and fruit, from which they are mainly distinguished by the use of butter or a similar shortening, and milk.

Butter, Coloring

Butter is frequently tinted pink or green, the former obtained by the addition of paprika or ground shellfish shell, the latter by that of well-pounded spinach.

Buttered

A term applied to any dish to which butter is added, not as an ingredient as in cakes, but as a sauce or seasoning as in hot vegetable dishes; also, to crumbs heated in butter and used as a garnish.

Butterfat

The yellow fat cells which make up butter, and which may be either numerous or scarce in any milk product. Usually, unless it has been artificially colored, the yellower the product, the richer it is in fat cells.

Butterfish

Another name for the dollarfish or gunnel.

Butter, Flavoring

Butter may be flavored with a variety of ingredients, for instance, herbs, shallots, shrimp, or nuts, which are thoroughly pulverized before being blended into the butter.

Butter Frosting

A sauce rather like hard sauce in that it is not cooked and is made basically of butter and sugar. However, egg yolks and various flavorings are often added.

Butter, Fruit

Fruit pulp and sugar cooked to a rather thick consistency and usually not so sweet as jam.

Butter Lettuce

Another name for Boston or salad bowl lettuce. See LETTUCE.

Buttermilk

The liquid which remains after sweet or sour milk or cream has been churned and the butter separated from it.

Butternut

The nut of the white walnut tree used in the manufacture of candy to which it lends a pleasant, buttery flavor.

Butternut Squash

A winter squash, spoon-shaped with a long, narrow neck, a light orange rind, and a weight of two or three pounds. It is not as highly recommended as the Hubbard, since its orange meat is frequently dry and mealy.

Butter Sauce

Any of various sauces containing a large amount of butter.

Buttery (Eng.)

Now a place where food is served, i.e. a restaurant, but originally a place for storage, particularly of butts of wine.

Button Onion

A very small variety, like the pearl onion, but about half its size, i.e., one-half to one inch in diameter. These little white onions are very mild and are usually served creamed or buttered.

Cabbage Palm

See PALM CABBAGE.

Cabernet Grape

A variety of black grape originated in Europe and now also grown in California used in making wine; also, the name given by some United States manufacturers to a wine made from these grapes.

Cabinet Pudding (Eng.)

A dessert also once popular in America consisting of sponge cake and custard baked together with candied cherries or some other fruit.

Cabrilla

A small fish sold as golden bass in California markets.

Cacciatore, Alla (It.)

Literally, "hunters' style"; applied to meat or poultry cooked and served in a sauce containing wine, herbs, seasonings, and usually tomatoes.

Cacciucco (It.)

A soup made of various kinds of fish and shellfish and strongly seasoned. A specialty of Leghorn.

Cacik (Turk.)

A soup made of cucumber, Yogurt, and oil of sesame, and served ice cold.

Caciocavallo Cheese (It.)

A hard, sharp cheese with a salty, smoky flavor, usually used grated.

Caesar Salad

A unique salad originated in California and having as its hallmark a dressing which includes a raw or coddled egg and, generally, anchovy fillets and croutons.

Café au Diable (Fr.)

See CAFÉ BRÛLOT.

Café au Lait (Fr.)

Very strong, hot coffee and scalded milk in equal proportions.

Café Brûlot (Fr.)

Spiced strong black coffee with brandy or rum and lemon or orange peel.

Café Noir (Fr.)

Black coffee.

Cake Flour

A flour low in gluten, giving a fine-textured product, extremely soft, light, and white.

Cala (U.S., Creole)

A small, yeast-raised cake or doughnut containing spiced and sweetened cooked rice and fried in deep fat.

Calabrese

An improved variety of broccoli.

Calalou (West Indies)

A stew of sliced calalou, spinach, greens, bacon, salt pork, and fried fish, a dish deriving its name from its chief component, calalou, a vegetable very similar to okra.

Calamondin

A kind of orange with a delicate pulp, the appearance of a small tangerine, and the flavor of a lime; native to the Philippines.

Calavo

The trade name for a California avocado.

Calf's Foot Jelly

A delicate jelly made by cooking the calf's feet for their gelatin and broth, flavoring it with spices, sugar, etc., and allowing it to set. Tasty and nourishing, it was once a favorite gift for invalids.

California Black Sea Bass

A large food and game fish sometimes weighing as much as eight hundred pounds. Its white, flaky, well-flavored flesh is sold in steaks.

California Kingfish

An excellent fish native to the Pacific coastal waters, generally taken at a weight of three-quarters to one and a quarter pounds and baked or broiled whole.

Caloric Punsch (Scan.)

A liqueur based on rum and syrup.

Calorie

The unit by which the energy value of a food is measured; technically, the amount of heat required to raise the temperature of one kilogram of water one degree centigrade.

Calvados (Fr.)

A potent cider brandy.

Calzoni (It.)

Dough stuffed with meat, cheese, and seasonings, and baked.

Cambric Tea

Weak tea with an equal amount of hot milk and a little sugar.

Cambridge Sausage (Eng.)

A beef sausage with a small amount of pork included. It is pinkish in color and has a dry, chewy, lean meat.

Camembert Cheese (Fr.)

A soft cheese, pungent in flavor, with a soft crust and creamy white center. It is eaten at room temperature, often with fruit as a dessert.

Camomile

A low, spreading herb with dark-green foliage and little daisy-like flowers whose fragrance resembles that of an apple from which it may have derived its name which means "apple of the earth." Camomile is little used except in the making of herb tea.

Campari

A brand of bitters made from an extract of capsicums.

Camp Biscuit

A biscuit made from the usual baking-powder biscuit recipe but rolled to a thickness of a quarter of an inch and cooked in a skillet over low heat.

Canapé (Fr.)

A small piece of toast, or a cracker, topped with a tidbit of cheese, fish, meat, or some savory mixture and served as an appetizer.

Cancalaise Salad (Fr.)

A salad made with poached oysters, potatoes, and truffles.

Candy

As a verb, to preserve by boiling in a sugar syrup and allowing a sugar coating to remain on the food, often pieces of fruit, so treated.

Cannelon (Fr.)

A roll of pastry stuffed with minced meat or some sweet filling and baked or fried.

Canneloni (It.)
Boiled squares of pasta filled with a meat or cheese mixture, baked, and served in a sauce.

Cannoli (Sicily)
Carefully rolled up pastry tubes, deep-fat-fried, and filled with sweetened ricotta cheese or a similar filling.

Can Sizes
Those numbers given cans of food by the companies canning and marketing them. Although not entirely consistent, can sizes and the amount of their contents will usually be as follows:

#	¼	(flat)	=	½	cup
#	½	(flat)	=	1	cup
#	1	(flat)	=	2	cups
#303			=	2	cups
#	1	(tall)	=	2	cups
#	2	(tall)	=	2½	cups
#	2½		=	3½	cups
#	3	(cylinder)	=	5¾	cups
#	5		=	6	cups
#10			=	13	cups

Cantaloupe
A round muskmelon with a laced or veined skin which is greenish-yellow in color. The meat is light to dark orange, sweet, aromatic, and juicy, being pleasantly firm but very tender.

Canton Oolong Tea
A fine oolong tea, i.e., one made with partially fermented leaves, used in various blends, particularly scented ones.

Caper
The pickled flower bud of a southern European shrub. It is round in shape, usually smaller than a pea, blackish in color, and sharp and distinctive in taste. The so-called English caper, however, is not from this plant but is a pickled nasturtium pod.

Capercailzie (Scot.)
A game bird common in Scotland; the largest member of the grouse family. Also spelled capercaillie.

Capilotade (Fr.)
A hash or stew of cooked meat.

Capirotada (Mex.)
A bread pudding made with bananas, apples, almonds, peanuts, and cheese, and baked with a sweet spicy syrup.

Capon
A castrated male chicken, usually under ten months old and weighing from six to nine pounds. It is more meaty and tender than an ordinary chicken.

Caponette
A hormone-treated chicken of either sex sold younger than the capon and lighter in weight, but just as meaty and tender.

Cappelletto (pl. *cappelletti;* It.)
A circle of noodle paste containing a chopped chicken mixture, folded into a cap shape, and cooked in broth.

Capricot
The trade name of a golden-colored apricot brandy liqueur. Others are Abricotine and Apry.

Capsicum

The botanical name for any of a genus of plants bearing red fruits generally known as peppers. Those of certain species produce the fruit called chilis (a Spanish word derived from the Indian name) which, when ripe, are bright red and very hot and are ground for cayenne pepper or crushed for other uses. They should always be used with great caution and may not be used interchangeably with paprika or chili powder. The bonnet pepper, the source of paprika, is of this genus, as is the large, mild, bell pepper, actually called capsicum in England.

Carambola (Orient)

A smooth, thin-skinned fruit ranging from the size of an egg to that of an orange. It may be acid or sweet in flavor, has a very pleasing fragrance, and is eaten raw or cooked.

Caramel

1. A smooth, waxy, chewy candy made with sugar, cream, and corn syrup.
2. Burnt sugar, which see.

Caramelize

The process producing burnt sugar, which see.

Caraway

An aromatic herb with feathery green leaves and yellowish-white flowers. The root, which is cooked like a parsnip for use as a vegetable, has a taste that is delicate and sweet and does not at all resemble the flavor of the pungent seed. The leaves, which are also milder than the seed, though the taste is essentially the same, are used in vegetable dishes, soups, salads, etc. The small, curved, brownish seeds are used either whole or ground in breads, especially rye bread, cakes, cookies, and pies, as well as in vegetables, soup, and meat dishes.

Carbohydrate

A chemical term designating certain compounds, including starches and sugars; thus, any food containing a large proportion of either of these.

Carbonada (S. Am.)

A thick meat stew made with rice, potatoes, pumpkin, green corn, and onions, and especially popular in Chile.

Carbonated Drink

A beverage charged with carbon dioxide under pressure, a process which produces a liquid which bubbles, fizzles, or sparkles when opened, like the common soda water.

Carbonate of Soda

Chemically, a type of soda having one-half the carbon dioxide gas content of bicarbonate of soda. In older recipes it is sometimes suggested that a little of this soda be used as a meat tenderizer, as a means for keeping juice in fruit pies, and as an addition to the water in which green vegetables are to be cooked.

Cardamom

The plump, rounded, bleached-ivory colored seed of a plant belonging to the ginger family. The flavor is penetrating but sweet, and cardamoms are often used either whole or ground in Scandinavian pastries and in East Indian cookery. At one time, cardamoms were called "grains of paradise," a name also applied to mignonnette pepper.

Carde (Fr.)
The edible portion of the cardoon, which see.

Cardinal Sauce (Fr.)
A béchamel sauce tinted red by the addition of lobster butter.

Cardoon
A coarse, prickly plant which looks rather like a cross between celery and artichoke and actually related to the latter. Its edible stalks are used raw or cooked, particularly in France.

Carob
A Mediterranean tree, also called locust bean or St. John's bread, whose beans, though bitter, grow in a long, sweet, succulent pod which is eaten fresh or dried, and is the source of a molasses-like syrup and of a meal or flour.

Carolina Tea
The "black drink" of the Cherokee Indians, this plant's leaves contain fair amounts of both caffeine and tannin.

Carp
A very prolific and long-lived fish having soft fins and a single dorsal fin and commonly found in ponds or sluggish streams. Its meat is lean or dry, and not particularly good if the carp is old. Otherwise, a sometimes muddy flavor can be overcome by seasoning, and a whole baked and decorated carp can make a really handsome dish.

Carrageen
See IRISH MOSS.

Carte, à la (Fr.)
To be chosen from a list, item by item; the opposite of *table d'hôte*.

Casaba Melon
A large, almost globular melon which, when ripe and ready to eat, has a yellow rind, often slightly furrowed lengthwise, and a juicy meat which is soft in texture and creamy white in color. There is, however, no aroma.

Case Knife
Either a sheath knife or a table knife.

Cashew Apple
A pear-shaped fruit with a thin yellow or scarlet skin. It is used for preserves, and its seed is the well-known cashew nut.

Casing
A covering into which sausage meat is tightly packed. Originally, animal intestine was always used for this purpose, but various commercial substitutes are now employed.

Cassabanana (S. Am.)
The large, crimson, cucumber-like fruit of a tall climbing vine. The meat has a peculiar, penetrating, but not unpleasant aroma and is sometimes eaten raw. Also called the musk cucumber.

Cassareep (West Indies)

A condiment made from the cassava plant and used to flavor a West Indian pepperpot as well as in various sauces.

Cassava

Any of several tropical plants whose tubers are the source of tapioca and are useful as vegetables. A bitter variety is poisonous, though often the poison is extracted in the cooking process to make this form usable also. An alternate name is *manioc*.

Casserole

A heavy dish often of glass or earthenware in which food is baked and served; also, the food so prepared and served, described as "en casserole."

Cassia

An evergreen tree native to Burma and China whose bark has a flavor similar to that of true Ceylon cinnamon. The buds are used in potpourris or in pickling, while the ground bark is used in conjunction with allspice, cloves, etc., wherever such spices are appropriate. Whole sticks or quills of the inner bark are used to stir tall drinks, to flavor fruits, puddings, main dishes, etc. Most of the so-called cinnamon used in the United States is really cassia.

Cassis (Fr.)

An almost-black liqueur made from black currants.

Cassoulet (Fr.)

A complex stew usually having beans and pork among a large variety of ingredients. There are many regional versions of this dish.

Cassoulet Mould

A small, handleless pot or mould.

Castagne (It.)

A mixture of well-cooked, mashed chestnuts, sugar, and whipped cream thoroughly chilled before serving.

Castor Sugar (Eng.)

White, finely granulated sugar.

Catalan (Fr.)

In the manner of Catalonia, Spain; for example, with tomato sauce and sausages.

Catawba Grape

An Eastern grape of excellent flavor and medium sweetness, dull purple color, and medium size, often with a lavender bloom or "frost." These grapes, almost round in shape and growing in large, compact bunches, are used in wines.

Catfish

A smooth-skinned, blackish-colored, fresh-water fish with fleshy whiskers resembling those of a cat, from which it gets its name. Choice Mississippi Valley channel cats weigh around five pounds and make excellent eating as they have none of the unpleasant, muddy taste other catfish may have.

Catnip

An herb with pretty, pale-blue flowers and a pleasant, mint-like aroma; around the fifteenth century catnip was used in soups and stews, though nowadays its only culinary use is in tea.

Catsup
A highly seasoned, semi-liquid sauce usually made of tomato pulp. The name is possibly derived from a Chinese word for pickled fish, "kitsiop," or "koechiap," and is also spelled catchup and ketchup.

Caudle (Eng.)
A hot, spiced drink based on red wine, ale, or tea with oatmeal gruel. In ancient times it was given to invalids.

Caul
An old word for the membrane covering the intestinal organs. Pig's caul, for instance, is used in various meat preparations in Europe.

Cavatoni Rigati (It.)
A ribbed, curved, tubular pasta about two inches long and half an inch in diameter.

Caviar
The salted roe of fish, especially sturgeon, which may be large or small, and red, black, grey, dark green, brown, or yellow in color. In Russia, home of caviar, gold is considered the best color and Beluga caviar is the most highly esteemed.

Cayenne Pepper
An extremely hot and pungent seasoning, made from ground or crushed chilis, which is still not as hot as Tabasco sauce, made from another, but smaller, chili. Cayenne is also known as red pepper. See also CAPSICUM.

Ceci (It.)
Chick-peas (in Spanish, garbanzos), a common food in Italy, Spain, and South America, especially in stews and thick soups.

Cédrat (Fr.)
Candied citron peel; the citron tree.

Celeriac
The edible turnip-like root of a kind of celery.

Celery
An herb plant native to southern Europe, where it is more often eaten braised than raw. The whole plant is edible, from root to seed, and is served in numerous ways.

Celery Cabbage
See CHINESE CABBAGE.

Célestin (Fr.)
Denoting dishes of an exquisite character.

Cellulose
The woody substance which forms the solid framework of plants; those having a high cellulose content provide bulk in the diet.

Century Plant
See AGAVE.

Cèpe (Fr.)
A large mushroom, often six inches across, of a yellow or reddish-brown color, occasionally exported canned in olive oil or a sauce.

Cerasella (It.)
A cherry-flavored brandy.

Ceriman
See FALSE BREADFRUIT.

Cervelat (Fr.)
A sausage made of pork and beef, highly seasoned and smoked, and relatively hard and dry. It is generally sold in rings or lengths.

Ceylon Green Tea
An unfermented tea with a light but pungent flavor.

Ceylon Tea
A black tea, i.e., one made from fermented leaves, which has a fine flavor and aroma if made from leaves grown high in the hills, or a nondescript flavor if made from those grown lower down.

Chablis
Correctly, a white Burgundy wine; in practice, any of several white wines marketed under this name. Either is properly served chilled with white meat, poultry, or fish.

Chafing Dish
A vessel supported on legs and having a burner underneath it; used to cook or warm food at the table.

Chahkee (Ind.)
The general name for any curry made with vegetables.

Challah (Jew.)
A yeast-raised egg bread. The dough is usually divided and rolled into three lengths which are then braided together and sprinkled with poppy seeds before baking.

Chalupa (Mex.)
A corncake, either plain or fried and filled with chorizo, grated cheese, shredded lettuce, and sauce.

Champ (Ir.)
Another name for stelk, i.e., a colcannon without cabbage.

Champagne
An effervescent white wine produced in a region of France northeast of Paris by a process which involves fermentation in the bottle; also, any of various wines made elsewhere by this process. Some sparkling wines not fermented in the bottle are referred to by the same name, but are not true champagnes. All such wines are served well chilled, often in an ice bucket, and are the traditional wine in which toasts are drunk.

Champignon (Fr.)
Mushroom.

Champurrado (Mex.)
A drink, usually served with tamales, containing water or milk, brown sugar, cloves, chocolate, and masa, or corn meal. It is not popular outside Mexico.

Channel Cat
See CATFISH.

Cha-No-Yu (Jap.)
The traditional tea drinking ceremony.

Chantilly (Fr.)
Denoting a dish made or served with sweetened and/or flavored whipped cream.

Chapati (Ind.)
A staple native bread made of whole wheat flour, water, and salt. The dough is rolled paper-thin and shaped into rounds which are fried on an ungreased griddle.

Chapon (Fr.)
A crust of bread rubbed with garlic and tossed with a green salad in order to impart the garlic flavor to the salad.

Charcoal
Porous carbon prepared from either animal or vegetable substance by partial burning. A popular fuel for the barbecue, it is now available commercially in several forms, a favorite one being the brick, or brickette.

Chard
See SWISS CHARD.

Charlotte or Charlotte Russe
A custard or gelatin dessert, often made with fruit and/or whipped cream, generally poured into a ring mould lined with slices of sponge cake or jelly roll, or into a casing made of bread, cake, or crumbs, and frequently topped with lady fingers.

Charlotte Mould
A doughnut-shaped ring mould. Also called a custard mould.

Charoses (Jew.)
Apples, nuts, and wine mixed together and served with matzos as a ceremonial Passover preparation. Also spelled *charoseth*.

Chartreuse (Fr.)
1. A fine French liqueur made with herbs and usually yellow or pale green in color, originated by the Carthusian monks near Grenoble.
2. A name sometimes given to food prepared and served in a casserole, specifically to a meat dish poached in a mould.

Chasseur (Fr.)
Literally, "hunter's style." In cooking, served with a brown sauce, generally containing tomatoes, mushrooms, and white wine.

Châteaubriand Butter (Fr.)
A seasoning containing butter, white wine, and green herbs used in sauces.

Châteaubriand Sauce (Fr.)
A steak sauce made with veal stock and seasoned with Châteaubriand butter, as in preceding entry.

Châteaubriand Steak
A steak cut from the tenderloin of beef, or fillet of the loin, which is the tenderest portion though not necessarily the most flavorful.

Château Potatoes
Quartered potatoes with corners rounded off, cooked briefly in butter and then roasted, usually with meat.

Chaud-Froid (Fr.)
Literally, "hot-cold," a term referring to cooked and jellied poultry, game or fish with a cold sauce and aspic, or with mayonnaise; also, a sauce made with aspic for jellied cold dishes.

Chaurice (U.S., Creole)
A pork sausage in a casing, quite similar to, and undoubtedly named from, the Mexican or Spanish chorizo.

Chausson (Fr.)
A large turnover made of puff paste.

Chawan-Mushi (Jap.)
A steamed custard containing chicken, shrimps, mushrooms, chestnuts, and vegetables, cooked briefly and served with lemon.

Chayote (Mex.)

A short-necked squash which may reach several inches in diameter. The rind is green and the pleasantly flavored meat is tinged with green. It retains a certain firmness of texture after cooking, and may thus be prepared in a variety of ways.

Checkerberry

See WINTERGREEN.

Cheddar Cheese

A solid yellow or orange, or very rarely, white, cheese of mild, medium, or strong flavor, originally made at Cheddar, England. Now also made in the United States and often called American cheese, especially when mild.

Cheesecake

One of the relatively rare cheese desserts; a cake made of a batter containing cottage cheese and with a crumb topping of zwieback, cinnamon, sugar, and butter. The tender, moist consistency and fine texture of the cake are achieved by thorough beating and, finally, by putting the batter through a fine sieve.

Cheesecloth

Very thin and loosely woven white cotton material for such culinary purposes as the straining of fruit juices.

Cheese Straw

A long, narrow strip of pastry into which cheese has been folded prior to its baking.

Chef's Knife

See FRENCH KNIFE.

Chelsea Bun (Eng.)

A sweet, yeast-raised bun made with lemon juice, which is rolled out twice, spread with butter and sugar, rolled up like a jelly roll, baked, and sliced.

Cheltenham Cake (Eng.)

A round, yeast-raised, unsweetened bun originated in Gloucestershire, England.

Cherimoya

An apple-like, tropical American fruit, brownish-yellow in color and anywhere from three to twelve inches in diameter. The pulp is white and juicy, with a custard-like center, and a fine flavor. It is also called vegetable ice cream and may be spelled chirimoya.

Cherrystone Clam

A small quahog, or littleneck clam, exceptionally good on the half shell.

Cherry Tomato

A miniature tomato, almost round, and often no more than an inch in diameter.

Chervil

A delicate-looking herb with lacy leaves and tiny white flowers, having a mild parsley-like flavor with a faint suggestion also of tarragon and licorice. It is used in the French "fines herbes" blend, with eggs, cheese, meat, vegetables, soups, and salads. Also called straight-leaf parsley.

Cheshire Cheese (Eng.)

The oldest of English cheeses. It generally resembles Cheddar, but there is also a Cheshire which is veined like Stilton. The white or creamy variety is much milder in flavor than the red, which is artificially colored.

Chester Bun (Eng.)

A plain, yeast-raised sweet bun glazed on top with sugar and water. These buns have been made in Chester, England, for many, many years.

Chestnut

The edible nut, enclosed in a smooth brown case within a prickly burr, of a tree belonging to the oak and beech family, which may be roasted, boiled and puréed, or used in dressings, or candied, as in the French confection *marron glacé*. *Marron*, the French word for chestnut, is often used in culinary context.

Chianti (It.)

A tart red wine served with the pasta course of a meal.

Chicasaw Plum

A poor quality of plum native to the southern states. Also called mountain cherry.

Chicken-Fried

Dredged in flour and seasonings, panfried, and, usually, smothered in gravy. Often applied to steak.

Chicken of the Sea

See TUNA.

Chick-Pea

The seed of a pea-like plant, larger than a regular pea and growing only one or two to a pod. They are a staple in many soups and stews of Europe and South America and are said to be the "pulse" of the ancient Hebrews. Also called *ceci* (Italian) and *garbanzos* (Spanish).

Chickweed

See WORT.

Chicory

A common plant whose roots are sliced, dried, and roasted to be used as a flavoring with ground coffee or as a coffee substitute. Its leaves are sometimes used in salads, and are also called curly endive.

Chiffonade (Fr.)

Finely shredded lettuce or sorrel added to certain soups; or the shreds of any other vegetable, such as cabbage, used as a garnish.

Chiffon Cake

A relatively new type of cake which uses vegetable oil in place of a more usual shortening.

Chiffon Pie

A pie made with beaten egg whites and/or gelatin, and often having a whipped cream topping. The filling is most often cooked separately, poured into a pre-baked pie shell, and chilled.

Chilaquile (Mex.)

A kind of hash made from tortillas cut up and fried with onions, peppers, tomato, chorizo, etc., and then cooked with cheese in either a casserole or a skillet.

Chile Con Carne (Mex.)

A popular dish consisting of highly seasoned beans and ground meat in a tomato sauce.

Chili Pepper

See CAPSICUM and RED PEPPER.

Chili Powder

A blend of ground chili peppers, herbs, and spices much used in Mexican and South American cookery. It may vary from sweetly mild to hot, and thus may not be used interchangeably with ground red pepper or cayenne.

Chili Sauce
A condiment made with tomatoes, vinegar, sweet peppers, onions, spices, and other seasonings.

Chill
To cool to a fairly low temperature but not to the freezing point.

China Green Tea
Any of various unfermented types of tea originating in China, among which are Country green, Hoochow, and Pingsuey.

Chincoteague Oyster
An excellent oyster from Chesapeake Bay.

Chine
The backbone of an animal, or any part of the backbone. In a young pig, the two undivided loins of pork corresponding to a saddle of mutton; in an older pig, the backbone and two inches of the meat on each side.

Chinese Cabbage
A very pale, mild-flavored cabbage which grows in elongated heads somewhat resembling celery. The leaves are tender and crisp, and may be cooked or used raw in a salad. Also called celery cabbage.

Chinese Mustard
A plant whose large leaves are used in salads or cooked as greens. The tuberous root resembles an elongated turnip and may be cooked in the same way as a turnip.

Chinese Pea
See SNOW PEA.

Chinese Red Cheese
A name sometimes given to bean curd, made by fermenting soy beans. It is slightly salty, and pungent.

Chinquapin
An edible nut; also, a New England name for the crappie.

Chipolata (It.)
A ragout of sausages, mushrooms, and onions; or, the sausages themselves, which are small and often served as hors d'oeuvres. Also spelled cipollata.

Chitling
An elided form of chitterling.

Chitterling
The edible entrails of pork or beef, cleaned, boiled, and, especially in the South, deep-fat-fried.

Chive
A small relative of the onion whose slender, hollow, green leaves are used as a seasoning in many dishes.

Chivry Butter (Fr.)
Half-melted butter blended with a purée of parboiled herbs, for use in sauces.

Chivry Sauce (Fr.)
A velouté sauce made with poultry stock and such herbs as tarragon, chervil, and pimpernel, to be served with boiled or poached fowl.

Chlodnik (Pol.)
A soup whose ingredients include cooked veal, beets, prawns, cucumbers, sour cream, and hard-boiled eggs. It is served ice-cold.

Chocolate

The product manufactured from ground cocoa beans. It is richer than cocoa, dark brown in color, and may be bought sweetened or unsweetened.

Chokecherry

A small wild cherry, well-named for its puckery taste, which may induce choking. It is edible, though perhaps best used in a jelly.

Cholent (Jew.)

A meat and bean dish resembling Boston baked beans in that it is slowly cooked in a banked oven, but without their sweetening. It was originated to avoid cooking on the Sabbath. Aslo spelled *chulent*.

Chop

1. A small cut of meat containing a portion of rib bone, usually with a "T" cross, thus providng a section of both fillet and loin.
2. To cut into small, but not minute, pieces by striking repeatedly with a sharp blade; see MINCE.
3. A term used in grading tea, first chop being the best.

Chop Suey

Supposedly Chinese, this dish was, in fact, originated in San Francisco in the 1800's; it contains water chestnuts, bamboo shoots, onions, mushrooms, etc. cooked with sliced meat and served with rice.

Chorizo (Mex.)

A sausage made of pork, chili powder, garlic, vinegar, and other seasonings, and enclosed in a casing.

Choron Sauce (Fr.)

A béarnaise sauce containing tomato purée, to be served with grilled meat or poultry.

Choux (Fr.)

A rich paste made with many eggs and used in making cream puffs, éclairs, etc.; also, a cake made from this paste.

Chowchow

1. A conglomerate vegetable pickle relish containing tomatoes, cucumbers, peppers, cauliflower, celery, string beans, onions, etc., cut into small pieces, marinated in salt water, and then cooked till soft in a solution of vinegar and spices.
2. Also, any mixture of chopped food.

Chowder

A thick soup or stew originally made in New England and containing fish, potatoes, and milk or cream.

Chow Mein (Chin.)

A thick stew of shredded meat, celery, onions, bean sprouts, etc., similar to chop suey but served with fried noodles, from which the dish takes its name. Also spelled *chao mien* and *chou min*.

Christmas Cake

A white fruit cake, i.e., one not containing molasses. In England, it is, by custom, given a white icing and often elaborate decorations in the holiday motif.

Christmas Melon

An oblong melon with a green rind, broadly banded with faint netting. The juicy but firm flesh is yellow-green and has a fine aroma. A winter melon, it is picked green, but keeps well and ripens slowly till the rind is slightly yellow. Also called Santa Claus melon.

Christmas Pie (Eng.)

1. Traditionally, an enormous pie containing a large variety of domestic and game birds. Pieces of hare and woodcock were placed in the corners of the huge pan and the whole was covered with a pastry crust and baked.
2. A sweet mince pie containing mutton, candied peel, currants, and raisins.

Christmas Pudding (Eng.)

A plum pudding, quite rich and full of fruit, most often steamed but sometimes boiled.

Chub

A fish related to the carp but much smaller and thinner, with extremely soft flesh. Chub are among the minnows often used as bait; however, if they do grow to cooking size, they are treated like whitefish.

Chuck Roast

A cut taken from high on the chuck, or front section, of the beef. It should be cooked long and slowly, for example, as a pot roast.

Chuck Steak

A reasonably good steak if the beef is absolutely prime; otherwise it should be marinated or tenderized.

Chufa

A European plant of the sedge family whose small, edible underground tubers are eaten raw, baked, fresh, or dried. Also called earth almond.

Chuk (Chin.)

A breakfast or late supper dish consisting of rice gruel cooked with pig liver and intestines and meatballs made of finely chopped pork. To this a variety of ingredients may be added at the table, for example, shredded lettuce, pickle, or sliced raw fish.

Chulan Blossom

A flower having an aroma similar to that of jasmine, with which most perfumed teas are scented.

Chuleta (Mex.)

A mixture of ground beef, onions, and garlic, shaped into steaks and served with a tomato sauce.

Chupatty (Ind.)

See CHAPATI.

Churro (Mex.)

A simple flour-and-water batter pressed in small amounts out of a pastry tube into deep fat in which a slice of bread and half a lemon have been browned, thus giving the resulting fritter a distinctive flavor.

Cider

Juice pressed out of apples and often very slightly fermented.

Cider Vinegar

A vinegar made by fermenting cider; generally rather mild.

Cinnamon

True cinnamon comes from a tree grown in Ceylon and along the Malabar coast of India. The flavor of its bark is sweet and delicate, and the ground product is a rich golden brown in color. Its uses in pies, cakes, cookies, and many main dishes, as well, are innumerable. However, most of the "cinnamon" used in the United States is actually made from cassia bark. See CASSIA.

Cioppino
A stew made with fish, shellfish, tomato sauce, and a large variety of seasonings. It is a San Francisco specialty, having originated on Fisherman's Wharf.

Citrange
A hybrid fruit, derived by crossing a common sweet orange and a hardy but inedible Japanese orange, most often used in preserves and drinks as it is rather tart.

Citrange-Quat
A hybrid fruit, the cross between a citrange and a kumquat, having a bitter skin and acid juice, and used in the manufacture of marmalade.

Citron
A large, thick-skinned fruit similar to a lemon but not so acid, whose preserved or candied rind (*cédrat*) is used in fruit cakes and mincemeat.

Citron Melon
A small, round watermelon, inedible raw, whose rind is used in preserves.

Citrouillat (Fr.)
An unsweetened pumpkin pie with a top rather than a bottom crust. Through a hole in this crust, heavy cream is added after the pie is baked. This is a country dish.

Civet (Fr.)
A ragout or stew of game or poultry usually containing wine and blood of the freshly killed animal with which it is made.

Clabber
Milk which has become thick in the natural process of souring but which has not reached the point at which curds and whey separate.

Clam
A double-shelled mollusk, of which there are many varieties, ranging from very small to quite large. The meat is firm but tender and usually a creamy white, and may be eaten either raw or cooked.

Claret
A red wine made in the Bordeaux region of France and somewhat lighter in body than Burgundy; or, by usage, any of several red wines made elsewhere, having the nature of claret, and sold under that name. In either case, the wine should be served at room temperature as an accompaniment to red meat.

Clarify
To make clean and clear by slow heating and removal of cloudy solids which collect during the process; often a term applied to butter.

Clary
A strong-scented mint which also has a tang of sage about it. It is used as a seasoning, especially in egg dishes, and for a tea. It sometimes replaces woodruff in wine drinks and substitutes for hops in beer and ale. In seventeenth- and eighteenth-century England, it was used in soups, fritters, etc.

Clementine
A practically seedless hybrid fruit, the cross between a tangerine and a wild North African orange.

Cling Peach
A peach which is hard to slice, since, as the name indicates, the flesh clings to the stone, but which is often juicy and sweet and otherwise quite desirable.

Clot
A very soft lump or globule such as that formed in a liquid by evaporation or coagulation; or to employ a process which will bring about such coagulation. See following entry.

Clotted Cream
The thick, coagulated cream derived from the application of very slow heat for quite some time to whole milk from which the cream, now coagulated or clotted, is then removed.

Cloudberry
A golden yellow or reddish, round, soft raspberry common in such cool areas as New England and Scandinavia.

Clove
1. One of the separate portions or segments of a bulb, such as garlic or the shallot.
2. The unopened flower bud of a tropical evergreen tree. Whole cloves are shaped like tiny wine glasses; they are brownish-red in color, delightfully pungent and sweet in aroma, and somewhat hot and burning in taste. They are used in pickling, in baking hams, or, stuck into an onion, as a seasoning for many meat dishes. Ground cloves are more common and are widely used as one of the most popular flavorings.

Club Sandwich
A sandwich consisting of three slices of bread most commonly with one filling of sliced chicken, ham, or turkey with mayonnaise and a second of bacon and tomato. The sandwich is often toasted and cut into four small triangular portions.

Club Steak
A boneless cut which, like minute steak, is usually fairly thin. The best ones are cut from the front rib and are essentially porterhouse with tenderloin removed and ends trimmed.

Coarse Fish (Eng.)
Any of various ordinary fish such as those to be found in streams or lakes and not particularly noted for their edibility.

Coat
To cover with a layer, usually thin, of some material or substance, for example, mayonnaise, aspic, flour, or the like.

Cobbler
1. A dessert consisting of sugared fruit covered with a single pastry or biscuit crust and baked, often, though not necessarily, in a large loaf pan.
2. A cooling, sweetened fruit drink, usually made with a wine or liqueur.

Cobnut
See FILBERT.

Cock-a-Leekie Soup (Scot.)
A soup made from leeks, stock from a boiled chicken, and part of the chicken meat. Prunes are often added or served as an accompaniment.

Cockle
A marine mollusk, i.e., a shellfish similar to a clam or an oyster, protected by two shells with ribs which ray out from the base. Cockles are also eaten like clams or oysters, though more commonly in Europe than the United States.

Cock's Comb
The comb of a rooster cooked and used, especially in France, as a garnish for certain rich stews, ragouts, etc., often in combination with cock's kernels, which see.

Cock's Kernels
The testicles of a rooster cooked and used for garnishing stews and certain other dishes, especially in French cookery and often in combination with the combs. The French name, *rognons de coq*, is the one most frequently given them.

Cocoa
The powdered form of the cacao bean from which some of the fat has been removed.

Coco De Mer
A large member of the coconut family which grows only in the Seychelles Islands of the Indian Ocean and which natives think is the forbidden fruit.

Coconut or Cocoanut
The egg-shaped fruit of a palm tree, having white meat and milk within a wood-like, hairy shell, which in turn is enclosed in a large husk. Dried, and shredded or flaked, the meat is used in many desserts, while the milk is also an ingredient in a variety of recipes, especially some from India.

Cocotte (Fr.)
A covered casserole of earthenware, porcelain, or cast iron. Food cooked in it is said to be *en cocotte*.

Cod
An elongated, soft-finned fish of the North Atlantic, with lean or dry meat, which may be sold pickled, smoked, salted, or fresh. It is generally taken at a weight of about ten pounds and is one of the most important of food fish, some one billion pounds being caught annually.

Coddle
To cook by allowing to stand in a tightly covered pan of water which has been brought to the boiling point and then removed from the heat; a method commonly applied to eggs.

Coffee Cake
A sweetened and flavored yeast bread, often shaped into rolls and frequently containing a filling or topping of apple slices, raisins, nuts, or the like. The name derives from its being eaten with coffee as a breakfast bread.

Cognac (Fr.)
A brandy distilled from wine and deriving its name from Cognac, a district of France, where it is made.

Cohune Nut (Cent. and S. Am.)
A palm tree nut, oval in shape and often two or more inches in diameter,

containing a high percentage of edible oil which is of considerable value in the manufacture of margarine.

Cointreau (Fr.)
A clear, colorless syrup-like liqueur made from oranges and wine spirits. It is used alone as an after-dinner cordial, or as a flavoring in other drinks.

Colander
A large, bowl-shaped metal sieve for draining foods such as vegetables or spaghetti which have been cooked in water, or for coarsely straining stewed fruit; usually made with short feet and side handles.

Cola Nut
An African nut growing several to a pod, and either red or white in color. It has long been known to be a stimulant and a thirst quencher, and was a staple of African diet before coming into use as an ingredient in Western cola drinks. It contains caffeine, is odorless, and has a taste resembling that of acorns. Also spelled *kola*.

Colbert Butter (Fr.)
Maître d'hôtel butter combined with meat glaze and seasoned with tarragon.

Colcannon (Ir.)
A well-known dish consisting of mashed potatoes into which pre-cooked onions and cabbage have been thoroughly pounded or "beetled." Colcannon is usually heated in the oven before serving.

Coleslaw or Slaw
A salad of finely cut cabbage and dressing; its name is derived from the Dutch words for cabbage and salad.

Colewort
The orginal wild plant from which all cultivated varieties of cabbage have been developed; or, any variety which does not form a compact head.

Collard
A leafy vegetable of the cabbage family, similar to kale, with large, curly-edged, dark green leaves. Also called collards and collard greens.

Collared
Denoting meat or fish prepared by being pressed tightly into a mould, cooked, and chilled. Collared eels are especially famous.

Collop
A small slice or piece, particularly of meat, dipped in egg and crumbs and then fried.

Coltsfoot
A wild plant whose flowers are used in England like those of the young dandelion for making wine.

Combine
To unite, especially unlike ingredients, by mixing thoroughly. See MIX.

Comfit (Eng.)
Originally, a small bit of spice or a spicy seed, such as caraway, covered with several layers of sugar; now usually applied to a sugar-coated candy, for example, a sugar-coated almond.

Comice Pear
A very fine autumn fruit, on a par with the Bartlett for dessert use, often with cheese.

Comino
The word in Spanish and Italian for cumin, which see.

Common Salt
Sodium chloride, for use in cooking; the ordinary salt marketed under various trade names, often in a cylindrical box.

Compote
A dish, often a large one holding several servings, of sliced fruit, which may be either fresh, cooked, or preserved in syrup, sweetened, and sometimes served with cream.

Compound Sauce
See SMALL SAUCE.

Compressed Yeast
A yeast preparation with a high moisture content, and thus rather perishable, sold in small squares which must be refrigerated. See DRY YEAST.

Concassé (Fr.)
Coarsely chopped or crushed; generally used in reference to chervil, shallots, and such.

Conch
A Southern shellfish, the inhabitant of the well-known conch shell. The meat is tasty but tough, and must be tenderized by beating or parboiling, though even then it is best ground and made into fritters or sliced very thin and fried.

Conchiglia (pl. conchiglie; It.)
A pasta shaped like a small conch shell. Also called *maruzzelle*.

Concord Grape
A North American variety, deep purple-blue in color, common on domestic vines and excellent for jelly and juice, though not generally esteemed for eating raw. The Concord, when ripe, characteristically slips out of its skin when gently squeezed, and is therefore called slip-coat or slip-skin.

Condé (Fr.)
1. Refers to stewed fruit served with rice.
2. A pastry strip spread with chopped almonds, egg white, sugar, etc., and baked.

Condensed Milk
Canned milk, thickened by evaporation, and sweetened.

Condiment
Any of various ingredients or substances used to throw a food's flavor into relief, or to heighten it. A condiment may be pungent, as, for example, onion and chives; hot, as for example, gherkins, capers, or chili; fatty, as, for example, butter and oil; or spicy.

Coney Island Clam Chowder
A vegetable clam chowder differing from Manhattan clam chowder in that it is thick and opaque rather than clear.

Confectioner's Sugar
The finest, smoothest, and whitest of granulated sugars, prepared with the addition of a small amount of cornstarch. It is primarily used in candies, uncooked frostings, and dessert sauces. Some manufacturers label it XXXX,

thus distinguishing it from powdered sugar, labeled XXX, with which it is often used interchangeably.

Congou Tea
A Chinese black tea, i.e., one fermented before firing. North China congou is strong, full-bodied, and fragrant with hard, black, aromatic leaves, while that from South China is lighter colored with a reddish leaf.

Congress Tart (Eng.)
A tart with a filling of almond paste and rice, or of almond-flavored rice.

Conserve
A preserve similar to jam in consistency, but generally containing more than one kind of fruit and occasionally raisins and nutmeats as well.

Consistency
The degree of density, firmness, or solidity of a food.

Consommé (Fr.)
A strong clear soup made by the long, slow boiling together of various meats, usually beef and poultry, followed by careful straining and clarifying of the resulting liquid.

Continental Breakfast
A breakfast of rolls and coffee or hot chocolate, as distinguished from the heartier "English breakfast" of porridge, eggs, bacon or sausage, toast, marmalade and such.

Converted Rice
Rice processed by a method of parboiling which permits the nutritious parts to remain with the grain after polishing.

Cooking Sherry
Any cheap sherry sold to be used in cookery. The best culinary opinion is against its use.

Cooky
A small, sweet cake either rolled flat and cut out or dropped from a spoon onto a pan, most often a thin, wide, sideless one called a "cooky sheet," to be baked. Also spelled cookie.

Cooter
A colloquial name for a terrapin found in Southern ponds and marshes.

Coq Au Vin (Fr.)
A famous casserole of cut-up chicken cooked in wine.

Coquille St. Jacques (Fr.)
Scallops, or a preparation of these served in their shells.

Coral
A name given to the unimpregnated eggs of the female lobster, which turn red when cooked and are used in making a sauce to be served with lobster.

Cordial
A sweet and aromatic alcoholic drink, by definition one intended as a stimulant to the action of the heart; now sometimes used to denote a sweetened spirit flavored after, rather than during, distillation, as distinguished from a liqueur. However, the terms are most often used interchangeably, especially as both cordials and liqueurs are taken in very small quantities after a meal, usually the evening one.

Core
1. The section at the center of an ap-

ple, pear, etc., containing the seeds and tough, or stringy, connective tissue.

2. To remove this center.

Coriander

The dried fruit of a delicate, lacy-looking, European or Asiatic herb. The "seeds," so called, are minute, round, and yellow-brown, with a warm flavor like a mixture of sage and lemon, and are generally used ground, in cakes and cookies, bread, puddings, etc., particularly in Danish pastry. In pickling, coriander is used whole, as it sometimes is in sausage. In England, whole coriander was often sugar-coated and sold as a comfit. A usual ingredient of most curry powders, it has been known and used from antiquity and is believed by some to have been the "manna from Heaven" that fed the Israelites.

Corn

1. In America, a name referring specifically to Indian corn, or maize; in Europe, the name given any of the principal cereal grains, for example, wheat, rye, or barley.
2. A grain, for example of salt.
3. To salt in a weak brine solution with preservatives, as in the preparation of corned beef.

Corncrake (Eng.)

A European bird, very popular as a game bird around the fourteenth century. It is now protected by law in England.

Corn Dodger

A simple bread made of corn meal, water, salt, and lard. The thick batter is dropped by spoonfuls onto a pan or cooky sheet and baked in a hot oven, or allowed to cool and solidify into a mush, which is then sliced and fried.

Cornish Game Hen

An alternate name for Rock Cornish hen.

Cornish Pasty (Eng.)

The most famous of all pasties (turnovers or small pies) and a characteristic dish from the Duchy of Cornwall, England. It consists of a round or square of piecrust with a filling of chopped beef, potatoes, and onions, or, alternately, of bacon and leeks, fish and potatoes, or some other combination.

Corn Meal

Coarsely ground corn, i.e., maize, which may be either yellow or white. Waterground meal, made of white corn, retains much of the rich skin and germ, and, though nutritionally excellent, tends to spoil more quickly than other kinds.

Corn Pone (U.S., South.)

A simple corn bread, generally made only of meal, water, and salt, without either milk or eggs.

Cornstarch

A very white, highly refined starch made from corn. Clear and virtually tasteless, it is a good thickening agent for clear sauces, puddings, fruit pies or stewed fruit, etc.

Corn Syrup

A golden syrup produced from the refining of corn sugar and which helps prevent sugaring or crystallization in sauces or frostings.

Cornucopia
A horn of puff pastry filled with whipped cream or custard. Also called horn-of-plenty.

Cortland Apple
A winter variety, i.e., one late in ripening, good for eating or baking, in salads, or in pies.

Cos Lettuce
Another name for romaine lettuce, which see.

Costilla (Sp.)
A chop.

Costmary
A somewhat unusual herb with a pleasant mint scent, but a bitter taste, whose flowers look like yellow buttons or daisies. The long, slender, light-green leaves, after infusion, have a lemon-like flavor which is exceptionally dominant, and thus they must be used sparingly, one leaf in the bottom of a cake pan usually being quite sufficient to flavor the whole cake. Costmary is also used with game, poultry, and meat, as well as for making herb tea. The plant, a native of Kashmir, is also called alecost from its use in flavoring ale, and bibleleaf, as its larger leaves were often used as book marks in the family Bible.

Côte (Fr.)
A piece of meat with a portion of the rib attached.

Cottage Cheese
A very soft white cheese which may have either large or small curds and a very mild flavor.

Cottage Fried
The name given potatoes which have been cooked whole, then diced or sliced and browned in a little fat.

Cottage Pie
See SHEPHERD'S PIE.

Cottage Pudding
A simple cake baked in a loaf pan and served with a sauce made with water, sugar, and flavoring, most often lemon, usually while it is warm.

Coulis (Fr.)
See CULLIS.

Coulommiers Cheese (Fr.)
A soft cheese similar to Brie.

Country Captain (Anglo-Ind.)
Chicken baked in a casserole with an assortment of condiments, raisins, almonds, etc., and enough liquid to cover.

Country-Cured Ham
See KENTUCKY, SMITHFIELD, and VIRGINIA HAM. The majority of country-cured hams require soaking and boiling before baking.

Country Green Tea
A China tea prepared in the gunpowder style, with rolled leaves which make a clear, rich-flavored cup of tea.

Coupe
A dessert, often confused with the parfait, consisting of ice cream topped with a sweet sauce or syrup, garnished with whipped cream, candied fruit, chopped nuts, toasted coconut, etc., and generally served in the tall, narrow glass typical of the parfait.

Court-Bouillon (Fr.)

A liquid in which fish is poached made up of water, wine or vinegar, onions, carrots, and herbs. Literally translated the name means short broth.

Couscous (N. Af.)

Coarsely ground grain, or meal, such as millet steamed in a little liquid to be served with many African or Near East dishes. Sweetened couscous is called *el mistouf,* which see.

Cowberry

Any of several berries which grow on bushes belonging to the large cranberry family and common to pastures and woodlands.

Cowpea

A small, pea-like, whitish bean with a black spot at the eye, the mid-point from which the bean sprouts. These highly nutritious beans are commonly used in Southern and Creole recipes. Also called black-eyed pea.

Cowslip

A plant of the crowfoot family with bright yellow flowers, common in the marshes of both Europe and America. The young leaves and stalks are excellent as greens while the blossoms are used for making wine. Also called marsh marigold.

Crab

A crustacean with a short, broad, covering shell, six jointed legs, and two menacing pincer-like front claws, with tender, tasty, white meat. See BLUE, DUNGENESS, KING, SOFT-SHELLED, and STONE CRAB.

Crab Apple

A miniature wild apple, tart and puckery in taste when raw but excellent for jelly.

Cracker

A thn, crisp, unleavened or only slightly raised biscuit either rectangular or round in shape and frequently sprinkled with salt.

Crackling

A crisp bit of connective tissue of pork, left after the fat has been rendered out.

Cracknel

1. A rich, light, yeast-raised roll, cut in long pieces about two inches broad.
2. (Eng.) A cooky, or biscuit, whose dough is boiled before it is baked.

Cranshaw Melon

A fairly new hybrid melon, the cross of a Persian and a Casaba melon, weighing from four to eight pounds and having a smooth, green or gold rind which deepens to gold as the melon ripens, and a salmon-colored meat. Also spelled Crenshaw.

Crapaudine (Fr.)

A term applied to chicken, squab, etc., which has been either very much flattened with a mallet before cooking or merely cut open and spread as flat as possible.

Crappie

A fish common in the Mississippi Valley but rarely caught commercially because of State regulations, seldom over a foot long or a pound in weight, and an excellent pan fish. One variety is also found in New England.

Crayfish or Crawfish

1. A fresh-water crustacean like a lobster but very much smaller, usually measuring only a few inches in length. It may be served plain after cooking in a court-bouillon or very elaborately. In French, *ecrevisse*.
2. A marine shellfish without the large claws of the lobster; also called rock or spiny lobster and, in French, *langouste*.

Cream

As a verb, to blend two or more ingredients, such as butter and sugar, until smooth, by rubbing them into each other with the back of a wooden spoon or with a blending fork.

Cream Cheese

A soft cheese, spreadable, white, and bland, made from sweet cream and often combined with chives, pimentos, etc.

Cream Horn

A cornucopia filled with whipped cream or sweetened meringue.

Cream of Tartar

Crystallized bitartrate of potassium, used as a leavening agent combined with bicarbonate of soda.

Cream Puff

A very light pastry that has expanded greatly in baking and then been filled with whipped cream or custard

Cream Puff Paste

Puff paste, which see.

Cream Sauce

A béchamel sauce made with cream and used with fish, poultry, eggs, or vegetables.

Crème Brûlée (Fr.)

A delicate custard made of heavy cream, eggs, and brown sugar and browned on top, either with a salamander or by placing under a broiler.

Crème de (Fr.)

When applied to liqueurs, denotes one having a greater than usual sweetness and followed by the name of the informing flavor, as *Crème de Menthe* (mint).

Creole

Originating in the Creole, i.e., mixed French and Spanish, cookery of New Orleans; used in referring to certain rice dishes, to a sauce containing tomatoes and green peppers, and also to sweet dishes with a chocolate covering.

Crêpe (Fr.)

A very thin, light pancake.

Crépinettes (Fr.)

A meat pasty or turnover made of sausage or other meat and, traditionally, wrapped in pig's caul and grilled.

Cress

See WATER CRESS and LAND CRESS.

Crevette (Fr.)

Shrimp.

Crimp

1. To indent or pinch together, as, for example, the edge of a pie crust with the thumb or tines of a fork in order to frill, flute, or pleat it.
2. Applied to fish, a process by which the sides of a freshly caught fish are gashed, the fish soaked thereafter in very cold water, and boiled.
3. In general, to make crisp.

Crisp

As a verb, to chill quickly, for example a vegetable such as lettuce, in order to make it firm and brittle.

Critten (Eng.)

A scrap of the very fat meat of pork, such as is used for making lard.

Croaker

Any of various fish, so named from the noises produced by the air bladder, and not highly regarded as food though some of them may be broiled or fried.

Croissant (Fr.)

A crescent-shaped roll.

Cromeskie (Rus.)

Minced meat wrapped in bacon, either dipped in batter or enclosed in a pastry crust, and fried. Also spelled *kromeskie*.

Crookneck Squash

A smooth, yellow summer squash whose shape is just what the name indicates. It may be cooked without peeling in a large variety of ways.

Croquant (Fr.)

A crisp, sweet, rich, almond cake; or, a gingerbread cooky.

Croquette (Fr.)

A ball or pyramid of minced meat, potatoes, etc., rolled in beaten egg and crumbs, and fried. Croquettes are usually of such a size that two or three make up an average serving.

Crosne (Fr.)

See ARTICHOKE, JAPANESE.

Croustade (Fr.)

A shell or case usually made by hollowing out bread to form a container which is then toasted and filled.

Croûte, en (Fr.)

Enclosed in a pastry shell or covered with a crust.

Crouton (Fr.)

A strip or cube of bread toasted or browned in melted butter and often flavored with garlic, cheese, or the like, to be served with soup or, occasionally, in a salad such as Caesar salad.

Crown Roast

A roast of lamb or pork cut from the rack, or rib, the mid-section in front of the loin. The roast is rolled, generally by a butcher, with the ribs binding it on the outside so that it does, in fact, resemble a crown.

Cruller

A sweet cake, generally made of dough cut in strips, two of which are twisted together and fried in deep fat.

Crumb

1. A very small bit or particle taken from a larger whole, usually a dry solid, as bread.
2. To dip or roll a food in crumbs until evenly covered.

Crumble

To break into small bits or pieces; said of a dry solid, such as bread, bacon, or the like.

Crumpet (Eng.)

A round, soft, flat, unsweetened tea or breakfast cake, pitted with many holes which allow it to absorb a great deal of butter when it is hot after toasting. Like the English muffin, crumpets are baked in individual rings on hot griddles.

Crush
To compress with considerable pressure so as to bruise, mash, or break into bits.

Crust
1. Any coating or covering, often of pastry.
2. A sediment of tartaric acid in wine, especially port, which adheres to the bottle. It is a sign of age and is not harmful, though care should be taken in decanting so that it does not come out.

Crystallization
To form into crystals, i.e., clear, transparent solid particles; often a term applied to sugar which has come out, or crystallized out, of a liquid or a semi-solid such as jelly. Sometimes a desirable condition, as in preserving fruit by impregnating with sugar and coating with sugar crystals. Also called sugaring.

Csipetke (Hung.)
Dumplings made of a very stiff dough and often served with goulash.

Cube
To cut into blocks or dice of medium size.

Cube Steak
A relatively thin steak cut from the sirloin tip or the top round and imprinted by heavy pressure with a pattern of small rectangles which breaks down some of the tough fibers and makes the meat more tender.

Cube Sugar
A fairly coarse sugar pressed into cubes, about half an inch square.

Cucumber Pickle
Cucumbers, whole or in slices, sometimes with dill or onions, marinated in salt water, boiled in vinegar to which sugar and spices are sometimes added, and packed in jars.

Cucuzza Squash
A light-green Italian squash.

Cullis
A soup or sauce made of meat, game, or fish stock with rice, lentils, panada, or some similar ingredient used as a thickening agent.

Cumberland Sauce (Eng.)
A cold sauce containing currant jelly, wine, and orange rind, to be served with game, especially venison.

Cumin
The dried seed of a small and delicate member of the parsley family. It is minute, yellow-brown, and shaped like a caraway seed, and has a strong, warm, bitter taste, also rather like caraway. Powdered cumin seed is much used in Indian cookery, especially in curry powder, and the whole seeds are an ingredient in much Oriental cookery, as well. In Mexico, chile con carne and similar dishes are flavored with *comino,* as it is called there. It is also frequently added to any rye or salty bread.

Cupboard
A closet or cabinet with shelves for dishes or food.

Curaçao (Hol.)

A liqueur originally made in Amsterdam with oranges brought from Dutch Guiana. It may be red, white, green, or orange in color, but always has the tang of the bitter-orange peel from which it is made.

Curd

A soft lump or mass formed in the process of coagulation or curdling, often of milk.

Curdle

To separate, or cause to separate, into curds, usually by heating, by overcooking, or by the addition of an acid.

Cure

A process by which meat, especially pork, or fish is preserved, for example, by smoking, by rubbing for some time with a salt and seasoning mixture, or by immersing in brine.

Curly Endive

A name sometimes given to chicory, which see. See also ENDIVE.

Currant

1. The small, dried, seedless grape, originally exported from Corinth, Greece, from which it takes its name.
2. A red, pale green, or black round berry, acid in taste, and the fruit of a shrub of the gooseberry family.

Curried

Denoting any dish of meat, poultry, fish, eggs, rice, or vegetables in which curry powder is used as a seasoning or in which curry flavors—turmeric, fenugreek, cumin, etc.—predominate.

Curry Powder

A mixture of powdered spices originated in India for use in cooking. As many as seventeen spices may be included to achieve a distinctive flavor which may be mild or hot. The name *curry* is from the Hindustani word *turcarri*.

Curry Sauce

A white sauce flavored with curry powder, used mainly with fish, poultry, and eggs.

Cush

A strange, old-fashioned soup, said to have been brought from England to America, and having as its ingredients fried mush or cornbread, onions, and milk.

Cusk

A salt-water fish related to the cod, whose meat is usually sold in fillets. It has a good flavor and texture and is prepared like fresh cod or haddock.

Custard

A dessert made of eggs and milk, sweetened and cooked, either by boiling, which produces a soft custard, or by baking, which produces a relatively firm one.

Custard Apple

An apple-like tropical American fruit, green or dark brown in color, with a soft, edible pulp which is sweet but insipid in flavor. Also called bullock's heart; the paw-paw (which see) is sometimes called a custard apple.

Custard Mould

See CHARLOTTE MOULD.

Cut

1. To separate into pieces with the blade of a knife or with scissors.
2. A portion removed from the whole, most often used in reference to meat.

Cut In

To combine, especially shortening and one or more dry ingredients, by using two knives or similar utensils, one in either hand, with a chopping motion.

Cutlet

Literally, a small rib (from the French word *cotelette*); used to refer to any small slice of meat from the leg or ribs, or to a croquette shaped like a chop or cutlet.

Cymling

Another name for summer or patty-pan squash.

Dab

1. A very small portion, i.e., a teaspoonful or less.
2. Flounder; specifically, one also called a sand dab, a good food fish from New England waters.

Dace

A small fresh-water fish.

Dagwood Sandwich

Any sandwich of large proportions and heterogeneous contents deriving its name from the comic-strip character whose nocturnal "snacks" consist of whatever happens to be in the refrigerator.

Dahi (Ind.)

Curds, or thickened sour milk, served with sugar as a sweet or eaten salted with rice.

Daikon (Jap.)

A giant white radish sometimes reaching three feet in length.

Dalken (Aus.)

Little tarts, usually jam-filled, baked in pans similar to those for poaching eggs, the rounded sides causing the edges to curve inward as they rise in baking.

Damascene

An inferior variety of damson plum; see following entry.

Damson Plum

The common purple plum, much used in cooking and having an amber-colored, firm, and juicy flesh.

Dandelion

Called a "tramp with a golden crown," the ubiquitous dandelion is a first cousin to chicory, endive, and lettuce. The young leaves make a fine addition to salad, and may also be cooked as a green. Italians are especially partial to dandelions in salad. The golden blossoms were once used to make wine, and the dried roots are often recommended as a remedy for a sluggish liver.

Danish Pastry

A sweet yeast bread or roll distinctive for its buttery richness.

Dap (Eng.)

An expression occasionally found in old recipes and apparently meaning to pat into shape with a bouncing motion of the hands.

Dariole (Fr.)
1. A small, plain, cylindrical, or nearly cylindrical, mould.
2. A cream-filled tart.

Darjeeling Tea
A black tea from India, often regarded as the finest and most delicately flavored of all.

Darne (Fr.)
A large slice, especially of salmon or some other large fish.

Dash
A small quantity; less than one-eighth of a teaspoonful.

Dasheen
A tuber of the taro plant with markings which resemble scars. Peeled after cooking, as the raw juice is an irritant to the skin, they are a greyish or violet hue.

Dashi (Jap.)
A popular seasoning sauce made with dried bonito and water. Fish, chicken, or beef bouillon are usable substitutes.

Daube (U.S., Creole)
A small beef roast, well larded, and cooked with seasonings as a pot roast; also, a large fish, or slices thereof.

Daube Froide (Fr.)
A stew of beef or mutton, wine, and seasonings, served chilled in its own jellied sauce.

Decant
To pour out, as, for example, wine from a bottle.

Deep-Fat-Fry
To cook in hot, gently bubbling fat which completely covers the food being so cooked or which is deep enough to allow the food to float.

Deep Sea Fillet
A commercial name applied indiscriminately to salted fillets of hake, cod, haddock, and other white fish.

Delaware Grape
A North American variety, originally wild but now cultivated in the East and next in importance to the Concord. Rather small and reddish in color, it has a good flavor and is used as a wine grape.

Delicious Apple
A good apple for eating raw or for use in salad, though its bland, sweet taste is too flat for cooking use. It is often dark red and is identifiable by the five bumps on its base. Its season, October to April, is longer than that of any other apple.

Delmonico Steak
A boneless chuck steak from the end of the loin; not as choice as porterhouse. It derives its name from a famous New York restaurant.

Demitasse (Fr.)
A small cup in which a strong, usually black coffee is served after dinner; or, the coffee itself.

Dente, Al (It.)
Medium well-done; cooked till tender enough to be cut with a fork, but rather chewy or bite-y. The term is used to describe a desirable quality in spaghetti or other pasta, which, ac-

cording to Italian taste, should be just slightly hard. *Dente* means tooth.

Denver Sandwich
A sandwich whose filling consists of eggs scrambled with bits of ham and, often, green pepper and onion. Also called a Western sandwich.

Derby Cake (Eng.)
A type of rolled cooky, containing currants, made in Derbyshire.

Devil
To season highly, usually with mustard, and invariably with pepper, often in the form of cayenne or tabasco sauce.

Devil-Doer
See GUARANA.

Deviled Sauce
A brown sauce containing shallots, white wine, and cayenne pepper, primarily for grilled fowl and left-over meat.

Devil's Food Cake
A rich, dark chocolate cake, usually made with sour milk or cream, and both baking powder and baking soda, and baked in two or more layers.

Devils on Horseback
See ANGELS ON HORSEBACK.

Devizes Pie (Eng.)
A cold meat pie made with layers of sliced cooked meat such as calf's head or lamb, with bacon, hard-boiled eggs and spices. A gravy or the jelly from the cooking of the calf's head is poured over it, and the whole is topped with crust.

Devon Cake (Eng.)
A little cake made of clotted cream, flour, egg, and sugar, and cut into any of various shapes and sizes.

Devonshire Cream (Eng.)
A very thick clotted cream, which in Devon, England, is served with strawberries, cake, and the like. It is made by allowing cream to rise on whole milk, which is then placed over an extremely low heat for an hour, and allowed to cool at least a day before the cream is removed.

Dewberry
A fruit resembling an elongated blackberry but having a different flavor, from a bush which, instead of growing upright, trails along the ground.

Dhall (Ind.)
Lentils, or occasionally, split peas, prepared with curry powder and, sometimes, onions.

Dice
To cut into very small blocks or cubes, usually about a quarter of an inch square. See CUBE.

Dijon Mustard
A fairly mild-flavored, brownish mustard containing vinegar, spices, and, usually, white wine, made in Dijon, France.

Dill
A tall, rather delicate-looking, but hardy herb native to the Mediterranean area. The stems are fairly strong in taste, but the fern-like leaves, while pungent, give a very pleasant flavoring to mild or sweet vegetables, fish, cheese, salads, and, of course, pickles. Also called dill weed.

Dill Pickles
Cucumbers, whole or in slices, soaked in fresh water overnight, and then scalded with a boiling solution of vinegar, salt, and water. A sprig of dill is added to each jar before sealing.

Dinner
The chief meal of the day, whether at midday or evening.

Diplomat Pudding
A pudding made of layers of ladyfingers dipped in Cognac or sherry, with jam between. The whole is sprinkled with liquor, weighted down, well chilled, and served with whipped cream.

Diplomat Sauce
A rich sauce containing cream, lobster, and truffles, and served with fish or shellfish.

Dish
1. A plate or bowl of china, porcelain, pewter, etc., in which food is served.
2. Any food preparation served in a dish.

Dissolve
To unite a solid with a liquid, usually by immersing it in liquid, with apparent loss of the individual identity of both solid and liquid; for example, a gelatin in hot water.

Ditali (It.)
Pasta in half-inch tubes about a quarter of an inch in diameter.

Ditalini (It.)
Small ditali, as in preceding entry; used in soups.

Dittany
See GAS-PLANT.

Divinity
A light candy, white or pastel-tinted, composed largely of sugar and egg white.

Dock
A coarse, bitter-flavored herb suitable for use as a pot-herb. The large dock family also includes sorrel and rhubarb.

Dolce (It.)
Any sweet, such as a dessert.

Dollarfish
A small, spiny-finned, smooth-scaled fish of the Atlantic coastal waters, having a narrow body, fat or oily meat, and a delicate flavor. Also called blenny, butterfish, and gunnel.

Dollop
A lump, spoonful, dab, etc., for example, of whipped cream.

Dolmas (Greece and Turkey)
Grapevine leaves folded around spoonfuls of a mixture of rice, minced onion, piñon nuts, mint, etc., and cooked slowly in layers in a large pot. Served cold with lemon as an appetizer. Also spelled *dolmadaka* or *dolmades*.

D.O.M.
The inscription appearing on all Bénédictine bottles, the abbreviation of a Latin phrase meaning, "To God most good, most great."

Domino Sugar
A fairly coarse sugar which has been pressed into rectangles, or domino shape.

Dop (S. Af.)
A brandy made from marc, which see.

Dopiaza Curry (Ind.)
A curry containing equal amounts of fried onions and ground onions, and made with more butter and less water than most curries. Also spelled *doh-peeazah.*

Doré (Fr.)
Glazed with a beaten whole egg or egg yolk. Pie crust is given a shiny golden finish in this way.

Dot
To distribute over a surface bits of some substance such as butter.

Double Acting Baking Powder
See BAKING POWDER.

Double Boiler
A double pot arrangement in which an upper pot, containing the food to be cooked, fits snugly down onto and slightly inside a lower pot, containing water whose heat or steam causes the food to be cooked.

Dough
A mixture of flour, or meal, and liquid, solid enough to be worked or handled.

Doughboy
Bread dough rolled quite thin, cut into a square or diamond, and fried in deep fat.

Doughnut
A ring-shaped, deep-fat-fried roll or small cake made of light, rich dough. Though the ring shape is character-istic, doughnuts may also be rectangu-lar, oval, or any of various other shapes. The dough may be cake-like or bread-like, and the doughnut may be plain, filled with jam or jelly, sugar-glazed, or iced. Also spelled donut.

Dovars Tea
A black tea from India used for blends because of its soft, mellow fla-vor when brewed.

Dove, Mock
A cabbage roll, i.e., a cooked cabbage leaf filled with any of various mix-tures such as ground meat, rice, and such, and simmered in a covering liquid.

Dover Beater
A patented device for beating eggs and whipping cream. Rapid, circular movement, by hand, of a side handle causes rotation of a wheel, which in turn causes rotaton of two interlock-ing sets of blades which, by their ac-tion, introduce air more rapidly and effectively into the food being whipped than a single fork or per-forated whisk could do.

Drachona (Rus.)
A cake-like dessert made with flour, milk, butter, eggs, and sugar.

Drain
To remove liquid by allowing it to run off.

Drambuie (Scot.)
A clear, pale brown, rather sweet li-queur made from Scotch whiskey, honey, and herbs.

Draw
To remove, as for example, the en-

trails from poultry, or the essence of tea by steeping; also, to clarify by melting.

Drawn Butter
The clear butter which separates after melting from the salt and paler, heavier curds. It is served as a sauce or is used as the basis of many other sauces. It is also much used in the cookery of India, where it is called *ghee*. Also called clarified butter.

Dredge
To cover with flour, sugar, etc., by sprinkling or by dipping the food into the substance with which it is to be covered.

Dress
1. To prepare for cooking by cleaning, trimming, etc.
2. Colloquially, to set and decorate a table.

Dressing
1. A sauce, especially one for a salad.
2. A stuffing for a fowl, fish, or roast.

Dried Beef
Lean beef cured by salting, smoking, and drying, and cut paper-thin. Dishes made with dried beef frequently need no further salting.

Drip Coffee
Coffee made in such a way that hot water passes once very slowly through ground coffee. Also called filtered coffee.

Drippings
Fat or juices which come out of meat in the process of cooking. Pan drippings are those caught in the cooking pan.

Drop Cooky
Any cooky whose uncooked dough is dropped by the spoonful onto a cooky sheet, rather than rolled and cut out.

Drupe Fruit (Eng.)
Any fleshy fruit with a seed or stone, for example, the peach, plum, or cherry.

Dry Mustard
Finely ground mustard seeds, a very pale yellow in color, and having a very intense mustard flavor. See PREPARED MUSTARD.

Dry Wine
Wine which contains a small proportion of sugar and thus is not sweet or heavy in its taste; it may be served during a meal. Also called *sec*, from the French word for dry.

Dry Yeast
A preparation of yeast with dry meal, which is lower in moisture content than compressed yeast and may easily be stored in any dry, cool place.

Duchess
Denoting potatoes prepared by mashing and then by adding to them some beaten egg yolks. Used for garnishing dishes such as steak.

Duchess Apple
A late summer variety, excellent baked or in pies.

Duff
An old term for dough, now applied to a stiff flour pudding either packed tightly into a bag and boiled, or, more often, steamed. Sailor's duff is made without fruit but with molasses, while plum duff is made with currants and raisins.

Duke Cherry

Any of several varieties, mainly grown for home rather than commercial use, having a light red color and a rather acid flavor.

Duk Sauce (Chin.)

A popular sauce, for which plum jam with chutney forms a fair substitute, served with dishes such as egg rolls.

Dulce (Sp.)

Granulated sugar and heavy cream cooked together until thick and stiff, and then poured into glasses. Mexican *panoche* is a coarser version.

Dulse

An edible seaweed, rich in iodine and common along almost all the coasts of the world. Almost unused nowadays in modern, commercialized countries, dulse was once used extensively in soups, stews, and as a treat for children. It is crisp, a little tough, brownish, and transparent when fresh, and is said to have a fine, distinctive flavor. It occurs in various forms around the world; see IRISH MOSS, LAVER, and SLOKE.

Dumpling

A ball of dough cooked by boiling, as in a stew or soup, or by steaming or baking, especially when it contains fruit or other filling. Dumplings are approximately round in shape and usually about an inch or two in diameter.

Dundee Cake (Scot.)

A simple cake made with currants and chopped candied peel, generally covered with almonds before baking and brushed over with orange syrup afterward.

Dungeness Crab

An excellently flavored crab from the West coast, often nine inches across and three pounds in weight.

Dunk

To dip doughtnuts, bread, etc., into coffee, milk, or the like while eating.

Durian

A large, East Indian fruit whose highly flavored, cream-colored pulp is covered by a spiny outer husk. When unripe, the fruit is cooked and eaten as a vegetable. It is said to have an odor offensive to those who encounter it for the first time. Rarely seen in American markets.

Durum Wheat

The hard wheat grown in North America, Southern Russia, and North Africa, which is particularly suitable for making into bread flour and also is the source of semolina, macaroni, and other forms of pasta.

Dust

As a verb, to cover lightly with a fine powder, such as flour or sugar.

Dust Tea

A grade of tea, either black or green, from India, Ceylon, or Java, inferior to the larger-leafed grades such as orange pekoe, pekoe, and souchong. The quality and flavor, however, vary with the kind of tea from which it is made.

Dutch Oven

A deep, heavy, covered pot, usually of cast iron or aluminum, with two short side handles. It is used for slow cooking of soups, stews, and the like.

Duxelle (Fr.)

A garnish or filling consisting of chopped onions, mushrooms, and seasonings.

Early Harvest Apple

A generally useful, yellow, autumn apple grown in the western and southwestern United States.

Earth Almond

See CHUFA.

Eau de Vie (Fr.)

Literally, "water of life." In practice, the name given any brandy or potable spirit, as *Eau de Vie de Framboise* (a spirit made with raspberries).

Eccles Cake (Eng.)

A cake made in Lancashire. A muffin or patty pan is lined with a rich crust, filled with a thin layer of golden syrup, currants, shredded coconut, almonds, etc., and topped with another crust.

Éclair (Fr.)

A light, bar-shaped pastry cake, filled with cream or custard and usually frosted with chocolate.

Écrevisse (Fr.)

The fresh-water crawfish (or crayfish).

Edam Cheese

Originally a Dutch cheese, now widely manufactured, having a smooth, solid texture and a mild, nut-like flavor. It is usually ball-shaped and coated with bright red paraffin.

Eel

A snake-like fish having a smooth shiny skin rather than scales and fat or oily meat. Eels figure more commonly in English and Continental cookery than in that of the United States. Smoked eel is considered especially delicious.

Eggfruit

The fruit of a West Indian tree, small and olive-shaped, orange in color, and decayed in appearance when ripe. Too sweet for eating raw, it makes good jams and jellies.

Eggnog

A drink made with milk or cream, raw eggs, spices, and, often, brandy, rum, or whiskey.

Eggplant

A large, egg-shaped, dark purple, sleek-skinned fruit used as a vegetable and so named because the fruit of one species is white.

Egg Roll

Authentic Chinese egg-roll batter is made of a mixture of water chestnut and wheat flour, cooked, but not browned, in the form of small pancakes, which are then filled with a minced mixture of bamboo shoots, roast pork, onions, etc., and fried in deep fat till they start to turn golden. They are then removed, cooled, and fried again until light brown in color.

Eglantine

A lovely old-fashioned rose whose petals are usable in cookery and whose hips, the fleshy swollen flower base that encloses the seeds, are valuable for their vitamin content. Also called sweetbrier. See ROSE.

Elberta Peach

The outstanding commercially grown freestone type, large, yellow with rose tinges, sweet, and juicy.

Elderberry

A common wild berry, smooth-skinned and deep purple in color, used in jams, jellies, pies, and once, with the blossoms, in a homemade wine. Many legends are attached to this tree: that a special spirit protected it; that Judas hanged himself on it; and that it was the tree upon which Christ was crucified.

Elecampane

An old-fashioned, rather bitter herb once grown for its root which was used to flavor certain candies and conserves.

Election Cake

A cake popular in the nineteenth century made of bread dough, butter, brown sugar, sour milk, raisins, figs, and spices. Also called Hartford election cake.

Elementary Preparations

See MISE-EN-PLACE.

El Mistouf (N. Af.)

Sweet couscous steamed and then flavored with ground pistachio nuts, almonds, currants, and orange rind. The whole is then sprinkled with softened chopped dates.

Elver

The young eel, about two inches in length and a transparent amber color. It may be fried in deep fat or, in quantity, packed into loaf form and steamed.

Émincé (Fr.)

Cut into thin slices; used as a noun, a meat hash.

Emmenthaler Cheese (Switz.)

The original Swiss cheese, having a somewhat hard texture, a mild, nutlike flavor, and perforated by large holes.

Empanada (Mex. and S. Am.)

A rather elaborate turnover with a spicy crust and a filling of chopped fruit, peas, peaches, chives, tomatoes, and chopped meat, baked in a hot oven.

Emrelettes (Fr.)

Peeled seedless grapes tinted green, flavored with crème de menthe, and used for garnishing.

En (Fr.)

In; for example, *en casserole, en croûte, en cocotte,* etc.

Enamelware

Metal or pottery which has been overlaid with a hard, glassy substance, which, in cooking utensils, is often white or blue, with a trim in some other color.

Enchilada (Mex.)

A tortilla dipped in a hot sauce, lightly fried, folded around a filling of meat, chorizo, cheese, etc., and topped with more sauce and grated cheese.

Endive

A leafy plant used in salads and as a vegetable. That known as French or Belgian endive, Witloof chicory, or often simply endive is grown in the dark and produces a pale-green or creamy white, tapering, closely packed head most used as a cooked vegetable. When grown in the open, the same plant is known as escarole or Batavian endive and has broad, flat leaves, much darker in color, and curled at the tips. The dark-green salad plant with somewhat curly leaves known as curly endive is actually chicory, a different, though closely related plant.

English Breakfast
See CONTINENTAL BREAKFAST.

English Breakfast Tea
A blend of China black teas, having a strong, fine aroma without bitterness.

English Monkey
A variation of Welsh rabbit, usually with egg and bread crumbs added to the cheese sauce.

English Muffin
A flattened, yeast-raised, unsweetened cake either allowed to rise in muffin ring or cut from rolled-out dough and baked on a griddle. Broken open, toasted, and buttered, it is eaten at tea or breakfast.

English Mustard
One of the hottest and sharpest of mustards, often consisting of dry powdered mustard seed mixed with a little vinegar or water and salt. Use with caution!

Enriched Flour
Flour which has had the bran and germ removed to make it white, but to which have been added various nutritional elements to compensate for the loss.

Entire Wheat
A term for whole wheat, often used in old recipes.

Entrecôte (Fr.)
The middle cut of sirloin steak or the rib of beef.

Entrée (Fr.)
In formal usage, a dish served between main courses of a dinner, for example, between the fish and the roast; less formally, any dish other than a roast served as a main course.

Entremets (Fr.)
A sweet course; hence, ordinarily, a dessert.

Epigramme (Fr.)
A small, boned cut or fillet, usually of poultry.

Escabecia (Sp.)
A dish made of partridges in a very highly seasoned sauce.

Escalope (Fr.)
A small, thin slice of meat or fish.

Escarole
See ENDIVE.

Espagnole Sauce (Fr.)
A brown sauce made with tomatoes.

Espresso Coffee (It.)
Strong coffee made in a special sort of pot or urn constructed so that boiling water is forced upward through specially roasted coffee into an upper section from which it is poured. Also spelled expresso coffee.

Estofado (Mex.)
A stew of beef, vinegar, red wine, spices, and, usually, vegetables.

Estouffade (Fr.)
1. Meat cooked in a covered casserole with very little liquid.
2. Another name for *fonds brun*, or brown stock.

Estragon (Fr.)
The French word for tarragon.

Étamine (Fr.)
A cloth or sieve through which to strain soups or sauces. In England called a tammy-cloth.

Evaporated Milk
Unsweetened canned milk thickened by evaporation. See CONDENSED MILK.

Everlasting Cake
A simple, old-fashioned cake flavored with almonds and citron. It is partially baked in flat rectangular pans, sliced, and then returned to the oven to finish baking. The slices, stored in a tightly closed tin box, will keep a year or more.

Expresso Coffee
See ESPRESSO COFFEE.

Extract
A preparation containing in concentrated form the flavor, color, or food value of the substance from which it has been made.

Eye of the Round Roast
A cut from the center of the round, i.e., the rear portion of beef just below the rump. It should be cooked long and slowly as a pot roast.

Faarikal (Scan.)
A dish of braised lamb and cabbage, with sour cream sometimes added just before serving.

Faggot (Eng.)
1. A small bundle, such as of herbs.
2. A baked meat loaf.

False Breadfruit
A fruit having a flavor resembling a combination of pineapple and banana. Also called ceriman.

Fameuse Apple
An apple good for eating raw or for making up into jelly, and in season October through December. Also called the Snow apple.

Famous Scholar's Abandon
The fanciful name for a Chinese dish consisting of bits of pork sausage and chicken cooked together as the meat course of a typical dinner.

Fan (Chin.)
Rice.

Farce (Fr.)
A forcemeat used for pies or stuffing.

Farci (Fr.)
Stuffed with forcemeat or some other filling.

Farfalletta (pl. *farfallette*; It.)
A decorative pasta in the shape of little bows; literally, little butterflies, and thus called by that name in English.

Farfel (Jew.)
Flour-and-egg noodles chopped into small bits and then boiled, generally in a soup.

Farina
A flour or meal made from wheat; also, a starch obtained from nuts, roots, or other similar source.

Farle (Scot.)
A quarter of a bannock in which the division has been marked before baking; also, a small scone. See also IRISH SODA BREAD.

Farm Cheese
The French equivalent of cottage cheese; also called, in French, *mou* cheese, or *ferme,* meaning soft.

Fat
Chemically, any of various organic compounds of glycerin with acid, such as are found in the tissues of animals and plants; thus, any substance largely or entirely made up of these compounds, for example, butter, lard, vegetable oils, margarine, suet, chicken fat, etc. See also VEGETABLE OIL and SHORTENING.

Fat Back of Pork
A cut from the back of the hog where the fat is concentrated, once used a great deal in southern cooking, but now generally converted into salt pork.

Fattigmand (Swed.)
A refrigerator cooky containing ground cardamom, brandy, and heavy cream. The dough is rolled thin and cut in diamond shapes. A slit is made in the center of each diamond and one corner is pulled through it. It is then fried in deep fat and dredged in confectioner's sugar.

Fava Bean
Another name for the broad bean, popular in England and becoming better known in the United States. *Fava* is the Italian word for bean.

Fave Dei Morti (It.)
Small candies, literally "beans of the dead," traditionally given to Italian children on November 2, All Souls' Day, or Day of the Dead, and made of almond paste, sugar, etc., rolled, cut out, and shaped to resemble beans.

Feathery
Very light, airy, flaky, and delicate.

Fecula
Pure starch, used for thickening, and often from such food plants as the potato or manioc rather than from a cereal grain.

Fell
The thin, tough, papery skin or membrane covering the outside of a leg of lamb; literally, the hide.

Fennel
A lovely herb with dark green, fernlike leaves and yellow flowers. The flavor is mildly reminiscent of licorice, and both stems and leaves are used in sauces, soups, salads, and as a garnish. Blanched, the stems are eaten raw; or cooked, like celery or Belgian endive.

Fenugreek
An Asiatic herb whose seeds have a bitter, distinctive, celery-like odor. It is an ingredient of good curry powders and, interestingly enough, is also used commercially to give candy a maple flavor. Its name derives from two Greek words meaning "Greek hay."

Fermentation

A chemical change brought about by the action of yeasts, such as occurs in the souring of milk, the conversion of grape juice into wine, of malt into beer, or of wine or cider into vinegar, and also in the leavening of yeast-raised dough; thus often a desirable process, though undesirable in many other cases, where a food is rendered unpalatable and is thus said to be "spoiled."

Fermière, à la (Fr.)

Farmhouse style, i.e., fresh, simply prepared, or garnished with young vegetables.

Fetticus

See LAMB'S LETTUCE.

Fettuccini (It.)

Small, bowknot-shaped noodles or pasta.

Feuilleté (Fr.)

An adjective describing a kind of puff pastry made in flaky layers by repeated folding and rolling; also, sometimes applied to an appetizer made from this pastry in an oval or round shape.

Fiddlehead Fern

A fern which, when young, has a tightly curled frond which is eaten fresh in northern Maine, where it grows, and is sometimes available canned elsewhere. Cooked like broccoli, it has a flavor resembling a cross between asparagus and mushroom.

Field Salad

See LAMB'S LETTUCE.

Figaro Sauce (Fr.)

A sauce for cold fish or poultry, made of mayonnaise mixed with a little tomato purèe.

Filbert

A European hazlenut, having a fringed husk longer than that of the North American variety.

Filé (U.S., Creole)

A powder made of young sassafras leaves; a commonly used seasoning in Creole cookery.

Filet Mignon

A small, thick fillet from the loin of beef. A cut prized for its tenderness and richness, though other steaks may be more flavorful.

Filled Cheese

Any cheese resembling Cheddar from which the butterfat has been removed, and another fat added during the processing. This practice is illegal in the United States.

Fillet

A boneless slice or strip of fish or meat. Also spelled *filet*.

Filtered Coffee

See DRIP COFFEE.

Fines Herbes (Fr.)

A combination of herbs, for example, onion or chives, parsley, chervil, and tarragon, used to flavor salads, omelets, etc.

Finnan Haddie (Scot.)

Cured and smoked haddock. Legend says the original came from the little fishing village of Findhorn in Scotland, hence the name.

Finocchio (It.)
The Italian word for fennel; also called Florentine fennel.

Firm Ball
In candy-making, the stage at which the syrup will form a firm ball when a bit is dropped into very cold water.

Fish and Chips (Eng.)
Deep-fat-fried fish fillets and potatoes cut in short, broad strips. Long a dietary standby of workmen who took them away wrapped in newspapers from the small shops or stands where they were sold.

Fizz
Any effervescent drink.

Flageolet (Eng.)
A variety of green bean.

Flake
As a verb, to break a food down into small, flat, thin, scale-like pieces.

Flaky
Denoting a texture such that the food so described breaks easily into thin, scale-like pieces, rather than, for example, into crumbs.

Flambé (Fr.)
Prepared by flaming, i.e., by pouring a warmed liquor, such as brandy, over a food, igniting, and serving while still alight.

Flame
See preceding entry.

Flan
In Spain, a burnt-sugar custard served with a flaming brandy sauce. Elsewhere, a name applied to a variety of custards, one made in a pastry shell, another with jellied fruit, etc.

Flank Steak
A triangular cut from the underside of beef, below the loin. To be good, the cut should be thin and made on the diagonal. Another name for this steak is London broil.

Flannel Cake (U.S., East.)
A pancake; specifically, a thin, tender griddle cake made with yeast.

Flan Ring
A narrow metal band, held by a clamp in a circular or rectangular form. It is set on a metal sheet, such as a cooky sheet, when the pastry shell for one kind of flan is to be baked in it.

Flapjack (U.S., North. and West.)
A pancake.

Flatfish
Any of a group of fish including flounder, halibut, turbot, and sole, which are flattened from side to side rather than from back to belly, and whose eyes are both on the upper side. The meat is generally lean, dry, and tasty.

Flead Cake (Eng.)
Flead, another name for flear or leaf lard, is used with flour and water to make small pastries. The mixture is also used for the crust of meat pies and turnovers.

Flear (Eng.)
Leaf lard.

Flensje (Hol.)
A very thin pancake spread with jam.

Flip
Originally, a sweetened mixture containing beer, wine, and rum, which was heated by plunging a red-hot poker into it. Today's flip is more often chilled, but both old and modern recipes frequently call for the inclusion of well-beaten eggs.

Flitch
A whole side of bacon.

Floating Island
A custard topped with whipped cream, or with puffs of meringue which have been cooked till firm in scalding milk.

Florentine
An adjective denoting various dishes containing, or garnished with, spinach, usually chopped fine or puréed; also, other dishes such as Florentine meringue either actually or supposedly typical of Florence, Italy.

Florentine Fennel
See FENNEL.

Flounder
Any flatfish, especially winter flounder or summer flounder (called plaice). Taken at one to five pounds, the meat is white and delicious.

Flour
To cover a food with, or roll it in, flour.

Fluke
Another name for flatfish, especially flounder.

Flummery (Eng.)
A dish of slightly fermented oatmeal boiled and served with cream or milk. Also, nowadays, a flavored pudding made with unfermented oatmeal or rice and served as a dessert; or, a fancy custard. Sometimes, though erroneously, called frumenty, which see.

Flute
To make a series of short indentations or channels, for example, around the edge of a pie crust. Also called crimping.

Foie Gras (Fr.)
Literally, fat liver; usually refers to goose liver, as in *pâté de foie gras,* which see.

Fold In
To combine ingredients by cutting down through the mixture with a spoon or fork on one side of the bowl, turning the utensil across the bottom, and bringing it up and over the top, just under the surface. The whole operation is repeated slowly, evenly, and gently, until the ingredients are thoroughly combined.

Folkestone Pudding Pie (Eng.)
A pudding of ground rice and currants baked in a small pan lined with a rich crust. These pudding pies are made in Kent, especially in Folkestone on the south coast.

Folly (Eng.)
Another name for "fool," which see.

Fondant
A plain, smooth, creamy candy, used for centers, coatings, icing, etc. From a French word which means "melting."

Fond de Cuisine (Fr.)
A basic stock sauce.

Fonds Brun (Fr.)
Brown stock; see STOCK.

Fondue
1. (Switz.) A hot dish made of melted cheese and wine, into which pieces of bread are dipped and eaten with the fingers. A baked version includes eggs and bread crumbs.
2. (Fr.) A vegetable reduced to a pulpy state by cooking.
3. (Eng.) Toasted or melted cheese.

Fool
A dessert consisting of sweetened fruit pulp mixed with whipped or plain cream or custard and served chilled. Gooseberry fool is particularly well known. The name is, perhaps, from the French *fouler,* to crush or press.

Foo Yong (Chin.)
Eggs combined with typical Chinese vegetables such as water chestnuts, bean sprouts, and bamboo shoots cooked like an omelet but browned on both sides rather than only one. Meat or fish may sometimes be added.

Forbidden Fruit (U.S.)
An American liqueur made from brandy and grapefruit.

Forcemeat
Meat or poultry reduced almost to a paste by pounding or grinding. Sometimes a binder is added. See PANADE and MOUSSELINE FORCEMEAT.

Formosa Black Tea
A standard black tea, i.e., one made from fermented leaves.

Formosa Oolong Tea
A partially fermented tea with a fine flavor and fragrance. Its varieties are known by district names and are sometimes used in blends with Gunpowder and Japan green teas.

Forno, Al (It.)
Baked or roasted; from the word for oven.

Fouettée Sauce (Fr.)
A foaming sauce of egg yolks, wine, and sugar.

Fou-Tou (Af.)
Boiled yams, peeled, pounded, and seasoned with salt and pepper, red pepper, and nutmeg.

Fowl
1. A stewing chicken a year or more old and weighing from three to six pounds or more.
2. Any bird whose meat is used for food.

Foxiness (Eng.)
A term sometimes used to describe the assertive aroma of American wines in contrast to the flowery, more discreet bouquet of European wines.

Foyot Sauce
A kind of béarnaise sauce with meat glaze added; the name is taken from that of a noted Paris restaurant.

Fraise (Fr.)
1. The strawberry.
2. Said to be an old name for omelet, perhaps from the fact that one meaning of the similar-appearing *frais* is "new-laid," and refers to eggs.

Framboise (Fr.)

The raspberry; also, a liqueur made with raspberries and known as *Eau de Vie de Framboise*.

Franconia

Applied to potatoes browned whole with a roast of meat.

Frangipan

A cream or custard made of flour, eggs, butter, and boiled milk. It is often flavored with almonds, and is used for filling éclairs, and as a topping for tarts. Sometimes it is sweet, sometimes not, depending upon its use. Also spelled *frangipane* or *frangipani*.

Frappé (Fr.)

An ice or sherbet frozen to the consistency of a mush.

Fraxinella

See GAS-PLANT.

Freestone Peach

Any peach whose flesh does not cling to the stone.

Freeze

To reduce the temperature of a food so drastically that the liquid particles are more or less totally congealed into ice; a process used to preserve food from decay. See CHILL.

French

1. To remove bone and fat, especially from a chop, or simply to remove fat and bare the end of the bone.
2. To cut in long, thin strips, usually referring to green beans sliced lengthwise.

French Bean

A green or string bean picked very young and tender; also, any green or string bean sliced lengthwise, as preceding entry notes.

French Bread

A yeast-raised bread made from a dough in which water rather than milk is used, and notable for its thick, crisp, well-browned crust. It is most often shaped in long, slim loaves with tapered ends.

French Dressing

A classic dressing for salads, made with salad or olive oil, vinegar, salt, and pepper.

French Endive

See ENDIVE.

French-Fry

To cook in hot fat deep enough to float the food to be cooked.

French Knife

A knife having a wide, rather thick blade which tapers from the handle to a sharply pointed tip; used for chopping or slicing. Also called a chef's knife.

French Toast

Slices of bread dipped in a mixture of eggs, sugar, and milk, and fried.

French Vinegar

A name sometimes designating white or distilled vinegar, although the vinegar used in France is wine vinegar.

Fricadelle (Fr.)

A ball or flat cake of meat, often made with egg yolks and crumbs as a binder. Technically, a hamburger is a kind of fricadelle.

Fricandeau (Fr.)
A larded cut of veal, usually from the rump or shoulder, cooked with vegetables in a covered casserole.

Fricassee
A dish consisting of pieces of poultry or meat stewed in a thick gravy.

Frijoles (Mex.)
Beans, usually of a red variety. A staple of the Mexican diet, they are cooked and served in a wide variety of ways.

Frijoles Refritos (Mex.)
Red beans cooked with salt, garlic, oil, and tomatoes, lightly fried, then mashed and refried. This is a typical Mexican dish.

Frill
1. To gather, pleat, crimp, or flute.
2. Part of the internal portion of a cod; old recipes suggest cooking it like the sounds or milt.

Fritter
A small batter cake fried in deep fat; also, a fruit, vegetable, or fish cut into small pieces and mixed, or covered, with batter and either sautéed or fried in deep fat.

Fritto (It.)
Fried.

Fritto Misto (It.)
Literally, "fried mixture"; i.e., pieces of meat or vegetables dipped individually into batter and fried in deep fat.

Frizzle
To cook on an ungreased or lightly greased skillet until crisp and curled at the edges. Often applied to dried beef or bacon.

Fromage (Fr.)
Cheese.

Frost
1. To decorate a cake with icing, so that it appears, when the icing is white as was once almost invariably the case, to be covered with frost.
2. To chill glasses, etc., rapidly, so that freezing moisture adheres to their outer surfaces.

Frühstück Cheese
A German or American cheese of the Limburger type, round and about three inches in diameter, meant to be eaten at breakfast (from which it derives its name, "break fast" in German), or lunch.

Fruit Cake
A cake which may be either light in color, i.e., made without molasses, or dark, i.e., made with molasses or, occasionally, chocolate. In either case, the cake contains a variety of currants, raisins, dates, candied peels, nutmeats, spices, and sometimes wine or brandy. Fruit cakes are frequently steamed as well as baked, and several hours are required to cook them completely. They keep well, and are often made several weeks ahead of the time they will be eaten, usually Thanksgiving and Christmas, and sealed in airtight containers to ripen.

Frumenty
A pudding somewhat resembling

flummery, but made with wheat rather than oatmeal. Also spelled furmenty.

Fry

1. To cook gently in hot, bubbling fat either in an amount sufficient only to cover the food one-third to one-half of the way up, or in deep fat, i.e., covering the food completely or allowing it to float.
2. To cook a fat meat, for example, bacon, in a skillet until the solid fat has been more or less completely liquefied.
3. A name given to the entrails or internal organs of animals. See LAMB'S FRY and PIG'S FRY.

Fryer

A chicken between three and a half and five months old, weighing from two to four pounds and suitable for frying.

Fudge

A soft, creamy candy, usually containing chocolate and, frequently, nutmeats.

Fumet (Fr.)

A fish, game, or meat stock.

Funny Cake (U.S., Pa. Dutch)

A cake batter and sauce baked in a pie pan with the sauce forming a layer underneath the cake.

Furmenty

See FRUMENTY.

Fusilli (It.)

A spiral or curly spaghetti.

Gage (Eng.)

Designating a type of plum which is almost spherical in shape and which has a small, circular stone. The greengage is the best-known example.

Gai See Chow Mein (Chin.)

Chow mein with chicken. As with so many Chinese terms which must be transliterated into English, there are various spellings, "gai," for example, is given also as "kai," "guy," and "chi." See CHOW MEIN.

Galantine (Fr.)

Meat, especially white meat, boned and chopped, spiced, tied, boiled, and served cold.

Galette (Fr.)

Any of various round cakes made of dough or pastry. Once, a very simple cake popular with the gamins, artists, and poorer people of Paris.

Galette, Pâte à (Fr.)

A very rich, sweet pastry.

Galuptze (Rus.)

Chopped meat rolled in cabbage leaves; a small dumpling, a specialty of the Ukraine.

Game Fish

Any fish sought primarily or partly for sport, for example, bass, trout, pike, or muskie. Many game fish are also good food fish.

Gammelost Cheese (Scan.)

A soft, brownish cheese made of sour milk and having a mild, sweetish taste. Opinion varies on its worth, but those who favor it recommend it as a spread or dessert cheese.

Gammon

Either a ham or a flitch of bacon which has been cured by salting and smoking.

Garbanzo (S. Am.)

See CHICK-PEA.

Garbure (Fr.)

A thick vegetable soup or hodge-podge.

Garlic

The bulb of a plant with tall, flattened, greyish-green leaves and delicate white flowers which form a head. The bulb is composed of sections, called cloves or toes, each of which is covered by a thin, white or pinkish skin, and which cluster tightly together enclosed in a white, paper-like outer skin. The cloves are peeled and used individually, whole, chopped, or grated. The flavor is onion-like, but much more pungent. It is pleasing when used with discretion, as in rubbing a salad bowl, in tomato dishes, with roast lamb, or in pickles, to mention a few of many uses. Eastern Mongolia, not Italy, is said to be the true home of garlic.

Garnish

To decorate or ornament.

Gaspar Clam

Another name for the soft clam.

Gas-Plant

A bushy Eurasian herb, related to the citrus plants, and once valued for its flavor, suggestive of lemon with a dash of almond and vanilla. It is so named as its flowers exude a heavy, volatile oil which will catch fire if a flame is held nearby. Also called burning bush, fraxinella, and dittany.

Gâteau (Fr.)

A cake, especially a rich, elaborately decorated one.

Gaufre (Fr.)

A wafer or light cooky; or a waffle.

Gaufre à la Flamande (Belg.)

Flemish waffles, made with yeast, cream, and brandy, and served with sugar.

Gaufrette (Fr.)

A little gaufre; i.e., a small, thin wafer used in desserts and for garnishing.

Gazpacho (Sp.)

A famous thick soup made primarily of cucumbers and tomatoes and flavored with garlic, other ingredients being oil, vinegar, onions, and bread, all mashed and sieved together and served very cold.

Gefuellte Fish (Jew.)

Balls of ground and pounded fish, carp, whitefish, etc., often including the heads and bones, with onions, soaked bread, egg, and seasonings, cooked in a fish broth with carrot strips, and served chilled with the jelled broth and slices of carrot, or baked, sometimes with a tomato sauce, and served hot. Also spelled *gefüllte* and *gefillte*.

Gelatin

A thickening agent for cooked fruits, aspics, and jellies, sold in powdered form, which, when mixed with a liquid and cooled, solidifies into a transparent jelly. It consists of purified protein obtained by boiling animal bones and tissues or from plants. Also spelled gelatine.

Gem
A type of muffin, generally not yeast-raised, baked in a gem-pan or gem-iron very much like the present-day muffin pan. The muffin as it is known today is more like the nineteenth-century "gem," than it is like the nineteenth-century "muffin," which was yeast-raised and baked in a ring on a griddle, as is the English muffin. The term "gem" is very seldom used nowadays; for example, no recipes for gems are given in the 1961 *Fannie Farmer Cookbook* though more than a dozen muffin recipes are included.

Genevoise Sauce (Fr.)
A meatless red wine sauce, made with fish stock.

Genipap
A greenish-white fruit, about the size of a small orange, native to the West Indies and South America, and having a purple juice and a slightly acid flavor. Its use is confined to marmalades and jams.

Genoa Sauce (Fr.)
A cold sauce seasoned with a paste of pistachio and piñon nuts and made like mayonnaise, to be served with cold fish.

Geodock
See GWEDUC.

Geranium
A plant which in its common form has a pungent, not unpleasant odor not associated, however, with culinary use; several other varieties have aromas which make their leaves suitable for use in teas, custards, drinks, jellies, and with fruit. The best-known of these is rose geranium, which has a delicate rose flavor. Others likewise named for their fragrance are apple, balm, camphor-rose, lemon-scented, nutmeg, orange, peppermint, and spicy geraniums.

German Mustard
A coarse-textured, brownish, rather hot mustard.

German Potato Salad
Potato salad without celery or hard-boiled eggs in which bits of bacon and hot bacon fat substitute for the usual mayonnaise dressing.

German Sauce
A frothy sweet sauce made of eggs, powdered sugar, Marsala, and lemon juice, heated and well beaten together.

Ghee (Ind.)
Clarified butter.

Gherkin
The small, soft, knobby fruit of a species of cucumber native to the West Indies, though now grown elsewhere, which is pickled, as cucumbers are. Immature garden cucumbers are sometimes also called gherkins.

Giblets
The heart, liver, and gizzard of poultry. The term may also include such parts as the neck, the feet, and, occasionally, the tips of the wings.

Ginger
The root of a tropical or semi-tropical herb, which is used dried and

powdered, crystallized, preserved in syrup, or fresh. While only the powdered form is much used in Western cookery, the whole root is used to flavor ginger ale and ginger beer. Gingerbread and gingersnaps are two of the most popular products using this spice, and it always appears in the long-time Christmas favorite, gingerbread men. It is excellent as a seasoning for apples and most stewed fruit, and often accompanies cloves, cinnamon, and nutmeg in pies, cakes, and cookies. Its unique, hot aroma and taste have been famous since ancient times, and, though the best ginger comes from Jamaica, other good grades are also produced widely in Africa and India.

Gingerbread

A dark, spicy, cake-like bread in which the flavor of ginger, along with that of molasses, is predominant. In former times in Europe, gingerbread was baked in fancy moulds, elaborately decorated, and used as a Christmas cake.

Gingersnap

A fairly thin, brittle molasses cooky spiced with ginger and almost invariably round in shape.

Gingko Nut

The seed of the foul-smelling yellow fruit of an Oriental tree. The nut is thin-skinned, sweet, and agreeable in taste. Generally eaten roasted, it is also used in various Oriental dishes.

Ginseng

A Chinese herb, which also grows in Canada and the eastern United States, and which has an oval root which is most used as a medicine.

Girdle (Eng.)

A variant name for a griddle, or frying pan. Thus, girdle cakes are the equivalent of griddle cakes.

Gjetost Cheese (Scan.)

A hard or semi-hard cheese made from goat's milk; it is considered the "national" cheese of Norway. Also spelled *gietost*.

Glacé (Fr.)

1. Having a smooth, shiny surface.
2. Covered with a sugar syrup icing, for example, candied fruits.
3. Frozen or iced.

Glaze

1. To give a shiny surface to meat, vegetables, etc., by coating them with caramel, meat juice, or transparent jelly.
2. A reduced brown stock obtained from meat, poultry, or fish.

Glögg (Swed.)

A hot New Year's drink made of almonds, raisins, cloves, whole cardamoms, and cinnamon marinated in wine for a week beforehand. When it is to be served, more wine and cognac are added and the drink is heated.

Gloucester Cheese (Eng.)

A mild cheese somewhat resembling Cheddar.

Glucose Syrup

An uncrystallizable syrup made by the incomplete conversion of starch into glucose, a sugar occurring naturally as dextrose and only about half as sweet as cane sugar.

Gluten

A naturally grey, sticky, nutritious substance in wheat. Gluten bread is made from a flour rich in gluten.

Gnocchi (It.)

A kind of dumpling made of farina, potatoes, or flour, rolled into rope-like strips about three-quarters of an inch thick, and cut into pieces three-quarters of an inch long. Usually gnocchi are served with Parmesan cheese.

Godcake (Eng.)

A triangular tart made in Coventry in former times for the New Year's day feast. It was sometimes very small, sometimes very large, and the shell of puff paste enclosed a filling of sugar, currants, butter, and spices.

Godiveau (Fr.)

A kind of veal forcemeat.

Goeduck

See GWEDUC.

Gofio (Sp.)

A staple food of the Canary Islands made of corn meal cooked with milk and used in many ways. Also sometimes spelled *gofro*.

Gohbi (Ind.)

See KOBI.

Golden Bass

A general name used in California markets for cabrilla and grouper, both small relatives of the California black sea bass.

Golden Buck

Welsh rabbit topped with a poached egg.

Golden Moons on a Silver Sea

The fanciful name for soup with pigeon's eggs, said to be the opening course of a fairly ordinary Chinese dinner.

Goldenrod

Refers to any dish topped with hard-boiled egg yolks put through a sieve.

Golden Syrup

A mixture of corn syrup and the syrups remaining after sugar is refined.

Goldwasser (Ger.)

A rather spectacular colorless liqueur containing particles of gold leaf which settle on the bottom but which rise into the liqueur and flash and sparkle when the bottle is shaken. It is quite strong and the fine taste of orange and anise is not at all affected by the presence of the gold leaf.

Goober

Another name for the peanut.

Gopher

The Southern name for a tortoise, i.e., land turtle, found in high sandy areas and pine woods. It is used mostly in stew.

Gorgonzola Cheese (It.)

A cheese resembling Roquefort in that it is creamy white, blue-veined, crumbly, and pungent.

Gouda Cheese (Hol.)

A variety of Edam; a smooth, solid, mild-flavored cheese in a red paraffin coating.

Goulash (Hung.)
A stew of beef or veal, vegetables, and seasonings, which, when made in its home country, also contains sauerkraut, paprika, and sour cream. Also spelled *gulyas.*

Goumi Berry (Orient)
A wild, reddish-orange fruit, a relative of the buffalo berry, having a pleasant, tart flavor which makes it suitable for use in preserves, though not for eating raw. In China and Japan it is used in many sauces, pies, etc., while in the eastern United States it is grown primarily as a decorative shrub.

Gourmet Powder
An alternate name for monosodium glutamate or ajinomoto.

Graham Flour
Another name for whole wheat flour.

Grains of Paradise
A name appearing in the recipes of a century ago, or more, and referring either to mignonnette pepper, or, in some cases, to cardamom.

Granadilla
A large, egg-shaped fruit growing on a vine related to the passion flower. The acid pulp is cooked as a vegetable while green, or, when ripened, it may be eaten raw or used in marmalade.

Grand-Marnier (Fr.)
A French liqueur, orange-flavored, rich, and golden brown in color, made from choice, aged Cognac.

Grand-Veneur Sauce (Fr.)
A brown sauce made with crushed peppercorns, red currant jelly, and cream, to accompany venison.

Granité (Fr.)
A thin fruit syrup frozen to the granular stage and resembling sherbet.

Granular Yeast
A dry yeast which keeps well without refrigeration.

Granulated Sugar
A much-refined white sugar which may be, however, either quite fine-grained or relatively coarse.

Grappa (It.)
An Italian brandy made from marc, i.e., the skins, pips, etc., of grapes.

Grate
To rub a solid food such as cheese or lettuce over a roughly punctured metal surface which allows bits or shreds to pass through the punctures to the other side.

Gratin, Au (Fr.)
Having a browned crust of bread or cracker crumbs, butter, etc. Grated cheese, while not an essential ingredient of this crust, is so often used that we have come to think of a dish *au gratin* as one necessarily topped with cheese.

Gravenstein Apple
A western apple, in season from July to September, of a greenish color distinctively streaked with red. May be used for eating raw, in applesauce, or in pies.

Gravy
A sauce for meat, especially one using the pan drippings as a portion of the

liquid. Gravy may be either clear or opaque, brown or white, depending upon the ingredients and the manner of preparation.

Grease
As a verb, to cover, as the inside of a pan, with a thin coating of oil or fat.

Grecque, à la (Fr.)
In the Greek manner; usually applied to vegetables cooked in oil and vinegar with seasonings.

Green Bean
A bean with a green pod eaten when it is young and tender. The mature bean itself is the kidney bean and is used dried.

Green Cheese
Another name for sage cheese, a Cheddar type either made with fresh sage or colored green and flavored with sage extract.

Greengage Plum
The prize dessert plum, if it is fully tree-ripened. It is then plump, greenish-yellow, and very sweet. See GAGE.

Green Herbs
Those herbs best used fresh, for example, chives, parsley, and mint.

Greening Apple
A green-skinned apple generally available and good for pies, applesauce, and other cooking purposes.

Greens
A cooked leafy vegetable such as spinach, dandelion, mustard, kale, collard, etc. See also SALAD GREENS.

Green Sauce
Mayonnaise seasoned with spices and tinted green with herb juice. Used with cold fish and shellfish.

Green Tea
A kind of tea made without fermenting of the leaves. It is chiefly from China and Japan, and is available in several varieties.

Grenadin (Fr.)
1. A small piece of meat, such as a small veal cutlet.
2. A fricassee.

Grenadine (Fr.)
A sweet, thick syrup made from pomegranates and used in flavoring many beverages.

Grey Salt
See SEA SALT.

Gribiche Sauce (Fr.)
A sauce made with olive oil base and hard-boiled eggs, mustard, and green herbs, to accompany cold fish.

Griddle
A heavy, shallow, or totally sideless pan, usually having a handle, though a handleless griddle frequently forms part of the top of a modern range. It is generally used with little or no grease, and cooking on it is correctly spoken of as "baking" rather than "frying."

Griddle Cake
A cake made by pouring a very thin batter onto a griddle or frying pan and browning it on both sides; often called a pancake. Also, more loosely, any cake baked on a griddle, whether

made of a thin batter or of a dough which is rolled out and cut into rounds prior to baking.

Gridiron
An iron grate used for broiling; also, in older usage, a griddle.

Griglia, Alla (It.)
Broiled or grilled.

Grill
As a verb, another term for broil; or for a dish so prepared, as a mixed grill. Or, a gridiron.

Grimes Golden Apple
An attractive golden-yellow apple; good for eating raw, or for use in general cooking. It is in season from October to January.

Grind
To reduce food to a very fine, almost pulverized, consistency.

Grits (U.S., South.)
Very coarsely ground corn, usually white, to which water or milk is added for slow cooking, often in the top of a double boiler. The word is related to the term "groats," and both are derived from an old word for fragment.

Groats
Hulled and sometimes crushed grain, especially oats. See preceding entry for derivation.

Groom's Cake
A cake made with a batter containing chopped almonds and well-beaten eggs alternated in the baking pan with a raisin and citron mixture. See BRIDE'S CAKE.

Ground Beef
Unless otherwise specified, meat from the plate, i.e., the lower section, of the beef.

Ground Cherry
The round, cherry-like fruit of a plant common to the lower Mississippi Valley. It is used in jams and preserves, and left in its husk will keep through the winter. Other names are winter cherry and strawberry tomato.

Groundnut
1. Another name for the peanut.
2. The tuberous root of either of two New England plants, both having a pleasant, nutty flavor, and both edible either raw or cooked. Much used by the Indians.

Grouper
A food fish similar to the sea bass, generally sold at a weight of from five to fifteen pounds.

Gruau
Sometimes used as the culinary term for husked grains such as pearl barley.

Gruel
A thin porridge, often made with oatmeal, and given to children and invalids.

Gru-Gru
See PALM CABBAGE.

Grunion
A small, delicate, flavorful fish common to the waters of the West coast and noted for its unique habit of climbing out onto the shore to lay its eggs in holes in the sand. When this event occurs, it is said that "the grun-

ion are running," and attempts to catch the fish while they are on the sand is called "grunion gathering."

Grunt (U.S. and Can.)
A dessert of berries, cherries, or peaches brought to a boil with cinnamon and sugar, topped with biscuit dough, covered tightly, and cooked over a low flame. When made with apples, this same dish is usually called slump.

Gruyère Cheese (Fr.)
A cheese made in France by the same process as Swiss cheese and having a similar flavor but smaller holes, sometimes none at all. See EMMENTHALER.

Guacamole (Mex.)
A salad, garnish, or cocktail dip made of avocado mashed together with onion juice, lemon juice, Tabasco sauce, pimento, etc.

Guanábana (Sp.)
A fruit used in ices or conserves, but rarely found in American markets. Also called soursop.

Guaraná (Brazil)
A plant whose seeds contain a high proportion of caffeine and thus are used as a substitute for coffee.

Guava
The round, yellow fruit of a tropical American tree, about the size of a small apple, and having a skin which may be either rough or smooth. The pinkish flesh is rather granular and filled with small seeds, but its taste, when cooked, is pleasant and distinctive, and it is used in jellies and jams.

Gugelhupf (Aus.)
A yeast-raised cake, often containing raisins and currants, which is baked in a fluted pan lined with almonds, and eaten with coffee. It is also popular in Germany.

Guinea Fowl
A small wild or domestic bird whose meat has a gamy, pleasant flavor, and a rather dry texture. Guinea hen is especially favored, and, generally speaking, may be prepared in any way suitable for a chicken.

Guinea Golden Apple
A winter apple which is best when baked.

Gulyas (Hung.)
See GOULASH.

Gumbo
1. Another name for okra.
2. A soup made in the South, thickened with okra and usually containing tomatoes.

Gunnel
See DOLLARFISH.

Gunpowder Tea
A green tea prepared by a method which produces a fine- to medium-sized, round, rolled leaf. Country green, Hoochow, and the poorer Pingsuey are gunpowder teas.

Gweduc
A very large clam, whose name, variously spelled, is pronounced "gooeyduck," native to the West coast. It has an excellent flavor but is not available commercially.

Hackberry
The small, sweet fruit of an American tree, resembling the elm, which is used in jam and jelly.

Haddock
A fish resembling the cod in having an elongated, soft-finned body and dry or lean meat, but smaller in size, usually weighing only two and a half to three pounds.

Haggerty (Eng.)
A dish of sliced potatoes, onions, and grated cheese, fried and then browned lightly under a broiler.

Haggis (Scot.)
A very famous dish whose merits are debated. It is made of the grated liver, heart, and lungs of a sheep combined with oatmeal, suet, and seasonings, stuffed into a pig's or a sheep's stomach, and boiled.

Hair Sieve
A sieve having small holes.

Hake
A relative of the cod, found in both the Atlantic and Pacific. It is large, elongated, and quite sharp-nosed, and has lean or dry meat.

Hale Peach
A standard variety of freestone peach having a very good flavor and yellow flesh.

Half-Glaze
A basic sauce made of brown stock, reduced by boiling, with sherry added.

Halibut
The largest of the flatfish, ordinarily caught at a weight of fifty to one hundred pounds. It has dry or lean flesh with deposits of fat which yield the much-used oil. It is usually sold in steaks or sometimes in fillets.

Hallaca (Venez.)
A turnover or small meat pie made of a corn meal dough with a filling of onion, suet, pimento, minced meat, raisins, olives, and seasonings.

Halva (Turkey and India)
A confection made with syrup, honey, butter, raisins, almonds, sesame seeds and various other ingredients heated together and then poured into moulds to harden. Cinnamon and cardamom are often added. Also spelled *halwa* and *halvah*.

Hamanabe (Jap.)
A dish resembling sukiyaki, but made with oysters or clams rather than beef.

Hamantashen (Jew.)
Sweet, yeast-raised turnovers filled with poppy seed or prune butter, or some other filling. Supposedly named for Haman, an enemy of the Jewish people. Also spelled *Hammentashen*.

Ham Hock
The portion of the front leg of a pig between the foot and the ham.

Hand Cheese
A soft, sharp, pungent cheese made from sour milk, often with caraway seeds added, and shaped by hand.

Handy Pudding (Eng.)
A nineteenth-century recipe describes this pudding as much like a roly-poly, but having sweetened lemon or orange pulp and juice as its filling.

Hangtown Fry

Usually, scrambled eggs into which oysters are mixed, although there are variations.

Hard Ball

Candy syrup at the point in cooking at which it forms a ball, pliable yet hard enough to hold its shape, when a bit of syrup is dropped into very cold water.

Hard Clam

Another name for the quahog.

Hard Crack

Candy syrup at the point in cooking at which it spins into hard, brittle threads when a bit of syrup is dropped into very cold water.

Hard Sauce

A sauce of creamed butter and either granulated or confectioner's sugar, with a flavoring of rum, brandy, or vanilla. The sauce is not cooked, but is chilled before use, so that it becomes fairly hard, hence the name. It is often served with fruit cake or plum pudding.

Hardtack

The hard biscuit eaten on shipboard in earlier days, and also called pilot bread or biscuit and ship's bread.

Hard Wheat

Wheat having a very hard grain and yielding a flour rich in gluten. See BREAD FLOUR.

Haricot

1. A ragout or stew, usually of mutton.
2. (Fr.) A kidney bean; a green bean is called *haricot vert*.

Harlequin

A name sometimes given to ice cream consisting of several flavors so frozen together as to give a ribbon effect. Also called Neapolitan.

Hartford Election Cake

See ELECTION CAKE.

Hartshorn

Another name for baking ammonia, a powerful leavening agent much used in baking in the nineteenth century. Still sometimes used by bakers, it may be purchased in the form of crystals which have to be totally dissolved before use.

Harvard Beets

Cooked beets, sliced or cubed and steeped in a hot mixture of sugar, vinegar, and water.

Hasenpfeffer (Ger.)

Jugged hare, to which sour cream is often added at the end of the cooking. Stewed fruit and toast usually accompany it.

Hash

A dish of chopped or diced cooked meat, potatoes, onions, pan drippings, etc., baked, or cooked on top of the range. Hash is generally made from leftover meat.

Hashed Brown Potatoes

Boiled potatoes cut up or diced very small and cooked in a little butter in a covered pan. They are turned once, or folded over like an omelet.

Haslet (Eng.)

The chopped edible entrails of a pig or other animal seasoned with herbs and spices and baked in individual cakes.

Hasty Pudding (U.S., New Eng.)
An old-fashioned American dish consisting of corn meal cooked in boiling salted water (nowadays in a double boiler) until the mixture thickens. It is served with maple sugar and butter. A European version is a thin, sweetened oatmeal porridge.

Havercake
An oatcake.

Hazel Hen
A small European wild fowl, common in Russian cookery. It is very plump-breasted, and is cooked like quail.

Hazelnut
A tasty, grape-sized nut with a smooth shell, which grows enclosed within a fuzzy outer husk. Those sold commercially are called filberts and come from a tree of European origin; but there are some native American species.

Head Cheese
A potted meat dish made from the head of a hog, thoroughly cleaned and simmered till the meat falls from the bones, after which it is drained, shredded, seasoned with salt, pepper, and sage, packed tightly in a bowl, and heavily weighted. It is allowed to chill for several days, and thus becomes highly compressed and ready for slicing. It is generally eaten as a snack with crackers.

Head Lettuce
Another name, and the more correct one, for the so-called iceberg lettuce, a variety having firm, crisp, pale green or white leaves, closely packed to form a solid, almost round head. The shape and crispness of the leaves make them suitable for serving under salads.

Health Food
See ORGANIC FOOD.

Heart of Palm
See PALM CABBAGE.

Heavy Cream
Cream with a high butterfat content and a thick consistency.

Herb Bunch
A small bunch of herbs, usually parsley, bay, and thyme.

Herb Juice
The extracted juice of herbs, for example, of parsley, chervil, tarragon, and chives.

Herb Mustard
A prepared mustard containing herbs.

Herb Sauce
According to *The Escoffier Cook Book*, a white wine sauce with shallot butter, parsley, chervil, etc., served with fish. In practice, any sauce containing herbs.

Herb Vinegar
Wine vinegar to which any of various herbs have been added.

Herkimer County Cheese (U.S.)
An aged Cheddar, made in New York State.

Hermit
A cooky containing brown sugar, chopped nuts, raisins, and several spices and either dropped onto a cooky sheet, or, more usually, cut in squares after baking.

Herring
A soft-finned, narrow-bodied, fork-tailed fish, quite abundant in the North Atlantic and caught in great numbers for its tasty, fat meat.

Hervido (Venez.)
A soup-like stew of meat and vegetables including peas in their pods, cabbage, and corn.

High Tea (Eng.)
See TEA.

Hip
The fleshy, swollen, red seed capsule of any of various roses, but especially of the wild rose. It has been found to be rich in Vitamin C, and is used to make a kind of jelly.

Hodge-Podge (Scot.)
See HOTCH-POTCH.

Hoecake (U.S., South.)
A simple bread made of corn meal and water and originally baked on a hoe in front of an open fire, or in the ashes.

Hogmaw, Maryland Stuffed
A dish resembling the Scottish haggis in its preparation, being made with a hog's stomach which is cleaned, scraped, and stuffed with a mixture of dried bread, onions, potatoes, sausage meat, and seasonings. The stomach is then sewed up and baked in a tightly covered pan containing a little water.

Hog Pudding
See BLACK PUDDING.

Hollandaise Sauce (Fr.)
A sauce of egg yolks, cream, lemon juice, and butter to be used with vegetables, fish, or eggs. It is very tricky to prepare and does not keep well, so it should be made just before it is to be used, and served immediately.

Homard (Fr.)
The lobster.

Home Fried Potatoes
Cooked potatoes sliced and fried with seasonings.

Hominy
1. Whole hulled kernels of white or yellow corn expanded by boiling.
2. Hulled corn kernels coarsely ground or crushed, and boiled.

Homogenized Milk
Whole milk which has been so treated that the cream will not rise to the top, but will remain in solution.

Honey
1. The sweet nectar collected by bees from blossoms and stored in the honeycomb.
2. A name sometimes used for a sweet fruit butter, as, for example, "apricot honey."

Honeydew Melon
A globular melon with a creamy yellow rind, usually quite smooth, but sometimes netted. The ripe flesh is sweet, succulent, of a melting texture, and a pale green color.

Hoochow Tea
A green tea from China, often prepared in the Gunpowder, or fine- to medium-sized, rolled-leaf style. The brew is light in flavor and of a pleasing color.

Hopping John (U.S., South.)

A New Year's day dish of dried cow-peas, salt pork, and rice, eaten in keeping with the superstition that eating cowpeas on New Year's will insure good luck for the rest of the year.

Horehound

An herb of the mint family, native to Europe and North America, with fuzzy, wrinkled, grey-green, oval leaves, and little, tubular, white flowers. It is pleasantly and distinctively bitter in taste, and is used to flavor a hard, brittle candy called by the same name. The crushed leaves and juice used in its preparation are also sometimes used in sweet dishes, sauces, hot drinks, cookies, etc., and horehound honey is much favored by gourmets.

Horn

An abbreviated name for the horn-of-plenty, or cornucopia, made of puff paste and filled with whipped cream or custard.

Hors d'Oeuvre (Fr.)

Any hot or cold appetizer other than one placed on toast or cracker. See CANAPÉ.

Horse Mackerel

See TUNNY.

Horseradish

The pungent root of a tall, coarse member of the mustard family, which, grated or scraped, and often creamed, is used as a sharp-flavored condiment, often with meat, and especially with roast beef.

Hoska (Eur.)

A sweet bread containing almonds and raisins, baked in the form of two or three braids placed on top of each other.

Hotch-Potch (Scot.)

A soup or stew made with diced mutton and any vegetables which are in season, such as carrots, turnips, peas, etc., also diced. Also called hodge-podge.

Hot Cross Bun

A sweet, yeast-raised bun containing raisins and citron and marked with a cross in white icing. Traditionally eaten in England on Good Friday, or, in the United States, throughout the Lenten season.

Hot Pot (Eng.)

Slices of mutton or beef with potatoes and other vegetables placed in a deep, tightly covered pot and either simmered for some time on top of the stove, or, preferably, cooked in an oven. Several regions are known for their variations of this hot pot, one of the more popular being that from Lancashire.

Howtowdie (Scot.)

Boiled chicken served with spinach and a poached egg.

Hubbard Squash

A large winter variety, often weighing five pounds, which may usually be bought by the piece. Its rough skin is dark green touched with orange, and is pared off if the squash is to be cooked and mashed, or left on if it is to be baked. The consistency of the meat is rather like that of a sweet potato.

Huckleberry
An edible, shiny, black or dark-blue berry, darker and more acid than the blueberry, but about the same size, and closely related to it. Also known as the whortleberry, and, in Europe, the bilberry.

Huffkin (Eng.)
A very light crumpet which originated in Kent, England, and derived its name from the fact that it was eaten so hot that one had to "huff" on it to cool it.

Huish Cake (Wales)
A cake made of flour, sugar, eggs, and shortening, but distinguished by its use of ground rice.

Hull
An external covering, often dry; also, the act of removing this covering. To "hull" corn, however, is to remove the grains from the ear.

Humble Pie
See UMBLES.

Humita (Chile)
A tamale with a filling of grated fresh corn, pepper, and onions.

Hungarian Sauce
A velouté sauce with white wine, onions, herbs, and paprika, which gives it a pink tinge. Served with lamb, veal, eggs, poultry, or fish.

Huntingdon Pudding (Eng.)
A steamed suet pudding made with gooseberries and served with a sweet sauce, originating in Huntingdonshire in the East Midlands.

Hush Puppy (U.S., South. and East.)
A fritter of corn meal and chopped onion, cooked in the fat left after the frying of fish. The name supposedly is derived from the need to appease the appetite of hungry dogs that hung around riverbank fish-fries. Balls of corn meal batter were fried, and thrown to them with the command, "Hush, puppy!"

Husk
The dry, outer envelope or covering of certain fruits, corn, etc.; also, to remove this covering.

Hussar Toast
Stale bread, fried, sprinkled with salt, and rubbed with a clove of garlic.

Hutspot (U.S., Mich. "Little Holland")
Onions, carrots, and potatoes, diced, cooked together, and then mashed with milk and butter.

Hydrogenated Fat
An oil or soft fat solidified by charging with hydrogen.

Hydromel
A mixture of honey, herbs, spices, and water, which in ancient days was fermented to produce mead.

Hyson Tea
A kind of China green tea having a pungent, light flavor, and so prepared that the leaves have a twisted or curly appearance.

Hyssop
A rather bushy member of the mint family, whose long, slender, dark-green leaves and blue flower spikes are used in Europe as a seasoning for

sausages, fish, game, salads, and, occasionally, fruit pies.

I'A Lawalu (Haw. and Poly.)
Fresh fish, cleaned, seasoned, wrapped in ti leaves or parchment, and baked.

Ice
1. A dessert consisting of sweetened and flavored crushed ice, especially one containing little or no milk.
2. See FROST.

Iceberg Lettuce
See HEAD LETTUCE.

Icebox Pudding
A dessert made by lining a bowl with sponge cake, lady fingers, or the like, over which a sweetened and flavored filling is poured, or alternated in layers with the cake, after which the whole is chilled for several hours.

Ice Cream Salt
A coarse rock salt used to chill the mixture in making homemade ice cream, although occasional recipes also call for the use of this salt as an ingredient.

Icicle Pickle
A lengthwise strip cut from a large cucumber and scalded with boiling water, vinegar, and salt after being packed upright in a jar. These pickles must be ripened for six weeks before use.

Icing
Frosting.

Icing Sugar
Powdered or confectioner's sugar.

Imbottiti (It.)
Stuffed; the more frequently used term, however, is *ripieno*.

Imbu (S. Am.)
A pale yellow fruit resembling a ripe greengage plum. The soft juicy pulp tastes like that of an orange and may be eaten raw or used in jelly.

Imperial Tea
Green tea prepared by a method which yields a large, round, rolled-up leaf.

Incanestrato Cheese (It.)
A very sharp, white, hard, Sicilian cheese generally grated for use.

Indian Corn
Corn meal; occasionally old recipes call for "ground Indian corn."

Indian Cress
Nasturtium.

Indian Meal
Another name for corn meal.

Indian Pickle
An alternate name for piccalilli.

Indian Pudding (U.S., New Eng.)
An old-fashioned pudding made of corn meal, which was either boiled, with molasses, suet, and spices, or baked, without these ingredients.

India Tea
Any of several varieties of tea produced in India, most of them black, named according to the district in which they are grown, such as Darjeeling (the finest), Assam, Travancore, etc., and further identified with the

name of the estate or garden within the district. They are also graded according to leaf size, for example, orange pekoe, pekoe, and souchong.

Infuse

To steep in a liquid in order to extract soluble properties such as flavor and color. Thus, a liquid which has derived its flavor and color from something steeped in it is called an infusion.

Ingram Apple

An apple exclusively for use in cooking and in season from January to May.

Iodized Salt

Salt to which a minute quantity of iodine has been added, a type often recommended for use by those who do not eat seafood, the more natural source of the tiny amount of iodine needed for the proper functioning of the body.

Irish Delight

A sort of blancmange, chilled and cut into blocks which are rolled in egg and bread crumbs and fried in very hot fat. Sometimes, for a savory, salt, pepper, and cheese, rather than vanilla and sugar, are used as flavoring.

Irish Moss

An edible seaweed common along the Irish coast, where it is also called carrageen or dulse. It is used as a gelatin base in several desserts; in one of these it is boiled with milk, sugar, and lemon juice to make a sort of custard. The same name is also applied to the dessert so made.

Irish Rabbit or Rarebit

Cheese with gherkins, mustard, pepper, and salt, chopped together until they are almost a paste, and then broiled briefly on toast.

Irish Rock

A dessert candy made with butter, sugar, ground sweet and bitter almonds, and brandy, pounded to a paste, formed into egg shapes, and piled high to form a pyramid which is decorated with slivered almonds, crystallized greengages, or preserved green fruits.

Irish Soda Bread

A bread leavened with soda, sometimes flavored with caraway seeds and raisins, shaped into a round loaf, and baked on a griddle, in which case it is called a soda farl, or in an oven. It is served cut into triangles.

Ironware

Cooking utensils made of cast iron. Although naturally black, they are often finished with a colored glaze.

Isinglass

A gelatin obtained from the swimming bladder of certain fish and ordinarily sold in the form of thin, almost transparent sheets. It has now been almost entirely replaced by commercial gelatins.

Italian Bean

The broad or fava bean, which in Italy is usually cooked with a little garlic and oil.

Italian Ham

A ham cured by salting and drying, which may be eaten without further cooking and whose production is, therefore, carefully regulated. Thin slices are a popular antipasto. *Prosciutto* is the Italian name.

Italian Onion
A large, mild onion with a purple or reddish-purple skin, often used in salads as the purple color of the rings is quite decorative.

Italian Paste
Any of various products made from semolina, including macaroni, spaghetti, etc., but not noodles or any other such product made with eggs.

Italian Prune Plum
A small, purplish-black, juicy plum with a thin, tough skin and a faintly aromatic, yellow pulp; it is excellent either cooked or raw.

Italian Sauce
Any of various sauces made with tomatoes.

Italian Squash
See ZUCCHINI.

Ivory Sauce (Fr.)
A cream sauce tinted ivory by adding a pale meat glaze; to be served with poultry. Also called Albufera sauce.

Jack Cheese (U.S.)
A cheese of the Cheddar type, usually of a pale ivory color, originally made at Monterey, California, and sometimes called Monterey Jack.

Jackfruit (Ind.)
An enormous, yellow-pulped fruit, often weighing forty or more pounds, and similar to breadfruit. In Asia, the entire fruit is made use of, either raw or cooked, in a variety of dishes.

Jade Growing Out of Coral
Cabbage shoots on crab roe; the romanticized name of a dish said to be a typical third course in a Chinese dinner.

Jaffa Orange
A fine, seedless orange much favored as a dessert fruit in Europe.

Jagger
See PASTRY JAGGER.

Jaggery
A coarse, dark, East Indian sugar made from the sap of the coconut palm.

Jam
Whole fruit, such as berries, cherries, peaches, etc., slightly crushed and boiled with sugar to a thick consistency. Generally the fruit is more broken down than it is in a preserve.

Jamaica Pepper
An alternate name for allspice.

Jambalaya (U.S., Creole)
A rice dish containing bits of ham, shrimps, or oysters, with tomatoes, garlic, and various other seasonings.

Jan in die Sak (Un. of S. Af.)
A boiled pudding made with raisins, currants, etc.; the name means, literally, "John in the bag."

Japan Black Tea
A black tea produced in Japan; most Japanese teas, however, are green.

Japanese Crab
See KING CRAB.

Japanese Gelatin
An alternate name for agar-agar.

Japanese Oyster
A giant oyster, so big it could not possibly be eaten on the half shell. Originally from Japan, it has now been planted along the West coast.

Japan Green Tea
Any of various unfermented teas named for the style of preparation and also by the district in which they are produced.

Jar-Cooked Method of Canning
Two methods of putting up fruit and vegetables, both of which involve boiling or steaming of the jar containing the product. In the cold pack method, used for fruit and tomatoes, the product is put cold into a sterilized jar and boiling water or syrup is poured over it, after which the jar is boiled or steamed. In the hot pack method, the product is pre-cooked briefly and packed hot in a sterilized jar, which is then either boiled or steamed in a pressure cooker.

Jardinière, à la (Fr.)
Containing or garnished with vegetables; literally, "in the manner of the gardener."

Java Tea
Any of several black teas named after the estates which produce them, generally of medium strength and a reasonably good flavor.

Jeff Davis Pie (U.S., South.)
A plain custard pie.

Jell
To cause a liquid to become a solid, often one of a tender, quivering consistency, usually by adding gelatin or pectin and allowing it to set.

Jelly
A solid, more or less transparent preparation with a soft, bouncy nature, characteristic of gelatin; often refers to a compound of boiled fruit juice and sugar, solidified by pectin.

Jelly Roll
A kind of sponge cake baked quickly in a special, shallow pan about ten inches by fifteen inches, and then removed, spread with jelly, rolled into a cylinder, cooled, and sliced for serving.

Jerked Beef
Beef preserved by being sliced into strips and dried in the sun or before a fire. This method was much used in pioneering days, especially as the beef so prepared would keep very well and was easy to take on long treks through the wilderness.

Jewfish
A salt-water fish related to the sea bass, common in Florida coastal waters, and valued more as a game fish than for food.

Jing Gai (Chin.)
A steamed custard containing chicken and various seasonings.

Johnny Cake
A crisp bread made of corn meal, water or milk, salt, and, sometimes, an egg. Also called journey cake, possibly, it is conjectured, because it kept

well and could be taken as provision on trips.

Joint (Eng.)
The main, or meat course of an ordinary meal, or the fifth course of a formal dinner, i.e., that preceded by hors d'oeuvre, soup, fish, and entrée; so named from the fact that it usually comprised an entire joint of beef or mutton.

Joinville Sauce (Fr.)
A fish sauce made with shrimp and crayfish butter.

Jonathan Apple
A bright red apple in season throughout the United States from late autumn until February. It is fine raw or cooked.

Jordan Almond
The finest cultivated almond, from Malaga, Spain, especially favored for salting, sugar coating, etc. Next in preference is the Valencia almond.

Journey Cake
See JOHNNY CAKE.

Juane Mange (Hol.)
A dessert made with eggs, gelatin, lemon, and wine.

Jug (Eng.)
To stew for a long time in a tightly covered pot, usually in a liquid containing vinegar, wine, and herbs.

Jugged Hare
A hare, i.e., a near relative of the rabbit, cooked in the manner described in the preceding entry.

Jujube
A European shrub whose fruit is used in making candy, or the candy itself; also, any of several bite-sized, chewy candies resembling it.

Jule Kaga (Scan.)
A sweet, yeast-raised Christmas bread.

Jules Verne
A garnish of small braised turnips and potatoes, often stuffed, and mushrooms.

Julienne (Fr.)
Vegetables cut into long, match-like strips and used for a garnish, often in a clear soup; also, such a soup itself. The term may sometimes be applied to meat and vegetables cut into such strips and served other than as a garnish.

Jumbles
Small cakes or cookies containing grated citrus rind, dropped onto a cooky sheet and baked till crisp and golden brown; also, a rolled cooky often cut, or formed, in an "S" shape.

Juneberry
See SERVICEBERRY.

Juniper Berry
The small, round, dark-colored fruit of the juniper, an evergreen shrub or tree. Juniper berries and/or their juice are used to flavor gin, and also the liquid for basting goose, lamb, and the like, especially in French cooking.

Junket
A soft, milk dessert, sweetened and often fruit-flavored, which is coagulated with rennet.

Jus, Au (Fr.)
With its juice; usually referring to sliced roast meat, especially beef, served in this way.

Ju Yook Chop Suey
Chop suey made with pork. In this, as in many terms transliterated from the Chinese, variations in spelling occur. For example, "ju" may appear as "tsu" and "chu," while "yook" is frequently spelled "yuk."

Kabob (Turk.)
See KEBAB.

Kaffir Bread
A flour-like foodstuff obtained from the pith of various South African plants.

Kaiser-Schmarn (Aus.)
A cake made of flour, cream, and eggs and cooked in an omelet pan, in which it is turned over instead of being folded over, until it is brown on both sides. It is then removed from the pan and pulled into pieces, which are sprinkled with sugar for serving. Also spelled *Kaiser Schmarren*.

Kale
A green vegetable of the cabbage tribe, with ruffled leaves of a dark blue-green color.

Kalua Puaa (Haw. and Poly.)
Whole roast pig; the pig is stuffed with hot stones and buried in an underground pit, or oven, called an *imu*.

Kanten
An alternate name for agar-agar.

Karaage (Jap.)
See AGEMONO.

Kasha (Rus. and Jew.)
1. Buckwheat groats.
2. A simple dish made of buckwheat flour, fried lightly, and then cooked with water and seasonings in a covered pot; strips of meat may be added just before serving. Kasha is used in many other recipes. It is also spelled *kascha* or *kasza*.

Kasseler Rippespeer (Ger.)
Two pork chops flattened and made into a kind of sandwich with a filling of cooked prunes, apples, and seasonings, dipped in bread crumbs, and fried.

Katsuobushi (Jap.)
Dried bonito. See DASHI.

Kebab (Turk.)
A cube or small piece of beef, lamb, or some other meat, broiled or roasted on a skewer. Also spelled *kabob* or, occasionally, *cabob*, and called *shish kebab*, which see.

Kedgeree (Anglo-Ind.)
In Indian cookery, a dish of rice, lentils, eggs, onions and the like, while in European, and especially English and Scottish cookery, a similar dish made with fish, and a favorite for breakfast. Also spelled *kitchari*.

Keema (Ind.)
A curry made with minced meat and a variety of other ingredients such as shredded cabbage, tomatoes, and onions.

Kefir (Indo-European)
A liquor made from milk fermented by the action of bacteria or fungi, similar to kumiss.

Keiffer Pear
An oval, yellow pear with flesh that is sweet but rather granular, and thus better cooked than raw.

Kentucky Burgoo
See BURGOO.

Kentucky Ham
A ham cured somewhat like Virginia ham (which see), but from a fine hog such as the Hampshire, which is first allowed to feed wild and then is grain-fed.

Kernel
A euphemistic name for the kidney or testicle, as of a cock or a lamb. Also, a pit or seed.

Ketchup
See CATSUP.

Khari Moorghi (Ind.)
A curry made with chicken and various other ingredients.

Khoa (Ind.)
Sour milk curds, drained, mixed with sugar, and fried in butter.

Kibbe (Syria)
See KOBBE.

Kidney Bean
The kidney-shaped seed of the string or green bean, which, when mature, is dark red and large. It is generally used dried.

King, à la
Applied to chicken, etc., served with a rich cream sauce usually containing mushrooms and pimentos.

King Apple
A winter, or late ripening, apple suitable for baking.

King Crab
1. A gigantic crab from Alaska which is shipped to the United States either fresh or frozen. It sometimes measures over six feet from claw tip to claw tip, and is superb eating. A land crab, it was known before World War II as the Japanese crab, and at that time was only imported canned.
2. A name sometimes given the horseshoe, or casserole, crab, so called because of the shape of its shell, and common along the Atlantic and Gulf coasts. This is not a true crab and has little or no culinary use.

King David Apple
An apple for eating raw or for using in general cooking, in season during October and November.

Kingfish
A large game fish, sometimes weighing seventy-five pounds, caught off Florida and in the Gulf of Mexico during the season which lasts from November to March. The meat has a pleasantly distinctive flavor.

Kipfel (Aus.)
A raised, crescent-shaped roll said to have been first made by a Viennese pastry cook in the seventeenth century, after the victory over the Turks.

Kipper
To cure fish by splitting open, cleaning, salting, drying, smoking, or preserving in oil or sauce. Fish so pre-

pared, chiefly herring, are called "kippers."

Kirsch Sauce

Correctly, a sauce flavored with Kirschwasser, but in practice, sometimes a sweet cream sauce flavored with lemon.

Kirschwasser or Kirsch (Ger.)

A potent liquor distilled from the fermented juice of cherries; originally made in Germany, and especially in the Black Forest, it is now also made in Switzerland and other parts of Europe.

Kishke (Jew.)

A boiled pudding made with matzo meal, onions, flour, seasonings, and chicken fat, and served with meat or poultry. Traditionally, it was boiled in a beef casing and then finished off by baking. Also called stuffed derma.

Klops (Ger.)

A meatball or patty.

Kloss (Ger.)

A dumpling; meat, fish, or poultry may be added to the basic ingredients of rice, potatoes, eggs, etc.

Klotzki (Rus.)

Little balls, or dumplings, made of pasta with chopped ham and shallots, or with chopped apples, etc. They are cooked in soup, or poached and served as an accompaniment to it.

Knaidlach (Jew.)

Little ball dumplings, sometimes plain and sometimes containing cheese, potatoes, or sugar. They are cooked in either soup or boiling water, and are served in soup, with meat, or as a dessert. Also spelled *kneidlach*.

Knead

To work and press with the palms and heels of the hands, turning up and over a small portion after each outward-from-the-center push. Especially applied to the preparation of bread dough.

Knee-Action Knife

A narrow knife about six to eight inches in length which resembles a large sewing needle, in so far as the blades form an "eye," the cutting edges being on the inside. Rather than cutting into or through a food, this knife is used in peeling thin-skinned fruits and vegetables, and the "eye" allows peelings or parings to drop free. The blades are set in a handle in such a way that they can turn on a short radius, which gives ease in following the contours of the food being peeled. Also called floating blade knife.

Knishes (Jew.)

A main dish made of dough, which after being kneaded and rolled out is either spread with a filling of cheese, meat, chicken, or the like and rolled up like a jelly roll; or is cut into individual circles, each of which is then spread with a filling, folded like a turnover, and baked.

Koaftah Curry (Ind.)

A curry consisting of meat balls in a seasoned sauce. Also spelled *kofta*.

Kobbe (Mid. East)

A casserole of ground lamb or mutton, meal or flour, oil, onions, piñon nuts, etc. Variously called *kobeda, kubbe,* and *kibbe,* in the countries of this region.

Kobi (Ind.)
The Hindustani word for cauliflower, though in recipes it frequently refers to cabbage, which in India is cooked in a large variety of ways, for example, with tomatoes, diced coconut, or eggs, but without exception accompanied by onions, chilis, and other seasonings. Also spelled *gohbi.*

Kohlrabi
The very much enlarged stem of a cabbage-like plant which is eaten like cauliflower. It is also called turnip cabbage, as the stem has a mild turnip flavor.

Kolacky (Czech.)
1. Rich, round buns with a filling of fruit, cheese, or poppy seed, and a syrup and nut icing.
2. Tarts or turnovers filled with jam or poppy seed paste.

Kolduny (Pol. and Lith.)
Filled dumplings, poached and served with soup. A usual filling is chopped meat, onion, and egg.

Korma (Ind.)
A highly seasoned curry prepared with meat or fish, a large amount of butter, and yogurt.

Kosher (Jew.)
Ceremonially clean; that is, prepared according to Jewish religious law.

Kottbullar (U.S., Scand.)
Very small meat balls, made of ground pork and beef, and fried in butter.

Koulibiak (Rus.)
A two-crust pie generally containing a filling of fish.

Koulich (Rus.)
See KULICH.

Kreplach (Jew.)
The equivalent of Chinese wonton or Italian ravioli; i.e., squares of noodle dough rolled thin and filled with meat, cheese, or chicken, and either fried or boiled.

Kringle (Den.)
A yeast-raised coffee cake.

Krupnich (Rus. and Pol.)
A barley soup made with various vegetables and a little sour cream.

Kubbe (Lebanon)
See KOBBE.

Kuchen (Ger.)
A cake or coffee cake.

Kuchitori (Jap.)
Appetizers.

Kugel (Jew.)
A casserole, which may be either a main dish containing fish, potatoes, onions, and cabbage, or a dessert made of rice, raisins, sugar, and nut meats.

Kulich (Rus.)
A sweet, light bread containing raisins, rum, and saffron, and marked with the initials XV, meaning "Christ is Risen," as it was traditionally served on Easter Sunday.

Kumiss
An intoxicating beverage made of

fermented mare's or camel's milk; sometimes, nowadays, an imitation made from cow's milk. Also spelled *koumiss*.

Kümmel (Hol.)
A Dutch liqueur also made in Germany and other north European countries, as an aid to digestion. It is white in color, flavored with caraway and other spices, and sweetened with varying amounts of sugar.

Kumquat
The Chinese word, meaning "golden orange," for a fruit the size of a small plum, oblong in shape, and like an orange in color and flavor, though much more tart. Skin and pulp are both edible raw, while preserved kumquats are considered a great delicacy.

Kvass (Rus.)
A light beer, generally home-brewed from rye flour, malt, and mint.

Kvorost (Rus.)
Strips of pastry made with flour, sugar, water, and rum or vodka, and fried in deep fat.

Lady Baltimore Cake
A cake using only the egg whites, while the Lord Baltimore cake uses only the yolks. The filling between the layers is similar to that of the Lord Baltimore, but frequently simpler, omitting nut meats and candied fruit. See LORD BALTIMORE CAKE.

Lady Finger
Spongecake baked in a narrow, finger-shaped, individual form and dusted with powdered sugar.

Lady Finger Grape
A long, thin, green grape, attractive in a fruit display.

Laekerli (Switz.)
A long-keeping spice cooky containing candied peel and almonds and baked in a rectangular shape. Also spelled *leckerle*.

La Fabada (Sp.)
An elaborate traditional dish made with salt beef, ham, beans, blood pudding, and sausages. It is cooked like a stew and is generally served as two courses, the beans and soup first, the meat second.

Lambert Cherry
A dark-red cherry, though not as dark as the Bing, especially popular in the northwestern United States.

Lamb's Fry
Originally, lamb's testicles; but may also refer to the head, tail, kidneys, heart, tongue, etc.

Lamb's Lettuce
A local New England name for a wild green, used either raw or cooked, having toothed, spoon-shaped leaves, which in some cases are clustered into loose heads. Also called field salad, lamb's quarters, fetticus and pigweed.

Lamb's Wool (Eng.)
A hot, spiced drink made of baked apple pulp and strong ale and often served on Epiphany with Twelfth-Day Cake.

La Mediatrice (U.S., Creole)
A fresh, warm loaf of bread, or a large roll, split open, scooped out to form a

case, and filled with fried oysters, after which the "lid" is put back on. This dish, "the peacemaker," is said to derive its name from the custom late-returning husbands had of bringing it to their wives.

Lamprey
An eel-like fish once very popular in England. It is difficult to prepare in that two filaments in the back contain a poison and must be removed before the fish is eaten.

Lancashire Hot Pot (Eng.)
See HOT POT.

Land Cress
A land plant resembling water cress and used in the same way. It is also called simply cress, or by its alternate name, peppergrass, as the taste is sharp and tangy.

Langouste (Fr.)
The rock or spiny lobster. See CRAY-FISH.

Langue-de-Chat (Fr.)
Literally, "cat's tongue"; the name given to a candy or chocolate-covered biscuit moulded in the shape of a tongue.

Lard
1. Pork fat which has been rendered and clarified; especially good for certain pastries. It is an opaque white solid, almost without odor. Leaf lard is the best quality.
2. To insert narrow strips of fat into gashes made in a lean cut of meat; this procedure is most correctly done with a special implement called a larding needle. Or, to lay such strips on the meat.

Larder
A room or large closet where food is kept. It is unheated and often has a stone or a concrete floor and stone or concrete shelves, which help to keep the food cool.

Larding Needle
See LARD.

Lardy John (Eng.)
A plain rolled cooky, which may contain currants, in which lard is the shortening.

Lasagne (It.)
1. Pasta or egg noodles, cut in widths about two inches wide, sometimes with a ruffled edge.
2. A baked dish of cheese, meat, tomato sauce, and herb seasonings in alternating layers with lasagne noodles.

Latkes (Jew.)
Pancakes made with cracker or matzo meal. Potato latkes, a popular variety, also contain grated potato and a little onion.

Laulau (Haw.)
An individual portion of pork and fish wrapped in leaves and steamed or baked in a pit.

Laurel Leaf
See BAY LEAF.

Lavender
Lavender is not ordinarily thought of as a culinary herb, but can be used to obtain an unusual effect in flavoring wine drinks, jellies, soft drinks, and desserts. Only very minute quantities of the flowering tips or petals should

be used, as their fragrance, though sweet and delicious, is extremely penetrating and lingering.

Laver
A dulse, or edible seaweed, used in the Orient as a vegetable and in soups; it also provides the diet of the swifts whose nests contain the gelatin used in birds'-nest soup. It is also common along the southern coast of Wales, where it is cooked and seasoned, or pickled for use.

Leaf Lard
See LARD.

Leaf Lettuce
Any lettuce whose leaves do not cluster to form a head.

Leavening Agent
Any ingredient added to dough, batter, etc., to produce a gas which will expand during heating, thus raising and lightening the food. See YEAST; BAKING POWDER; BAKING SODA ; and CREAM OF TARTAR.

Lebkuchen (Ger.)
1. A spice cake made with honey.
2. A spicy, frosted cooky, similar to gingerbread, and served during the Christmas season.

Leckerle (Switz.)
See LAEKERLI.

Leek
An onion-like vegetable with broad, flat leaves and an enlarged but only slightly bulbous white stem and root, which has a mild, sweet, onion flavor.

Leekie Pasty (Eng.)
A typical Cornish pasty containing sliced leeks, bacon, and seasonings.

Lees
The sediment or solid bits which settle out of any liquid, but especially wine or liqueur.

Lemon Balm
See BALM.

Lemon Curd or Lemon Cheese (Eng.)
A custard or filling for tarts, made of sugar, eggs, butter, and lemon juice, in a double boiler. It actually does not form curds, except when cooked too fast and not stirred.

Lemon Jelly Cake
A simple cake batter baked in layers and spread with a boiled lemon jelly or custard.

Lemon Verbena
See VERBENA.

Lenten Sauce
Any of various sauces made without meat, to be served with fish and other meatless dishes during Lent.

Lentil
A small, light-colored legume resembling a flattened pea. Lentils are very nutritious and inexpensive and are widely used in Indian and European cookery.

Les Choesels (Belg.)
A meat stew containing, among a variety of meats and other ingredients, sweetbreads. It was once a usual Thursday dish as slaughtering was done on that day and the sweetbreads could be had absolutely fresh.

Les Grillades (U.S., Creole)
Steaks, or rounds of beef or veal, cooked slowly in stock and tomato sauce and usually served with rice or hominy.

Les Oiseaux Sans Têtes (Fr.)
Thin slices of ham or of round steak, rolled around a mushroom and herb stuffing, fried, and served in broth or red wine. The name literally means "birds without heads."

Lesso (It.)
Boiled.

Lettuce
Any of several species of leafy plants having milky juice, and commonly used as salad greens. They include such varieties as Bibb, romaine, leaf, Boston, and head or iceberg lettuce. The name butter lettuce is somewhat loosely applied to distinguish any of the softer and tenderer varieties from head lettuce.

Leveret (Eng.)
A young hare.

Leyden Cheese (Hol.)
A hard cheese flavored with cumin seed.

Liaison (Fr.)
A thickening agent; for example, egg yolks, cream, or roux (i.e., butter and flour cooked together).

Licorice
An herb belonging to the pea family, native to Europe, having blue flowers and a distinctive, strong, sweet, rather pungent flavor resembling that of anise. The root after being dried and treated is used in medicines and in a chewy black candy.

Liederkranz Cheese (U.S.)
A soft cheese, creamy white with an edible golden crust, somewhat resembling Camembert. It has a full, pungent flavor, and should be eaten at room temperature with fruit and crackers.

Light
Not heavy; porous. Having a high percentage of air in relation to the volume of the whole; a term used to describe a desirable quality of such foods as cakes, breads, whipped potatoes, and the like.

Light Cream
Cream which is relatively low in butterfat content.

Lights
Originally, the name applied only to the lungs of an animal, as these filled with air and floated in the brine tub where the meat was being processed; but now often used for the kidneys, liver, heart, etc., as well as for the lungs.

Lima Bean
A kind of flattened bean eaten either fresh, when it is green, or dried, when its color is ivory white. The pods are papery and inedible.

Limburger Cheese (Belg.)
The emphatic odor of Limburger is misleading, as it is actually a rather mild, though full-flavored cheese. It is semi-soft, creamy-yellow, and smooth in texture, but should be served only to known fanciers as the odor is offensive to many people.

Limequat
A hybrid fruit having the juiciness and firm pulp of a lime and the flavor of a kumquat.

Limestone Lettuce
See BIBB LETTUCE.

Limpa (Swed.)
A yeast-raised, cake-like bread made with rye flour, ale, milk, and molasses, and flavored with orange peel and fennel seed.

Ling Cod
A West Coast fish, no relation to the true cod, having greenish scales and flesh. It usually weighs about twelve pounds and is sold either whole or in steaks and fillets; a European ling is generally salted. Also called long cod.

Lingonberry (Scan.)
A sweet cranberry, popular in Swedish pancake sauces, jellies, and jams.

Linguini (It.)
Plain noodles about one-eighth of an inch wide.

Linzer Torte (Aus.)
A rich cake, made with various ingredients, but usually containing powdered almonds, spices, and a filling of raspberry jam, and covered with a latticed crust.

Liptauer Cheese (Hung.)
A sharp, salty, sour-milk cheese variously flavored with capers, anchovies, mustard, and onion, but especially paprika. The name is the more frequently used German version of the Hungarian *lipto*.

Liqueur
A sweetened, alcoholic, after-dinner drink, especially one flavored during the process of distillation rather than after it, and originated primarily to act as an aid to digestion. See CORDIAL, with which this term is now used interchangeably.

Liquor
In culinary usage, often refers to the liquid in which something has been, or is to be, cooked.

Litchee Nut
See LITCHI NUT.

Litchi Nut (Chin.)
A dried, raisin-like fruit enclosed in a fragile shell and eaten like peanuts or almonds.

Littleneck Clam
Another name for the quahog.

Livarot Cheese (Fr.)
A soft, skim-milk cheese, usually cylindrical in shape and of a dark red or brown color. The flavor is strong and piquant.

Liverwurst
A liver sausage very much like Braunschweiger, though it contains less liver and is usually smoked. It is also ready-to-eat.

Llapingacho (Sp.)
A potato cake containing cheese, served in an onion and tomato sauce, and topped with a poached egg.

Loaf Sugar
Sugar, often fairly coarse, which has been pressed into cubes or rectangles.

Lobster

An elongated crustacean with ten small, jointed legs and two large pincer claws, native to northern waters around Maine and Nova Scotia. The meat is available frozen or in tins, while whole fresh lobsters may be purchased already boiled. Almost all lobster dishes, with the exception of broiled or baked live lobster, which is killed just before cooking, are made with boiled live lobster, i.e., lobsters dropped alive into boiling water, thus giving the shell its distinctive bright pink color. Two rules apply in the use of lobster: never buy a dead one, and, the larger it is, the more likely it is to be tough.

Loganberry

Possibly a natural hybrid between the blackberry and red raspberry, this fruit has the shape of the former and the color and flavor of the latter, and is rarely sold outside its native western states as it is quite perishable.

Loin

A choice portion of a meat animal consisting of the front part of a hind quarter with the flank removed.

Lollipop

A lump of hard candy on the end of a short stick.

Lomi (Haw.)

To crush; a popular way of preparing salted or smoked fish such as cod or salmon, with green onions, tomatoes, etc., which is then called lomi lomi.

London Broil

Flank steak broiled quickly and carved in thin, diagonal slices.

London Bun (Eng.)

A round, sweet, yeast-raised bun containing bits of candied orange peel, and glazed with a mixture of egg and sugar.

Long Cod

See LING COD.

Long Island Oyster

Any oyster grown wholly or partially in the waters around Long Island, supposedly designating one of a fine flavor, such as the Blue Point. Actually, the waters vary greatly in the amount of salt, and the like, which they contain, and oysters from them differ also, as, for example, in having a very mild or a very strong coppery taste.

Long-Neck Clam

See SOFT CLAM.

Loquat

An Asiatic fruit resembling a pear in shape and color, and cultivated in the southern states for preserves. Its meat is soft, slightly acid, and cherry-like.

Lord Baltimore Cake

A faintly lemon-flavored cake containing beaten egg yolks, and baked in layers which are spread with a cream filling of stiffly beaten egg whites, sugar, water, nut meats, candied cherries, and lemon and orange flavoring. See LADY BALTIMORE CAKE.

Lorgnette (Fr.)

Garnished with fried onion rings.

Lotus

A water lily which grows in many parts of the world and whose root is used as a vegetable in certain Oriental recipes.

Louisiana Mustard
A mild-flavored mustard similar to that of Dijon.

Lovage
A tall-growing herb of the parsley family, also called love parsley, and having pale green leaves which look and taste rather like those of celery. In New England it is occasionally used as a vegetable, but more often to give a celery flavor to soups, salads, sauces, and stews. The seeds are used in candy.

Love Apple
An old-fashioned name for the tomato.

Love-in-a-Mist
A garden plant whose seeds have a curious, aromatic fragrance and were once sprinkled on cakes and cookies.

Love Parsley
See LOVAGE.

Lox (Jew.)
Smoked salmon.

Luau (Haw.)
A feast or celebration; also, taro leaves.

Lukewarm
Tepid. For practical purposes, a temperature at which a drop of the liquid placed on the underside of the arm feels neither hot nor cold.

Luncheon
A usually light midday meal. The word is derived from "lump," and

dates back to a time when a lump, or chunk, of bread, cheese, etc., was eaten between breakfast and dinner. "Lunch," an abbreviated form, is frequently used.

Lutfisk (Scan.)
Dried, cured fish, which is soaked several days in lye water, and then is placed in fresh water to prepare it for cooking. It is little used outside Scandinavia.

Lyonnaise (Fr.)
Seasoned with onions; for example, lyonnaise potatoes.

Lyonnaise Sauce (Fr.)
A sauce in which onions are the main ingredient.

Macadamia Nut
A golden-brown nut, about half an inch in diameter, having an almond-like taste and an aroma resembling that of freshly roasted coffee. It is widely cultivated in Hawaii, where it was first discovered by John Mac-Adam in the late nineteenth century, and is salted and sold as a cocktail snack.

Macaroni
An Italian pasta, made from wheat flour and shaped into tubes one-half inch or less in diameter which are often broken or cut into shorter pieces.

Macaroon
A chewy cooky containing almond paste or ground almonds, egg whites, sugar, and flavoring. Other nuts are sometimes substituted for almonds, and coconut is used in making a popular variety.

Mace

A spice derived from the fruit of the evergreen tree whose kernel is the nutmeg. When this fruit ripens it splits open and reveals three layers: one green, one orange, and, next to the kernel itself, a scarlet one, which is dried and ground to produce mace. The aroma and taste is like nutmeg, but much stronger. It is often combined with cloves and ginger and may be used where nutmeg is suitable, though a lesser quantity is needed.

Macedoine (Fr.)

A mixture of vegetables and/or fruits, usually evenly sliced; or any mixture of finely cut ingredients.

Macerate

To soften or separate the parts of a food by steeping it in a fluid.

Machli Curry (Ind.)

A fish curry, of which there are many variations. Also spelled *machchi*.

McIntosh Apple

A crisp, tangy, red-skinned apple, grown throughout the United States. Fine for eating raw and for salads, applesauce, and pies, it may also be baked if size is of no importance, for it is rather small. It is in season from October through January.

Mackerel

A fat or oily North Atlantic food fish, green with blue bars on back and sides, and silver below. The meat is excellent, especially that from the first catch of the season, when the fish are about sixteen inches in length.

Macon (Eng.)

A synthetic bacon made from mutton.

Macoon Apple

An apple good for eating raw or for pies.

Mad-Apple

An alternate name for the eggplant.

Madeira Cake (Eng.)

A kind of sponge cake made with shortening and occasionally decorated on top with a large slice of preserved citron. It was traditionally served with Madeira wine.

Madeira Sauce

A brown sauce containing Madeira wine.

Madeira Wine

A fine wine fortified with spirits, from the island of Madeira off the African coast. There are many kinds of Madeira, ranging from pale and fairly dry to dark, sweet, and heavy.

Madeleine (Fr.)

A light cake baked in a small mould shaped like a scallop shell.

Madrilène (Fr.)

Literally, in the manner of Madrid; but usually referring to a tomato consommé served either hot or cold (jellied). Jellied madrilène is usually broken up into pieces for serving.

Mafalde (It.)

Long, crimped or twisted ribbon noodles.

Maguey

An alternate name for the agave, which see.

Maiale Ubriaco (It.)
Literally, "intoxicated pork"; refers to pork cooked in red wine.

Maiden Blush Apple
An excellent apple for pies and general cooking, distinguished by its rosy color, and in season from August through November.

Maid of Honor (Eng.)
A small, rich cake baked in a muffin tin lined with puff pastry. It originated in the county of Surrey in the time of Queen Elizabeth I, and old recipes included curds, butter, brandy, sweet and bitter almonds, eggs, lemon, and potatoes.

Maigre (Fr.)
Literally, "lean," but denoting a dish prepared without meat, for example, a Lenten sauce.

Maintenon (Fr.)
Designating a dish or sauce which (supposedly) is prepared in the manner of Madame Maintenon who, it is said, devised many tasty foods to tempt the appetite of Louis XIV during his failing years.

Mais "Tac-Tac" (U.S., Creole)
A kind of candy made of parched corn and molasses and hardened in paper cases about three by six inches square.

Maître d'Hôtel (Fr.)
Denoting a seasoning of melted butter, chopped parsley, and lemon juice. Literally, the phrase means "chief cook."

Malaga Grape
A large, sweet, pale-green grape, native to southern Spain. It is used to make white raisins and white wine and is now cultivated in California.

Mallobet
A refrigerator dessert, usually consisting of marshmallows partially melted, with fruit or a fruit flavoring, and beaten egg whites folded in. The whole is frozen in a refrigerator tray.

Malmsey
A kind of Madeira wine, typically dark, sweet, and heady, with a delightful bouquet.

Malt
Grain put into a liquid and allowed to germinate. The malt used in brewing consists of barley which is steeped in water at a warm temperature, kiln-dried, sifted, cleaned, and mashed. Both wheat and barley are used in preparing the malt for malted milk, and the mixture is dried in a vacuum.

Maltese Sauce (Fr.)
A variant of hollandaise sauce made with the juice of blood oranges and served with asparagus.

Mamaliga (Romania)
Corn meal mush which is made, or served, with cheese, and either hot or cold.

Mammee (S. Am.)
A large, oval, tropical fruit, with soft crimson or yellow pulp and a brownish rind. Also native to Africa, and sometimes called mammee apple.

Mammoth Black Twig Apple
See ARKANSAS APPLE.

Manchet (Eng.)

The ancient name for a loaf of fine bread baked for the lord of a manor or for a person of quality; or, in some regions, a loaf shaped by hand and baked on a metal sheet rather than in a loaf pan.

Mandarine

A sweet, tangerine-flavored liqueur.

Mandarin Orange

A small, Oriental orange, of which the tangerine is one variety, having a loose, easily removed skin, small, neat segments, and a sweet, mild flavor.

Mandelbrodt (Jew.)

A loaf cake made with almonds; it is partially baked, removed from the oven, and cut into slices which are then returned to the oven to finish browning.

Mandlen (Jew.)

Small strips of dough which are baked, or, rarely, fried, and served with soup.

Mangel

An alternate name for the mangold.

Mango

1. A fruit grown in tropical regions, varying in size from that of a peach to one weighing five pounds, and in color from green or yellow to red, the most common being orange. The best mangoes have sweet, juicy, aromatic pulp, of the texture of a peach. They are best eaten when just picked, canned, or in chutney.
2. In old cookbooks, a name sometimes given to the cantaloupe.

3. A pickled pepper, stuffed with a mixture of cabbage and vegetables.

Mangold

A large field beet, which must be used when young and small if it is to be at all tender. Also called *mangel* and *mangel-wurzel*.

Mango-Squash

See CHAYOTE.

Mangosteen

A fruit having a hard rind like a pomegranate and about the size of an orange. The rosy, sweet, slightly tart meat combines the virtues of grape, pineapple, peach, and strawberry and is divided into sections as is the orange. It is sometimes imported from Australia, and the West Indies, and grows widely in India, China, and Malaya, its home.

Manhattan Clam Chowder

Clam soup made with tomatoes and other vegetables and differing from New England clam chowder particularly in the fact that it contains no milk or cream.

Manicotti (It.)

Squares of dough filled with a mixture of, for example, ricotta cheese, chopped ham, and egg, rolled up, boiled, and served with a tomato sauce.

Manié Butter (Fr.)

Butter and flour creamed and used as a quick binder.

Manioc Flour

A starchy flour made from the roots of a tropical plant, the manioc or cassava.

Manzanilla

1. The small, apple-like fruit of a thorny tropical tree, having mealy white or yellowish pulp and three large seeds.
2. A pale dry sherry having a pleasant, but unique flavor.

Maple Sugar

The crystallized product obtained by boiling down the sap of certain species of maple trees, especially the yellow-flowering one called the sugar maple.

Maple Syrup

The uncrystallized portion of boiled-down maple sap.

Maraschino (Yugo.)

A clear liqueur distilled from wild marasca cherries, a species grown in Yugoslavia.

Maraschino Cherry

A cherry, picked while unripe and artificially flavored and colored bright red; or, one preserved in Maraschino.

Marble Cake

A cake for which half the batter is white, the other half flavored and colored with chocolate. To achieve the marbled appearance, the batter is dropped by spoonfuls, alternating white and dark, into the baking pan.

Marbled

Having the appearance of marble, that is, veined or laced with a contrasting color or material, as a steak or roast is with fat.

Marc

The skins, pulp, seeds, etc., which remain after the making of wine. Sometimes a brandy, for example, the Italian grappa, is distilled from this residue.

Marchpane

See MARZIPAN.

Maréchale, à la (Fr.)

Garnished with vegetables or cucumber slices.

Marengo (Fr.)

The name given to a dish consisting of cut-up chicken or veal, browned in oil and simmered in a sauce of tomatoes, wine, mushrooms, garlic, and onions, which is said to have been originated by one of Napoleon's cooks before the battle of Marengo, in Italy.

Margarine

A butter substitute made with vegetable and/or animal fats, and having a rather high percentage of water. It is often sold fortified with vitamins, and is colored yellow with annatto.

Marguerite

1. A small, candy-like cake containing among its ingredients eggs, sugar, and nut meats.
2. A soda or graham cracker spread with either a simple icing of powdered sugar or marshmallow or a topping of boiled frosting, nut meats, and chocolate.

Marigold

A garden flower whose round gold or

orange petals may be used, though sparingly, to add a strong, unique tang to salads, stews, and soups. Powdered, the flowers are used to flavor and color various drinks, butter, cheese, cakes, and the like. Marigold may be used in place of saffron, usually in double quantity, as it imparts much the same color.

Marinade
The liquid mixture in which food has been marinated (see following entry); or the food itself.

Marinara Sauce (It.)
Literally, "sailor style," in practice, a sauce made without meat and containing tomatoes, onions, garlic, etc.

Marinate
To soak a food, for example, a roast of beef, or to allow it to stand, in a liquid mixture in order to flavor, tenderize, or preserve it. Often the marinade for meat contains pickles, vinegar, wine, and various spices.

Marinière Sauce (Fr.)
A white wine sauce made with mussel liquor and egg yolks, to be served with poached fish or mussels.

Marjoram
A Mediterranean herb, growing about a foot high and having small, grey-green leaves and tiny, creamy, flowers. Its flavor is spicy, pleasant, and rather sweet, much like sage, but less pungent. Its uses, green or dried, are manifold: with eggs, fish, game, roasts of meat and especially beef, poultry,

salads, vegetables, and sauces. Powdered marjoram is used in sausages and poultry seasoning. See WILD MARJORAM and OREGANO.

Marlow
A refrigerator dessert similar to mallobet, consisting of partially melted marshmallows, heavy cream, and a flavoring, often fruit, frozen together.

Marmalade
Fruit cut up and boiled with sugar to a thick, clear, jelly-like consistency. It is most often made of citrus fruits, and the flavor is generally rather tart. The term is derived from *marmelo*, the Portuguese name for quince, from which marmalade was first made.

Marmite (Fr.)
A vessel used as a stock pot or for cooking stews or soups. See PETITE MARMITE.

Marquise (Fr.)
A kind of frozen dessert made with whipped cream folded into a custard, sherbet, or some similar ingredient.

Marron (Fr.)
The French word for chestnut, a frequently used culinary term.

Marron Glacé (Fr.)
A sugar-coated cooked chestnut; a popular confection in France.

Marrow
1. The soft, rich substance in the central cavity of bones.
2. A squash-like, edible gourd common in England, and shaped like a large, elongated egg.

Marrowbone
A bone, usually large, which contains edible marrow and is used for making soups or stews.

Marrowfat (Eng.)
A large, rich variety of pea.

Marrow Sauce (Fr.)
A red wine sauce containing beef marrow and parsley, to be served with vegetables.

Marrow Spoon
A long-handled, narrow-bowled spoon for removing marrow from the bone.

Marsala (It.)
A semi-sweet, white dessert wine resembling sherry. It is made with Sicilian grapes, and is probably the most popular of Italian dessert wines, having enjoyed especially great vogue in nineteenth-century England.

Marsala, alla (It.)
Cooked with Marsala.

Marsh Marigold
See COWSLIP.

Maruzzelle (It.)
See CONCHIGLIA.

Mary Ann Tin
A large or small cake pan having a convex bottom, so that any cake baked in it has a concave (i.e., hollowed out) top when it is turned out of the pan. Into this depression is put fruit, ice cream, or the like.

Marzipan (Fr.)
A candy made of almond paste and sugar and often moulded into the shape of tiny fruits and vegetables and colored.

Masa (Mex.)
Mexican corn meal, specially ground and, ideally, used when very fresh and moist.

Mash
To reduce to a pulp by crushing, pounding, or beating; or, the food so prepared.

Masha
See ROSELLE.

Mask
To cover completely with a thick sauce, jelly, or mayonnaise.

Maté (S. Am.)
A bush belonging to the holly family, the dried leaves of which are brewed into a beverage sometimes drunk in place of tea or coffee. Also known as *yerba maté*.

Mateca Cheese (It.)
A combination of cheese and butter, consisting of a small brick of butter covered with Mozzarella cheese, eaten sliced and not used in cooking.

Matelote (Fr.)
Literally, "sailor's style"; in cooking, a fish stew, usually one which includes several kinds of fish, together with onions and wine. Also, a sauce very similar to this.

Matignon (Fr.)
A preparation of minced and seasoned vegetables which is sometimes spread over certain cuts of meat or poultry in

order to flavor them during the cooking process.

Matzo (Jew.)
An unleavened bread, made of flour and water. Matzo meal, i.e., the specially ground flour used, is also made into small dumplings for soup, called matzo balls. Also spelled *matzoth*.

Maultasche (Ger.)
Literally, "mouth pockets"; puff pastry turnovers filled, for example, with a very sweet jam made of apples, plums, and currants.

May Apple
The egg-shaped, small-plum-sized yellowish fruit of a wild plant of the same name. It is quite seedy, but is sometimes eaten raw or used for marmalade in the area east of the Mississippi, where it is common.

Mayonnaise
Egg yolks, vinegar, oil, lemon juice, and seasonings well combined with a little boiling water to ensure their cohesion. The mixture is rather liquid at first, but later congeals.

May Pie (Eng.)
A pie containing chopped spring vegetables such as peas, lettuce hearts, turnips, and onions.

May Wine (Ger.)
A light-bodied white wine flavored with woodruff. A product of Germany.

Mazarin (Fr.)
1. A French liqueur, similar to Bénédictine.
2. A small almond cake or pastry.

Mead
An ancient drink made of fermented honey and water.

Meal
1. The occasion of taking food, or the food so taken.
2. Coarsely ground, unsifted grain, as distinguished from flour.

Mealy
Soft, dry, powdery, unpleasantly grainy or crumbly; generally used in a derogatory sense when applied to food.

Meat Bird
A thin slice of meat folded and pinned around a spoonful of stuffing, seasoned and browned in fat to which milk is added, and the whole covered and simmered or baked till tender.

Medallion
A small, round shape; in cooking, usually a meat fillet prepared in this shape.

Medlar
A small fruit like an apple, brown or russet in color, and extremely sour unless eaten when almost decayed. It is very good in jams and jellies.

Medley Pie (Eng.)
A two-crust pie containing cold roast pork and apples arranged in layers and sprinkled with ginger and other seasonings, to which a good quantity of ale is added.

Mélange
An uncooked preserve made of a variety of fruits with an equal weight of sugar and some brandy. It is prefer-

ably kept in a stone jar, more fruit and sugar being added as the first are used.

Melba

A dessert of vanilla ice cream topped with fruit and Melba sauce, a raspberry syrup. Peaches were used in the original version, named in honor of the singer Nellie Melba.

Melba Toast

Very thin, very dry toast, usually served unbuttered or with melted butter lightly brushed on. Named for the singer Nellie Melba.

Melon-Baller

See PARISIAN POTATO SPOON.

Melon Mould

An oval mould having a separate top and bottom to facilitate filling. The French *bombe* mould is similar.

Melt

1. The spleen, a soft and pulpy gland.
2. To change a solid, for example, butter, to a liquid by heating.

Melted Butter Sauce

Melted butter combined with salt and lemon juice and used at once, before it clarifies, with fish.

Melton Mowbray Pie (Eng.)

A jellied pork pie served either warm or chilled and named for a town in the North Country in which it is said to have originated.

Meringue

1. Egg whites beaten stiff, often with sugar, and placed on top of a pie or pudding.

2. A baked shell of such egg whites, filled with ice cream or fruit.
3. A small cake made of such egg whites, often with nut meats, baked to a pale golden brown.

Merrythought (Eng.)

A name for the wishbone of a chicken or turkey.

Mescal (Mex.)

A very strong liquor made from the agave.

Meshimono (Jap.)

Rice with other ingredients.

Meunière (Fr.)

Fried in butter; most often refers to fish, which are then seasoned and garnished. Literally, "miller's wife."

Meunière Butter (Fr.)

Melted butter combined with lemon juice and chopped parsley and used with fish.

Mezzani (It.)

A smooth, curved, tubular pasta about a quarter of an inch in diameter.

Mignonnette (Fr.)

Ground pepper; also a name sometimes given to a peeled peppercorn of the finest quality.

Milanese, alla (It.)

In the style of Milan; applied to a number of dishes prepared in various ways, but not to any particular method or ingredient.

Milcon (S. Am.)

A preparation of potatoes and pumpkin resembling spaghetti or macaroni.

Milk

See CONDENSED, EVAPORATED, HOMOGEN-IZED, PASTEURIZED, POWDERED, RAW, SKIM, TOP, and WHOLE MILK.

Mille-Feuille (Fr.)

A delicate pastry made of many thin layers of puff paste. Literally, "a thousand leaves."

Millet

A type of cereal grain grown in Europe, but especially in northern China, where it is eaten almost as commonly as rice. It is also often hulled like barley and ground into flour.

Milt

The male reproductive glands of a fish, which may be prepared like roe.

Mince

To cut, chop, or, grind into minute pieces; or, the food so prepared.

Mineral

A substance neither animal nor vegetable, which, however, may occur in animal and vegetable tissue; for example, calcium or iron.

Minestra (It.)

Soup.

Minestrone (It.)

A thick soup containing vegetables and herbs in a chicken or meat broth.

Minnehaha Cake

A layer cake popular around the end of the nineteenth century, consisting of a plain cake with a filling and icing made with raisins and/or chopped hickory nuts.

Minnow

Any small, soft-finned, fresh-water bait fish, such as chub, dace, or shiner.

Mint

1. A well-known herb, of which there are many varieties and uses. Probably the most common are peppermint and spearmint, each of which has rough, dark-green leaves, but its own special minty taste. Apple mint has smooth, grey-green leaves and a delicate, fruity aroma; curly mint has dull green, curled leaves. The fresh, new leaves are the best part of any mint. They are used in flavoring beverages, fruit cups and other fruit dishes, ice cream, jellies, candies, salads, and sauces; and, notably, of course, with lamb. See also BERGAMOT.
2. To flavor by sprinkling with mint sauce, by rubbing with mint leaves, or by marinating in a mint infusion.

Minute Steak

A boneless, fairly thin steak cut from the front ribs of beef, which is delicious if not too fat.

Mirabeau (Fr.)

Denoting an elaborate garnish of anchovy fillets, tarragon leaves, and olives or truffles; for example, sole Mirabeau.

Mirabelle (Fr.)

A small yellow plum with a fine flavor.

Mirabelle de Lorraine (Fr.)

A liqueur or spirit redistilled with extract of fresh mirabelle plums.

Mirepoix (Fr.)
A basic seasoning, consisting usually of diced carrots, onions, and celery, cooked with salt pork, bacon, or ham, and used in the preparation of brown soups and sauces and with braised meat.

Miroton (Fr.)
Cooked meat, sliced and heated, often with onions and pickles added, and served rather like a stew in a sauce.

Mise-en-Place (Fr.)
Those preparations and ingredients frequently used in cookery, and thus regularly kept on hand.

Miso (Jap.)
Fermented soy bean paste and rice, used with bean curd, in soups, etc.

Misoshiru (Jap.)
A thick soup made with miso, fish, meat, vegetables, and beans. Also sometimes transliterated *shiru-miso*.

Misto (It.)
Mixed.

Mix
To unite similar ingredients, for example, flour, salt, and sugar, by stirring. See COMBINE.

Mixed Grill (Eng.)
A combination of lamb chops, liver or kidneys, and link sausage or bacon, often accompanied by mushrooms and tomatoes, and broiled.

Mocha
Coffee-flavored; sometimes, but not necessarily, with chocolate added.

Mock Chicken Leg
Ground veal and pork with seasonings, shaped around a wooden skewer in a shape suggesting a chicken leg, coated with bread crumbs or their equivalent, browned in fat, and then simmered in water till tender.

Mock Duck
A lamb roast so cut, rolled, and garnished as to suggest, in appearance, a roast duck.

Mock Turtle Soup
A soup made from a calf's head, with beef, wine, and a variety of condiments.

Mode, à la
"According to the fashion"; usually, in the United States, indicating a dessert topped with ice cream. For the French usage of this phrase, see À LA.

Mokoto (Port.)
Tripe simmered, then browned, and simmered again in a highly seasoned tomato sauce.

Molasses
The thick, sweet, dark syrup produced as sugar is refined.

Mole Poblano (Mex.)
A sauce for chicken or turkey containing chilis, almonds, onion, garlic, bread crumbs, spices and seasonings, and an unusual but invariable ingredient, a small amount of chocolate. The chicken is cut up and served in the sauce.

Mongole Purée
A cream soup made with tomatoes and peas; often made of condensed tomato and green pea soups.

Monkey Fruit
An apple-like tropical fruit.

Monkey Nut (Eng.)
The peanut.

Monosodium Glutamate
See AJINOMOTO.

Monterey Jack Cheese
See JACK CHEESE.

Montmorency Cherry
A sour cherry of a bright, clear-red color and a fine flavor which make it excellent for canning. It is grown widely throughout the United States.

Montpellier Butter (Fr.)
Butter mixed with herb paste, boiled eggs, raw yolks, and oil; used as a decorative garnish for fish.

Moonshine
1. The slang term for home-brewed corn whiskey.
2. A dessert of whipped egg whites, confectioner's sugar, and peach preserve, thoroughly chilled; also, a lemon gelatin dessert.

Morel
A delicate mushroom (in French, *morille*) much prized by connoisseurs but not generally obtainable in the United States.

Morello Cherry
Any of several dark-red, sour varieties used as a garnish and in making cherry brandy.

Mornay Sauce (Fr.)
A béchamel sauce containing grated cheese.

Morro Crab
A large Pacific coast crab.

Mortar and Pestle
A deep, round-bottomed bowl (the mortar) of wood, porcelain, or glass, and a short, thick, club-shaped implement (the pestle) of the same material, with which herbs, etc., may be pulverized.

Mostaccioli (It.)
A smooth, tubular pasta, cut diagonally in two-and-a-half-inch lengths, and about half an inch in diameter.

Mothering Cake (Eng.)
An alternate name for simnel cake.

Mother of Vinegar
A slimy mass of yeast cells and bacteria such as develops in vinegar, wine, or cider during fermentation.

Mother Sauce (Fr.)
One of the basic warm sauces, i.e., brown, béchamel (white sauce made with milk), and velouté (white sauce made with stock).

Mould
1. To make into a certain shape; or, the product so shaped; or the cavity in which, or form upon which, the product is shaped.
2. Woolly or furry growth of fungi on food or other material.

Mountain Cherry
See CHICKASAW PLUM.

Mountain Oysters (U.S., South.)
Calves' testicles, fried in deep fat. Regarded as a great delicacy.

Mousaka (Mid. East)

A casserole containing meat and eggplant in layers, made in various ways throughout the Middle East. Also spelled *moussaka* or *musaka*.

Mousse (Fr.)

1. A dessert consisting of flavored cream which has been whipped and frozen, often in an elaborately shaped mould.
2. A jellied main dish made of chicken, sea food, etc., placed in a mould and chilled to a firm consistency before serving.

Mousseline (Fr.)

A mousse made in an individual mould.

Mousseline Forcemeat (Fr.)

A very fine forcemeat, with cream and, usually, egg whites used as a binder.

Mousseline Sauce (Fr.)

A hollandaise sauce with whipped cream added.

Mousseuse Sauce (Fr.)

A sauce made of manié butter combined with seasonings and whipped cream, to be served with fish.

Mozzarella Cheese (It.)

A white, rindless, rubbery, mild-flavored cooking cheese.

MSG

An abbreviaton for monosodium glutamate, or ajinomoto, which see.

Mud Clam

A very large West coast clam, especially prized among the many available varieties.

Muddle

As a verb, to mix together thoroughly.

Muffin

In contemporary usage, a light, quick bread baked in a pan having several individual cups in which the batter is placed, and resembling the earlier "gem," which see. The English muffin is a remaining example of an earlier type, i.e., a yeast-raised bread baked in rings which were set on a hot griddle or in an oven.

Muffin Pan

A pan having several individual depressions, or cups, in which muffin batter is placed and baked in an oven. See MUFFIN.

Muffin Ring

A small, round hoop of metal in which muffin batter may be placed for raising and baking, either on a griddle or in an oven. More used in the nineteenth century, and earlier, than at present. See MUFFIN.

Mugwort

An ancient herb related to tarragon and wormwood, now grown mostly for making tea, in which its yellow, clustered spikes of flowers are used.

Mulberry

A red to purple-black fruit resembling a blackberry though the tree on which it grows is a very different plant. In spite of the fact that it is quite good raw and is fine in cooking, it is so perishable that it is little used.

Mull

To make wine, beer, or, sometimes fruit juice into a hot drink with sugar, spices, egg yolks, etc., added.

Mullet

The most common food fish in the South is the striped or jumping mullet which most often weighs two or three pounds when caught, and which travels in schools, leaping out of the water so that fishermen locate them by the noise. Mullets are common in many parts of the world, and were known to the ancient Egyptians and Romans, as well as to the inhabitants of Polynesia and Hawaii.

Mulligan

A stew, generally made with fish or poultry and such vegetables as potatoes, carrots, and peppers.

Mulligatawny Soup (Ind.)

A soup whose name means "pepper water," having a flavor of curry and generally made from chicken stock.

Mulse

An old-fashioned drink made of mulled claret wine and honey.

Mung Bean

A bean whose sprouts are frequently used in Oriental dishes; compared with the soy bean, it has a low calorie count. Also spelled mungo.

Münster Cheese (Ger.)

A mild, semi-soft cheese, creamy-yellow in color and smooth in texture, with small surface holes, and often a flavoring of caraway or anise seeds. Also spelled Muenster.

Muscat Grape

A white, sweet, pleasantly scented grape grown largely for table use but also used in making muscatel wine.

Mush

1. A soft, sometimes sticky pulp.
2. Corn meal boiled with water, egg, seasoning, etc., and either eaten hot or allowed to cool and solidify and then sliced and fried.

Mushimono (Jap.)

Steamed foods. Also spelled umushimono.

Musk Cucumber

See CASSABANANA.

Muskie or Muskellunge

An especially large North American pike, much prized as a game fish.

Muskmelon

Another name for the canteloupe and similar melons with a strong, sweet aroma, as distinguished from the casaba melon, which has none.

Muslin

A thin cotton fabric of rather loose weave, often used as a straining cloth for fruit jellies, and in similar culinary operations; white muslin is always used for these purposes.

Mussel

A mollusk having a rather soft, ribbed shell, usually blue-black in color, and meat similar to that of a clam. Mussels are rarely eaten in the United States, just as clams are rarely eaten in Europe, although both mollusks are found in both places.

Must

Grape juice just before and during the process of fermentation necessary to produce wine.

Mustard

The powdered seed of the herb plant of the same name, available in either dry or paste (prepared) form. See BAHAMIAN, DIJON, DRY, ENGLISH, GERMAN, HERB, LOUISIANA, and PREPARED MUSTARD.

Mustard Sauce

A butter sauce containing mustard, to be served with grilled fish.

Mutton

The flesh of a sheep twelve months old or more. The best mutton is "yearling," i.e., from sheep between one and two years old.

Mutton Ham (Scot.)

A Highland breakfast specialty consisting of a shoulder of mutton cured like ham with salt, brown sugar, pepper, juniper berries, etc., and then smoked. It is boiled and cooked like ham, also.

Myrrh

The true, non-culinary Biblical myrrh is the gum of a tropical tree. Any culinary reference to myrrh is to the herb sweet cicely, which is often called by that name.

Mysost Cheese (Scan.)

A hard to semi-hard cheese with a somewhat buttery texture and a mild, sweetish flavor.

Nabemono (Jap.)

A general name for any food cooked in a saucepan.

Nalesniki (Pol.)

Pancakes filled with meat, cheese, or a sweet such as jam.

Nantua Sauce (Fr.)

A béchamel sauce with cream, crayfish butter, and crayfish tails.

Napoleon

Puff paste baked in a three-by-five-inch rectangle, which is then split lengthwise into four portions which are spread and put back together with a custard cream. A glaze of confectioner's sugar and butter is spread on the top.

Napoleon Cherry

See ROYAL ANNE CHERRY.

Nartje (S. Af.)

A tangerine used as the basis for the liqueur Van der Hum. Also spelled *naartje*.

Nasi Goreng (Indonesia)

Literally, "fried rice," this dish usually includes chicken, shrimp, onions, and a wide selection of seasonings such as chilis, coriander, cumin, and the like, cooked together over low heat.

Nasturtium

A bright, orange-and-yellow-flowered plant whose name means "to turn the nose," which, like marigold, is rarely regarded as a culinary herb, though for centuries in the Orient nasturtium petals have been used as a garnish for their peppery pungency. The dark-green, tender leaves are excellent in vegetable salads, and with canapés, while English capers are actually pickled nasturtium seed pods.

Naturel, au (Fr.)

Either "plainly cooked," or "served in a natural state."

Navarin de Mouton (Fr.)
A hot pot or stew containing lamb or mutton and vegetables, and considered a national dish of France.

Navel Orange
A large orange, deep golden in color and widely cultivated in California. It is usually seedless and divides easily into neat sections. The end opposite the stem is characterized by a navel-like formation, hence the name.

Navy Bean
A dried white pea bean often used in bean soup or baked with pork, ham, or bacon and various seasonings such as brown sugar or molasses, onions, green peppers, and tomatoes, and served as a main dish.

Neapolitan Ice Cream
Brick ice cream in layers of several flavors, most commonly vanilla, chocolate, and strawberry.

Neat's Foot
The foot of an ox or calf; a name used in old recipes for calf's foot jelly or soup.

Nectarine
A smooth-skinned variety of peach, suggesting a cross between it and a plum. The consistency of the flesh as well as the smoothness of the skin are plum-like, but the color and flavor are both those of a peach.

Nesselrode Pudding
A milk and egg pudding containing whipped cream, candied fruits, and, frequently, puréed chestnuts, raisins, and maraschino flavoring.

Nest
A small, shallow, circular cup of pastry, meringue, mashed potatoes, rice, noodles, and the like, containing a food appropriate to it, as ice cream, creamed chicken, etc.

Nettle
A green which, in Europe, is cooked like spinach and is considered not only nourishing, but tasty.

Neufchâtel Cheese (Switz.)
A cream cheese, white, soft, and bland in flavor.

Newburg Sauce
A rich cream sauce made with lobster, wine, brandy, and seasonings, and served either with the lobster itself or, occasionally, with other seafood.

New England Clam Chowder
The original clam chowder, a thick clam soup made with milk or cream, potatoes, and onions. See MANHATTAN CLAM CHOWDER.

New York Cut Steak
A long, narrow steak, actually a porterhouse with the fillet and usually the bone removed; the name is used in the West, though not in New York.

Niagara Grape
The leading eastern white grape, pale yellow-green in color, juicy, and varying in flavor from sweet to tart.

Niçoise Salad (Fr.)
A mixed salad containing green beans, potatoes, anchovies, ripe olives, capers, and tomato quarters, or a similar combination.

Nid (Fr.)
The French word for nest.

Nimono (Jap.)
Boiled fish, meat, and vegetables, served with a variety of Oriental sauces and seasonings.

Nockerl (pl. *Nockerln*; Aus.)
A kind of light dumpling made in any of several different ways. Salzburger Nockerl, a specialty of that city, is made of beaten egg yolks and whites and flour, and is often served as a dessert.

Noekkelost Cheese (Scan.)
A hard or semi-hard cheese with a mild, sweetish flavor, spiced with caraway seeds.

Nog
An old name for a strong ale or beer, chiefly surviving nowadays in "eggnog," but correctly it may be used to refer to any alcoholic drink which contains an egg. (Eggnog itself is occasionally served without alcoholic content.)

Noisette (Fr.)
Literally, a hazelnut; also, a small, choice part of meat, for example, from the tenderloin or eye of a chop. The name generally signifies the best part of something.

Noisette Sauce (Fr.)
A hollandaise sauce made with hazelnut butter, and served with fish.

Nonpareille (Fr.)
A tiny sugar candy usually sold in a multi-colored assortment, and used to decorate cakes and cookies.

Noodle
A flour paste made with eggs, rolled very thin and cut into long, flat, usually narrow strips.

Norfolk Dumpling (Eng.)
A dumpling which may either be yeast-raised or not (a recipe dated 1765, for instance, does not include yeast), made with either milk or water, and eaten hot with gravy or butter, or cold with butter and sugar.

Normandy Sauce (Fr.)
A sauce for fish or vegetables made with cream, fish stock, and seasonings and thickened with egg yolks.

Northern Spy Apple
An eastern apple, red with yellow streaking, eaten raw, or used in pies and in general cooking; in season from October through March.

Nougat
A candy made of almonds, honey, powdered sugar, and pistachio nuts.

Noyau (Fr.)
A sweet, white, almond-flavored liqueur.

Nut-Brown Butter
Another name for black butter.

Nutmeg
The seed or kernel of the fruit of a luxuriant evergreen tree native to the East Indies, about the size of the end of a thumb, ovoid in shape, and greenish-brown in color. Nutmeg is usually sold ground, but the kernels can be bought whole for home grating. Its flavor is pungent and spicy, and is excellent for bringing out the

hidden flavors of fruit and vegetables. It is also used in cakes and cookies, eggnog, and custards, often in combination with cloves, cinnamon, and ginger. Mace and nutmeg are usable almost interchangeably, although mace is stronger in aroma.

Nutrient
Anything having food (i.e., energy-producing) value.

Oast Cake (Eng.)
A small cake made with sugar, currants, and lard, rolled out and cut, fried in a little lard, and eaten hot from the pan.

Oatmeal
Oats, ground or rolled into flakes; useful and tasty as a cereal or in breads and cookies.

O'Brien
Fried with onion and chopped pimentoes and/or peppers; a method of cooking potatoes.

Ocean Perch
The name commonly used for fillets of rosefish, redfish, red perch, and sea perch. The meat is firm, rather coarse, and quite bland in flavor, and lends itself to being prepared in a number of ways.

Occa (S. Am.)
See OXALIS ROOT.

Odamaki-Mushi (Jap.)
A custard made with a macaroni-like product, fish paste, ham, mushrooms, leafy vegetables, eggs, and various sauces, steamed and served with lemon juice.

Oeuf (Fr.)
Egg.

Offal (Eng.)
Usually understood to refer to the waste parts of an animal, for example, the entrails; but in a culinary sense designates the edible inner parts, for example, kidneys, heart, and liver, as well as the head, tail, and feet. Also sometimes designates low-priced fish, for example, plaice, as opposed to sole or other prime fish.

Oil, Vegetable
See VEGETABLE OIL.

Oka (S. Am.)
See OXALIS ROOT.

Oka Cheese (Can.)
Canada's finest cheese, resembling Port du Salut, but less firm.

Okra
A vegetable seed pod commonly used in the southern United States. The tapering green pods, usually around two inches in length, have a gluey pulp which may make the vegetable, by itself, offensive to any but a true fancier. In soups or stews, and with tomatoes, it is more acceptable. Also called gumbo.

Oladyi (Rus.)
Pancakes or fritters.

Olallie Berry
A berry which grows in the West, especially in California, and most resembling a fat and elongated blackberry. It has a sharp, distinct flavor and thus is excellent in jams and preserves.

Oldenburg Apple
A cooking and baking apple in season from July through October.

Oleomargarine
See MARGARINE.

Oliebollen (Hol.)
Doughnuts containing raisins and dropped by the spoonful into deep fat.

Olio (Sp.)
A rich stew prepared for festive occasions, consisting of several meats, vegetables, and garbanzos. The term has now entered the English language and refers to a hotch-potch or mixed dish.

Olive
1. A small, oval, drupe fruit with a hard stone; it is pickled when green for eating as a relish or is allowed to ripen to a purple-black color and more tender consistency, when it is also used as a relish or as an ingredient in various cooked dishes.
2. (Eng.) A preparation similar to what in the United States is called a meat bird, although in England the thin slices of meat are usually folded around forcemeat rather than any other type of stuffing.

Olivette (Fr.)
A vegetable, usually a potato, cut into balls no larger than an olive and browned for use as a garnish.

Olla Podrida (Sp.)
A stew composed of sausages, garbanzos, beans, beef, etc., baked slowly in an earthenware pot, or olla. Considered a national dish.

Øllebrød (Scan.)
Beer bread, a popular Danish and Norwegian dish differing considerably in various methods of preparation. In one Danish recipe, it is a porridge of sugar, diced rye bread, and beer, which is served with heavy cream; while in a Norwegian recipe it consists of a light sauce of sugar, beer, cream, and eggs, which is served with fried bread.

Olympia Oyster
A tiny Pacific coast oyster, whose distinctive flavor makes it a favorite on the half shell.

Omelet
Beaten eggs cooked in a frying pan, or in a special omelet pan (a frying pan with somewhat rounded bottom and sides, and of a heavy material, such as cast aluminum), and folded over on itself, often with a filling of herbs, cheese, jelly, or meat.

One-Berry
See PARTRIDGEBERRY.

On the Half Shell
Used to describe any mollusk, usually an oyster or a clam, served raw in its natural juice and in half of its own shell. A sauce, or lemon juice with salt and pepper, usually accompanies this delicacy, often served as the first course of a dinner.

Oolong Tea
A tea made by partial fermentation of tea leaves, and thus distinguished from the unfermented green and totally fermented black teas. Standard varieties are the Canton, China, Formosa, and Foochow oolongs.

Opalescent Apple
A winter apple, i.e., late ripening, which should be baked.

Open-Faced Sandwich
A sandwich consisting of only one slice of bread upon which is placed a spread or "filling," often in a decorative manner.

Open Kettle Canning
The oldest method of canning tomatoes and fruits. The product is cooked in water or syrup, packed hot, and sealed tightly in a sterilized jar.

Orach
An herb with red or green leaves, used as a vegetable or in soups or stews.

Orange Pekoe
A grade of black tea produced in India, Ceylon, or Java, having very small and delicate leaves. Other grades are the less fine broken orange pekoe, and the pekoe.

Oregano
A Mediterranean herb also called wild marjoram, growing as a bush two to three feet high. The little, grey-green leaves have a fine, pungent scent and flavor, especially good with tomatoes, onions, pork and lamb, and in sausages.

Organic Food
A food grown or produced without the use of inorganic (i.e., never alive; referring to minerals, chemicals, etc., in contrast to plants and animals) materials such as chemical fertilizers or insecticides. Also called health food.

Orgeat (Fr.)
A thick syrup of orange water, sugar, flour, and almonds; also, in an old American recipe, a dessert made of milk cooked with cinnamon, almonds, rose water, sugar, etc.

Oriental Sauce
A sauce containing curry powder and cream, and usually served with a rice dish.

O-Sembei (Jap.)
Little cakes made with rice or wheat flour and a variety of other ingredients. Also spelled *sembei*.

Osso Buco (It.)
A dish of veal shank seasoned with garlic, white wine, olive oil, tomato purée, chopped anchovy fillets, etc., and served with saffron-tinted rice.

Ost (Scan.)
Cheese.

Oswego Tea
A common name for red bergamot, a native wild mint which grows in the eastern United States, and which the Oswego Indians are said to have used for making tea.

Oven
An insulated chamber with one or more doors, which is heated for roasting or baking.

Oven Temperature
Many old recipes give oven baking temperatures as only slow, medium, or hot. *The Fannie Farmer Cookbook*, 1961 edition, lists the equivalents as 300 degrees, 350 degrees, and 400 degrees, while 25- to 50-degree varia-

tions make for a very slow, a moderately slow, a moderately hot, and a very hot oven.

Oxalis Root (S. Am.)
A small, potato-like tuber of one kind of sorrel native to Peru and Bolivia, and having a slightly sweet, but very mild flavor. They are best when kept a few days after gathering, when they may be cooked like potatoes. Also called *occa* and *oka*.

Oxford Pudding (Eng.)
According to a recipe dating from 1765, a pudding made from currants, suet, grated plain cookies, and egg yolks. The mixture was shaped into balls the size of a large egg and fried in butter.

Oyster
A mollusk with a rough, hinged, double shell. The meat is quite tender and usually pearly white and grey, and is served in a large variety of ways. Oysters may be very plump or rather flat, and vary greatly in taste, size, and tenderness. Some ninety million pounds are eaten in the United States each year. See CHINCOTEAGUE, JAPANESE, LONG ISLAND, and OLYMPIA OYSTER.

Oyster Crab
A tiny crab which occasionally lives in the gill cavity of an oyster, and which is considered a great delicacy.

Oyster Plant
See SALSIFY.

Oysters Rockefeller
A New Orleans specialty, consisting of oysters on the half shell topped with butter, crumbs, and a sauce of herbs and spinach, and baked on a bed of rock salt.

Paella (Sp.)
Rice, prepared with meat, shellfish, sausages, etc., and a variety of seasonings, two chief ones being garlic and saffron. It is cooked in a deep pot, and the various ingredients are added as the cooking progresses.

Paillette (Fr.)
A stick of puff paste.

Pain Perdu (Fr.)
Literally, "lost bread," a type of fritter made of stale rolls soaked in milk and sugar, dipped in egg yolk, and fried a light golden brown.

Palm Cabbage
The central leaf bud or head of various palms, which is eaten raw or cooked. Also called cabbage palm, heart of palm, or gru-gru.

Palm Leaf
Puff paste so rolled, folded, and cut as to form a confection in the shape of a palm leaf.

Pamplemousse (Fr.)
Grapefruit.

Pan
Originally, a shallow cooking utensil; now applied to one of any size or depth, for example, the saucepan.

Panada (Eng.)
A simple bread soup consisting of bread boiled to a pulp in milk and then flavored.

Panade (Fr.)

A mixture of milk or stock and flour, crumbs, or bread used to give force-meat or stuffing the proper consistency, or to thicken a sauce. It is often made by soaking bread in milk and squeezing out the excess fluid.

Pan Bread

A quick bread baked on top of the stove in a covered saucepan.

Pan-Broil

To cook uncovered in a hot, generally ungreased, skillet.

Pancake

See GRIDDLE CAKE.

Pancake Turner

A thin, flat square or rectangle of metal set at a slight upward slant at the end of a handle.

Pan Drippings

See DRIPPINGS.

Pandora (Sp.)

A toasted or fried bread strip spread with a meat mixture, dipped in butter and fried. A great delicacy.

Pané à l'Anglaise (Fr.)

Covered with bread crumbs.

Pan Fish

Any fish, though generally a fresh-water variety, which may be fried whole in a skillet.

Pan-Fry

To sauté; also, to slice and fry raw potatoes, then called pan-fried.

Pannequet (Fr.)

A pancake.

Panocha (Mex.)

A candy made of brown sugar, milk, butter, and nuts. Also spelled *penuche*.

Pantry

A small room off the kitchen or dining room, in which bread and other food, or glassware, china, etc., are kept.

Papaya

1. A tropical fruit which, when cultivated, may often weigh ten pounds, having a yellow-pink flesh and a pleasantly unique flavor, somewhat resembling that of the canteloupe. It is usually eaten like a melon.
2. A name sometimes given to the paw-paw, which see.

Papillote, en (Fr.)

Literally, "wrapped in paper." The use of paper cases or decorative frills is an old French culinary tradition. Foil may be substituted for parchment, the usual paper for cases.

Paprika

See RED PEPPER.

Paradise Nut

A sweet, oily nut resembling the Brazil nut and used in candies. It is said that few reach the market, as the urn-shaped pod which contains the nuts falls to the ground with a loud report which summons all the monkeys within hearing distance. Also called *sapucaia nut*.

Paradise Pepper

A name for the fine mignonnette peppercorn, which is also called shot pepper and grains of paradise.

Paratha (Ind.)

A native bread, made of whole meal and shaped into a thin, round pancake, like a chapati, but some times fried in butter rather than being baked on an ungreased griddle.

Parboil

To put into boiling water and to cook partially, usually not over five minutes.

Parch

To expose to heat till thoroughly dry and shriveled.

Pare

To cut away the outer covering, as of apples, potatoes, etc.

Parfait

1. (Fr.) A dessert made of custard or whipped cream and syrup frozen together.
2. (U.S.) Sometimes designates a dessert of several flavors of ice cream layered in a tall, thin glass and topped with syrup and whipped cream.

Parfait Amour

A sweet liqueur, colored and flavored with violets and a suggestion of vanilla.

Paring Knife

A small, single-edged knife for paring and miscellaneous cutting purposes.

Parisian Potato Spoon

A small, round-bowled, sharp-edged spoon designed for cutting potatoes, especially, into balls known as olivette potatoes, and corresponding to the American "melon-baller."

Parisienne Sauce

A sweet sauce of egg yolks, powdered sugar, and sherry whipped together over heat, and with a little cream gradually added.

Parker House Roll

A roll folded over before baking, originated at the Parker House, a hotel in Boston.

Parkin (Eng.)

A kind of oatmeal cake also using flour, sugar, spices, and molasses, which is allowed to stand for a while before baking and is best when ripened a few days afterwards. They are most popular in the North Country, and are often baked for Guy Fawkes Day, November 5.

Parmentier (Fr.)

Any preparation containing potatoes, so named in honor of Parmentier, who introduced the potato into France in 1786.

Parmesan Cheese (It.)

A sharp cheese with salty, smoky flavor, hard in texture and almost always used grated, made in Parma, and elsewhere.

Parmigiana, alla (It.)

Cooked with Parmesan cheese. Veal cutlets and eggplant are often prepared in this way.

Parratta (Ind.)

See PARATHA.

Parsley

An herb whose lacy, dark-green leaves are used as a garnish and as a seasoning in a wide variety of dishes such as eggs, fish, meats, and all vegetables, and as a part of the *bouquet garni* used in French cooking. There are some thirty varieties of this member of the carrot family varying in curlyness and color, among them being the double-curled, moss-leaved, fern-leaved, and turnip-rooted.

Parsnip
The long, pale yellow, tapered root of a plant belonging to the carrot family which may be served boiled and sautéed, or in fritters, stews, and souffles, and either whole (if young and tender) mashed, or cut into strips.

Parson's Nose
A name sometimes given to the part of the rump of a bird, such as a chicken or turkey, from which the tail feathers grow. Also called Pope's nose.

Partridgeberry
The pithy, sweet, scarlet berry of a trailing evergreen plant found in the eastern United States. Also called oneberry.

Paskha (Rus.)
A cheese cake made with sugar, almonds, and candied peel, chilled in a turk's head pan for at least half a day, and traditionally served at Easter with *kulich*.

Passion Fruit
A plum-sized fruit, cultivated in California, with yellow aromatic pulp suggesting a blend of the flavors of peach, apricot, and guava. The juice, which is used in flavoring cocktails, punch, etc., has a pleasant but very distinctive and lingering taste, so that a little goes a long way.

Pasta (It.)
See ITALIAN PASTE; also, ACINI DI PEPE; DITALI; DITALINI; FUSILLI; MACARONI; MOSTACCIOLI; PERCIATELLI; RIGATONI; SPAGHETTI; SPAGHETTINI; ZITI.

Paste
1. Dough, especially that containing a large proportion of shortening, as, for example, puff paste.
2. A foodstuff pounded or ground till creamy, as, for example, meat paste.
3. A mixture of flour and water used in the manufacture of macaroni, etc. See PASTA.

Pasteurized Milk
Milk, either whole or homogenized, or skimmed, which has been partially sterilized by heating and thus purified for use. Most of the milk and cream sold nowadays is pasteurized rather than raw.

Pastille
A tiny ball or lozenge, flavored and colored, or coated with coloring.

Pastina (It.)
Tiny disks of noodle paste, about half an inch in diameter, used in soups.

Pastrami
Meat from the underside of the beef, cured with spices, and smoked. It is tender, succulent, and spicy, and is served thinly sliced, either hot or cold, most often in sandwiches.

Pastry
1. A dough of flour, water, and shortening used in making pies and tarts.
2. Foods made from the above, or any sweet bread, cooky, cake, etc.

Pastry Bag

A cone or cornucopia-shaped tube of strong paper, metal, or plastic, with a small hole in the point of the cone, through which frosting is forced from above by hand pressure.

Pastry Flour

A very white and very soft flour made of soft wheat, and used for the finest cakes and pastries.

Pastry Jagger

A wheeled metal device for making a fancy edge on a pie crust or other pastry.

Pasty (Eng.)

A type of turnover; a portion of meat, vegetables, fruit, jam, or some other filling is enclosed in a puff paste or pastry crust and baked. See CORNISH PASTY.

Pâte (Fr.)

Paste, pastry, or dough.

Pâté (Fr.)

Pie or patty with a filling of meat or fish paste, or occasionally, with a fruit or vegetable mixture; also, the filling itself.

Pâte à Choux (Fr.)

Cream puff pastry.

Pâté de Foie Gras (Fr.)

A paste made partially or entirely of goose liver.

Patna Rice

The brown rice eaten in India.

Patty

1. A small, rounded, and flattened mass of dough, mashed potatoes, minced meat, etc.
2. A small pie, i.e., one baked in a patty-pan.

Patty-Pan

A miniature pie pan; see preceding entry.

Patty-Pan Squash

A summer squash, round, and rather flat in shape, with scalloped edges, and pale green or white in color. Generally cooked whole without peeling, unless old and dry. It may be cut in cubes and creamed, sliced, or sautéed. Also called cymling.

Paupiette (Fr.)

A thin slice of meat stuffed with a vegetable or other filling, rolled up and fried or braised; in English, a meat bird.

Paw-Paw

The oblong, yellowish fruit of a tree native to the middle and southern states. The flesh has the consistency of a banana and at its best is sweet and fragrant. Also sometimes called papaya, but is not to be confused with the tropical fruit of that name.

Paysanne (Fr.)

1. Cut into triangles.
2. Cooked in a plain manner; literally, "peasant style."

Pea Bean

A small bean, round rather than kidney-shaped, dried and used for Boston baked beans.

Pea-Leaf Tea

Green tea prepared by a method which yields a round, rolled-up leaf.

Pearl Barley
Husked barley which has been polished so that the grains are rounded and pearly in appearance.

Pearl Onion
A round onion, usually not over an inch and a half in diameter, with a thin, transparent white skin. Pearl onions are cooked either as a separate vegetable or with meat.

Pecorino Cheese (It.)
A medium sharp cheese, off-white in color, made from sheep's milk. It is grated and used for seasoning.

Pectin
A natural gelatin occurring in fruits and some vegetables and used in the making of fruit jelly.

Peel
To remove the skin of a vegetable or fruit, for example, of a tomato or banana; or the skin itself.

Pekoe
A grade of black tea from India, Ceylon, or Java based on the size of the leaf. See ORANGE PEKOE.

Pelmeni (Rus.)
A food resembling ravioli, consisting of noodle paste rolled thin, cut small, filled with a meat mixture, and poached, often in a soup.

Pemmican
A kind of sausage made of dried meat (now usually beef, though venison and bison were formerly used) pounded together with hot fat, dried berries, raisins, and suet, and packed into a waterproof casing, where it will keep indefinitely. It is very rich in food value, may be eaten with or without further cooking, and is still used during polar exploration.

Peneque (Mex.)
A corn pancake, cooked on an ungreased skillet and folded around a piece of cheese, then dipped in a flour and egg batter, fried quickly, and served with hot sauce.

Pennyroyal
A member of the mint family which trails along the ground rather than growing upright. It is used for herb tea and occasionally in soups and stews.

Penuche (Mex.)
See PANOCHA.

Peperoncini all' Aceto (It.)
An antipasto dish consisting of small green pickled peppers which are the equivalent of the American sour pickle.

Pepper
An aromatic and pungent condiment obtained from the dried berries of a climbing vine native to the East Indies. The peppercorns, or berries, are a brilliant red before drying, which turns them brown or black. The dried berries are round, rough-skinned, and an eighth to a quarter of an inch in diameter, with the well-known hot, pungent aroma and taste. They may be used whole, but are generally ground. White pepper is obtained by grinding only the inner seed after the dark outer coat has been removed, and it is favored for dishes where the dark flakes of black pepper might be

unattractive, or where the fuller, stronger flavor of black pepper might be undesirable, though both white and black pepper come from the berry of the same plant.

Peppercorn
The dried berry of the pepper plant.

Peppergrass
See LAND CRESS.

Pepperpot
1. (U.S., Pa.) A soup made with tripe, and heavily seasoned with pepper.
2. (W. Ind.) A soup made with fish, meats, chilis, and vegetables.

Perch
Any of several small, spiny-finned, fresh- or salt-water fish having a variety of markings. One frequently seen has an olive-green back with yellow, dark-banded sides, and vermilion lower fins. Generally considered a good pan fish. See OCEAN PERCH and YELLOW PERCH.

Perciatelli (It.)
A long, tubular pasta resembling spaghetti but slightly larger in diameter.

Percolated Coffee
Coffee made in such a way that boiling water is forced by its own steam pressure up a hollow stem and into a basket holding the ground coffee, through which it drips back down into the pot, to continue boiling and rising until the coffee reaches the desired strength.

Perfection Salad
A tomato aspic containing chopped onion, cabbage, celery, pimento, and green pepper.

Perigourdine (Fr.)
Signifying any dish made or served with truffles, for which the French region of Perigord is famous.

Perigueux Sauce (Fr.)
A brown sauce made with Madeira and truffles. Used with entrées, timbales, etc.

Periwinkle
A small sea snail with a pretty black spiral shell, common along the coasts of Scotland and England, and often used for food. A fresh-water periwinkle is found in the Mississippi valley, but it is not eaten.

Pernod (Fr.)
An anise-flavored liqueur, somewhat resembling absinthe, with a taste like that of licorice.

Perry
A drink made from the fermented juice of pears, as cider is from that of apples.

Persian Melon
A pale green, oval melon with pale pink flesh, grown in the Southwest.

Persillade (Fr.)
A seasoning or sauce containing chopped parsley.

Persimmon
A plum-shaped fruit, orange in color when ripe, and both tart and sweet in flavor. To be good, a persimmon has to have been frost-nipped, otherwise it is extremely puckery.

Pestle
See MORTAR AND PESTLE.

Petit or Petite (Fr.)
Small or little; often implying fresh and young, also, as in *petits pois*.

Petite Marmite (Fr.)
A soup made with chicken, beef, marrowbone, onions, carrots, and various herbs and spices, simmered for a very long time. It derives its name from the small earthenware casseroles, or marmites, in which it is served.

Petit Four (Fr.)
A small, frosted tea cake, or any of various sweet, rich cookies.

Petits Pois (Fr.)
Small green peas, especially those that are very young and tender.

Pettitoes
Pig's trotters.

Pfeffernuss (pl. *Pfeffernüsse;* Ger.)
Literally, "pepper nut," or "ginger nut"; a heavily spiced cooky, sometimes including black pepper. It is rolled, shaped into balls, and rested overnight. Before baking, it is moistened with a drop of fruit juice or brandy which helps the "nut" to pop, or expand. Pfeffernüsse are ripened before being eaten, which is usually during the Christmas holiday season.

Philadelphia Clam Chowder
Like Manhattan clam chowder, one made with tomatoes rather than milk.

Philpy (U.S., South.)
A rice "pie" containing both cooked rice and rice flour and served with butter. An old recipe.

Phosphate Baking Powder
See BAKING POWDER.

Picadillo (Mex.)
A hash, often made with chopped cooked beef, garlic, onion, vinegar, and raisins.

Piccalilli
A pickle relish based on chopped tomatoes cooked with horseradish, sugar, spices, and vinegar. Also called Indian pickle, from its origin in the East Indies.

Pickerel
A fish with lean or dry meat, belonging to the pike family, and ranging from one to two feet in length when mature.

Pickle
To steep in brine, vinegar, spices, etc., as a means of preserving and flavoring.

Pickle Meat
A country name for salt pork, which is excellent as a main dish if sliced thin, cooked slowly till a great deal of the salt and some of the fat are removed, and fried till golden and crisp.

Pie
Any baked dish of fruit, meat, etc., having at least one crust of pastry or dough.

Pie Bird
A small, hollow figurine, usually in the shape of a bird with an open beak, which is inserted into the upper crust of a two-crust pie to allow for the escape of steam and to serve as an ornament during serving.

Pièce de Résistance (Fr.)
The main dish; hence, often one con-

sisting of meat, poultry, or game, served with a sauce or stuffing, though sometimes the term may be applied to an elaborate salad or dessert.

Pieplant
A name for rhubarb.

Pignut
The bitter-sweet nut of a species of hickory.

Pig's Face (Ir.)
A national dish in Ireland, much as haggis is in Scotland, consisting of half a pig's head, well simmered and oven-toasted, placed on a large platter, and surrounded with cooked cabbage.

Pig's Fry
The edible entrails of a pig, usually cut in long, thin slices, and cooked in a rich stew.

Pigs in Blankets
1. Oysters wrapped in bacon and broiled. Also called angels on horseback and devils on horseback.
2. Little sausages wrapped in dough and baked.

Pigweed
See LAMB'S LETTUCE.

Pike
A slender, fresh-water fish with lean or dry meat. A fierce game fish, it often reaches four feet in length and is found under various names from New York to the mouth of the Ohio, and as far north and west as Alaska. The average market size is one-and-a-half to ten pounds, though it can reach twenty-five. One of the common species is the pickerel.

Pikelet (Scot.)
The Northern name for a type of crumpet; i.e., a small, thin, yeast-raised pancake baked on a griddle and served with butter.

Pilau
An Oriental, Indian, or Middle Eastern dish consisting mainly of rice, usually with meat, spices, etc., added. Also spelled *pilaf*, *pilaw*, and *pellao*.

Pilchard
A European fish much like the herring. The sardine is often a young pilchard.

Pilot Bread
An alternate name for hardtack.

Pimento
1. A mild, sweet red pepper, also called Spanish paprika, used in sauces or as a garnish. Also spelled *pimiento*.
2. Allspice, i.e., the dried aromatic berries of the West Indian pimento tree.

Pimpernel
A small annual plant which grows wild in wastelands, and is sometimes used as a seasoning.

Pineapple Cheese (U.S.)
A hard, moderately sharp cheese of the Cheddar type, made in a pineapple shape and hung and dried in a net which gives the surface a diamond-patterned corrugation.

Pine Nut
See PIÑON NUT.

Pine-Nut Sauce
A brown sauce containing toasted pine nuts, usually served with venison.

Pingsuey Tea
An inferior grade of China green tea.

Piñon Nut
A small, sweet, oval-shaped seed from an evergreen tree of the same name. Also called pine nut.

Pinot Blanc Grape
A variety of white or pale green grape from which white Burgundy wines are made; also used in some California white wines.

Pinot Noir Grape
A black grape, dark blue or purple in color, used in making red Burgundy wines, and also some of those made in California.

Pinto Bean
A pink, mottled bean grown in the western United States and Mexico.

Pinwheel
A name applied to any dish prepared from pastry, dough, or cake, which is rolled out, spread with a filling, which may be anything from ground beef to ice cream, and then rolled up into a cylinder and cut into slices for baking or serving. The name is derived, of course, from the spiral or pinwheel pattern of each slice.

Pip Fruit
See POME.

Pippin
Any of several varieties of apple, most of them used in cooking. Among the better varieties are the fall-ripening Holland and Fall pippins, good baked or in pies; the Albemarle, one of those which may be eaten raw; and the Missouri, a good cooking apple, in season from January to May.

Piquant
Agreeably pungent, sharp, or stimulating to the sense of taste or smell.

Piquante Sauce (Fr.)
A highly-seasoned sauce, made with vinegar, white wine, shallots, gherkins, capers, herbs, etc., to accompany pork or left-over meat.

Piroshki (Rus. and Jew.)
Turnovers, or pockets, rather like knishes but made of unleavened dough resembling pastry which is rolled into very thin, individual-sized rounds, spread with a liver, mushroom, cheese, or sweet filling, folded over and sealed, and baked or steamed. Also popular in Poland; sometimes called *pirogen* or *pierogen*.

Pismo Clam
A West coast clam, named for Pismo Beach at San Luis Obispo, California. It is highly prized and may be used in any clam recipe.

Pistachio Nut
A greenish, almond-like nut used for its delicate color and flavor, especially in sweet dishes and confectionery.

Pisto Manchego (Sp.)
A pork stew.

Pit
The hard seed or stone of a fruit, for example, a peach or cherry; also, to remove this stone.

Pizza (It.)
A kind of pie made of dough spread with tomato sauce, Mozzarella cheese, sausage, mushrooms, and the like, and baked.

Pizzaiola (It.)
The name given to a kind of tomato sauce, or to any of various dishes prepared with it.

Plaice
Any of several kinds of flatfish, especially the summer flounder.

Planked
Refers to fish or steak both cooked and served on a wooden board, or plank, or similarly prepared on a shallow baking dish.

Plantain
1. A common, short-stemmed weed, of which the young buds and leaves are eaten as greens.
2. A fruit similar to the banana, but larger, less sweet, and more starchy.

Plättar (Swed.)
Pancakes.

Pliofilm
A trade name for a kitchen wrapping paper having the clear, colorless transparency of cellophane, and the pliability of metal foil wrapping paper.

Plombière (Fr.)
A dessert of ice cream with candied fruit.

Pluche (Fr.)
The tip or unveined portion of a leaf, for example, of chervil, tarragon, or mint.

Pluck
1. To pick or pull off, as the feathers from poultry.
2. (Eng.) The heart, lungs, and liver of an animal as food.

Plum Pudding
A suet pudding which, like plum cake, actually never contains plums but is made with currants and, generally, raisins, and which is steamed or boiled.

Plum Tomato
A small, oval, Italian tomato, shaped like a plum.

Poach
To cook by immersing more or less completely in water or other liquid which may be either at or below the boiling point; or to cook in a *bainmarie*.

Pocket
A turnover.

Pod Bean
Any bean, especially one eaten pod and all.

Poelé (Fr.)
Roasted in melted butter, usually without the addition of liquid; from the noun *poéle*, meaning frying-pan.

Poffertje (Hol.)
A small yeast- or beer-raised fritter which may be baked in a muffin tin, or on a griddle, though a special poffertje-pan is much preferred.

Poi (Haw.)
A native dish consisting of pounded taro, fermented for anywhere from a few hours to several days.

Poisson (Fr.)
A fish.

Poivrade Sauce (Fr.)
A brown sauce seasoned with crushed whole peppercorns, to be served with meat.

Pokeweed
A strong-smelling perennial whose first, green shoots are succulent and may be cooked like asparagus, though the root and berries are poisonous.

Polenta (It.)
A porridge or mush which may be made of barley or chestnut meal, but is now most often made of corn meal, and which is used in Italy as a separate dish with meat or fish, or in place of bread.

Polished Rice
White rice, i.e., that from which the dark bran has been removed, and which has been put through a device which smooths and polishes the kernels.

Polish Sauce
A sweet butter sauce containing raisins, currants, almonds, spices, and red wine.

Pollock
A relative of the haddock and cod, the well-flavored white meat of which is often sold as deep-sea fillet.

Polpetta (pl. _polpette;_ It.)
A meat ball.

Polpettone (It.)
Meat loaf.

Polvorone (Mex.)
A small round cooky or tea cake covered with confectioner's sugar.

Poly-Unsaturated Fat
A liquid fat having a low number of hydrogen atoms on the fat molecule, and including corn, cottonseed, and fish oil.

Pome
A fleshy fruit, such as the apple or pear, having the seeds inclosed in cases (carpels) to form a core. Also called pip fruits.

Pomegranate
An African and Asiatic fruit having a brilliant red, hard rind and a tart, translucent scarlet pulp in which the many seeds are embedded. The fruit is about the size of a large apple, and the seeds, covered with the firm, juicy pulp, are an attractive ingredient in fruit salads.

Pomelo
A type of grapefruit.

Pompano
A delicious, oily-meated fish, native to the South Atlantic and Gulf of Mexico.

Pompion
An old name for the yellow-orange field pumpkin commonly grown and used for pies.

Pone
See CORN PONE.

Pont l'Evêque Cheese (Fr.)
A soft cheese somewhat similar to Brie.

141

Poona Cheese (U.S.)
A soft, mild cheese made in New York State.

Poor Man's Pudding
An old-fashioned pudding consisting of milk, a little uncooked rice, and sugar baked slowly together. Various flavorings or raisins are sometimes added.

Popcicle
A kind of frozen lollipop, or icicle on a stick, consisting of sweetened and flavored ice.

Pope's Nose
See PARSON'S NOSE.

Popover
A muffin made from a light batter similar to that used in Yorkshire pudding, which greatly expands during baking, causing the muffin to "pop over" the edge of its cup, thus forming a crisp, hollow shell.

Poppadum (Ind.)
A crisp pancake of wafer thinness, cooked on an ungreased, or only slightly greased griddle, eaten in a variety of ways, but always piping hot.

Popple
An old-fashioned Southern rice pudding made without raisins, but topped with cherries and meringue and served with a lemon or cream sauce.

Poppy Seed
The tiny, round, grey seed of an Oriental flowering plant. Those used in the kitchen have no narcotic properties, and form an ingredient in, or garnish for, cakes, cookies, eggs, salads, and vegetables. In Europe a mixture of ground poppy seed with milk, nuts, sugar, etc. is used as a filling for cakes and pastries. The flavor is rich, nutty, and oily.

Porcelain
A fine pottery or baked clay with a translucent glaze and delicate finish. See EARTHENWARE.

Porette
An ancient English name, from at least the fourteenth century, for greens.

Porgy
A food or game fish, generally weighing from three-quarters of a pound to two pounds, which is common along the Atlantic coast and, sometimes, in the Gulf of Mexico. Also called scup.

Porridge
Oatmeal, generally rolled or coarsely ground, cooked with water and salt and served with milk and salt or sugar, most commonly at breakfast.

Porringer
A small bowl, usually with a short handle, from which porridge was formerly eaten.

Port
A strong, sweet wine, most often dark red, although occasionally tawny or white, made in Portugal; or any of various similar wines made in the United States and elsewhere. It is traditionally a man's wine, served with cheese and nuts after a hearty meal.

Port du Salut Cheese (Fr.)
A soft cheese with a fairly strong aroma, creamy yellow inside, with an edible russet-brown crust. It is made

in both France and America, mainly by Trappist monks, and is sometimes called Trappist cheese, though there are also some commercial brands. Also called Port Salut.

Porter (Eng.)
A dark bitter beer made with roasted malt, which accounts for its color.

Porterhouse Steak
A choice cut of beef, taken from the loin of beef, and containing both loin and a good section of fillet. It is quite expensive, especially as it should be over an inch thick.

Port Royal Salad (Fr.)
A salad containing potatoes, apples, string beans, and hard-boiled eggs with mayonnaise.

Posset
A drink made of milk curdled with ale, molasses, wine, etc., flavored with spices, and served very hot.

Pot
A deep, round, cooking vessel without a side handle; or any kind of pan used in cooking, with the exception of a frying-pan. Also, as a verb, to place meat, fish, etc., usually with salt and seasonings, in a pot-like vessel to preserve them.

Potable
Drinkable.

Potage (Fr.)
Soup.

Potato Flour
A flour made from potatoes, which in making bread may be substituted for

wheat flour, using one part potato flour to three parts wheat flour. An excellent thickener for sauces and gravies.

Pot-au-Feu (Fr.)
Literally, "kettle on the fire," or stock pot; but usually refers to a stew of beef, vegetables, and seasonings in broth.

Pot Herb
Any plant whose leaves, stems, or blossoms are used in cooking to add flavor, and, occasionally, nutritious qualities.

Pot Likker (U.S., South.)
The juice left in the pot after greens have been cooked with pork.

Pot-Luck
A term now used to designate an informal dinner gathering, often one to which each person brings a dish of food; or, the idea of "taking things food-wise as you find them." This usage may have developed from an earlier one which appears in *Soyer's Cookery Book*, by Alexis Soyer, which was published in England in 1854, and in which he refers to the "immortal pot-luck," as any of several meat and vegetable soups or stews made in the three-legged iron pot.

Pot Marigold
Another name for marigold.

Pot Marjoram
See MARJORAM.

Pot Pie
A meat or poultry pie, usually with vegetables and potatoes, baked in an

uncovered casserole with a single or double crust of pastry or biscuit dough.

Potpourri

A stew of various meats and seasonings; or, any food mixture.

Pot Roast

A cut of beef, most often from the chuck or round, tending to be rather tough and thus requiring long, slow cooking in a covered pot, either on top of the stove or in an oven.

Potted

An adjective referring to various preparations, including food stewed in a deep pot, in which case the term is used interchangeably with "jugged"; or to that packaged or served in a small vessel or pot, for example, a custard cup or earthenware dish, usually a minced meat or a cheese product.

Pouchong Tea

An oolong tea which is scented with gardenia and jasmine; the best of these teas are from Formosa.

Poulette Sauce (Fr.)

A thick velouté sauce seasoned with lemon juice.

Pound Cake

A loaf cake made with whole eggs and approximately equal amounts of sugar and flour. It is yellow, firm, and fine-textured. Its name is probably derived from the fact that the ingredients were originally measured by the pound.

Pound Sweet Apple

A fall variety, which is good baked.

Pousse-Café (Fr.)

An after-dinner drink made by pouring various liqueurs, the heaviest first, the lightest last, into a small, thin, yet rather deep glass so that they form separate, differently colored layers. One recipe calls for grenadine, yellow Chartreuse, Creme de Yvette, Creme de Menthe, green Chartreuse, and brandy.

Powdered Milk

Either whole or skim milk which has been dehydrated and powdered.

Powdered Sugar

An extremely fine-grained white sugar, often labeled XXX to distinguish it from the even finer confectioner's sugar, often labeled XXXX, but which is frequently used interchangeably with it.

Prairie Oyster

A non-alcoholic cocktail, recommended as an antidote for a hangover, composed of an unbroken egg yolk with various other ingredients, for example, tomato juice and Worcestershire sauce.

Pralin (Fr.)

A sweet paste containing chopped almonds, used in the preparation of desserts.

Praline (U.S., South.)

A candy made of brown sugar and nut meats, generally pecans, boiled together and then dipped by the spoonful onto a cool plate and allowed to harden.

Prawn

A shrimp-like shellfish, generally

larger and more delicately flavored than the American shrimp, and more common in Europe than in the United States. Like shrimps, prawns are whitish when caught, but are generally boiled before they are marketed, a process which turns the shell red or pink.

Prepared Mustard
Dry mustard mixed with vinegar, water, and, sometimes, seasoning. Turmeric is often added to American mustard to give it a bright yellow color. The typical American prepared mustard is also quite mild in flavor.

Preserve
Fruit boiled with sugar to a thick consistency in order to preserve it; distinguished from jam or marmalade in that the pieces are usually left intact rather than mashed or cut up. See also CONSERVE.

Pressure Cooker
A large saucepan with a tightly sealed and valve-controlled lid, in which steam pressure is used to cook food quickly at a temperature well above that of boiling water.

Pretzel (Ger.)
A crisp, slender roll of dough, traditionally twisted by hand into a loose knot and heavily sprinkled with coarse salt before baking. Pretzels may be small or large and are now made also in the form of sticks, bite-size balls, etc.

Prickly Pear
The deep purple, pear-shaped fruit of various flat-jointed cacti. The pulp is refreshing but seedy, and is used in jam.

Primost Cheese (Scan.)
A hard or semi-hard cheese, light brown in color and sweet and mild in flavor.

Printanier (Fr.)
Literally, springlike or vernal; referring usually to a dish made or garnished with spring vegetables.

Printanier Butter (Fr.)
A purée of spring vegetables blended with butter.

Process Cheese
A natural cheese which has been shredded, melted, and packaged while still warm. Many commercial cheeses are of this kind, and many cheese spreads and other cheese foods are made from process cheese.

Profiterolle (Fr.)
A small shell of unsweetened puff pastry, stuffed with a purée of vegetables, chicken, or some other ingredient, and served with soup or as an appetizer.

Prosciutto (It.)
Italian ham, which see.

Protein
Any food containing a good proportion of the amino acid compounds which are an essential part of living matter, and which account for growth, repair, and replacement of living cells in the organism. Meat, fish, eggs, milk, cereal grains, and legumes are major protein foods.

Protose
A commercial product, also called "vegetable meat," made from nut

meats and cereal, popular with vegetarians at the turn of the century and usually served as a main dish as it was often shaped into cutlets and loaves. Other commercial products of this sort were called Nuttolene and Bromose.

Prove (Eng.)
To rest dough just prior to baking.

Provençale (Fr.)
In the style of Provence; most frequently, though not necessarily, made with garlic, oil, and tomatoes.

Provençale Sauce (Fr.)
A sauce containing tomatoes, oil, garlic, and seasonings.

Provence Butter (Fr.)
A mixture of garlic, oil, egg, and lemon juice, similar to mayonnaise. Also called *aioli* sauce.

Provolone Cheese (It.)
A hard, mild to moderately sharp cheese with a slightly salty, smoky flavor. Often used grated in the United States, though it is more often eaten sliced in Italy.

Prunelle (Fr.)
A sweet, aromatic liqueur, yellow-brown in color, made from sloes.

Puaa (Haw. and Poly.)
Pig; see KALUA PUAA.

Puchero (Sp. and S. Am.)
A soup-like stew of garbanzos, beef, and various other meats.

Pudding
A sweet dessert, which may have either the soft consistency of a custard or the dense and heavy one of a plum pudding. Soft puddings are baked or cooked in a double boiler; the others are baked, boiled, or steamed.

Puffer
See BLOWFISH.

Puff Paste
A very light, flaky pastry which expands considerably in baking. The art of making a good puff paste is a highly refined specialty of French cooks.

Pulled Bread
Fresh bread, with crust removed, broken or pulled into pieces and browned in an oven.

Pullet
A young hen chicken, four to nine months old and weighing from two and a half to five and a half pounds.

Pulp
1. A soft, moist, homogeneous mass, for example, that obtained by mashing.
2. The soft, fleshy part of a fruit.

Pulque (Mex.)
A fermented drink made from the agave.

Pulse
The edible seeds of any pea or bean plant; more specifically, an ancient Hebrew dish consisting of roasted or boiled chick peas.

Pulverize
To reduce to a powder, or to very small particles.

Pumpernickel (Ger.)

A coarse-textured black or dark-brown bread made of unbolted rye flour, and having a strong, pleasant, slightly acid taste. It originated in Westphalia in Germany, but is now popular in the United States. Also called *Schwarzbrot,* or black bread.

Punch

A drink made of any of several ingredients, for example, milk, tea, fruit juices, wines, liquors, and carbonated beverages, and flavored with sugar and spices. The name is possibly derived from a Hindustani word for a drink containing five ingredients.

Pungent

Used to describe a flavor or odor which affects the organs of taste and smell with a prickling sensation, or which is pleasantly strong and distinctive but just this side of being unpleasantly so.

Purée

1. A sieved fruit or vegetable, either raw or cooked.
2. (Fr.) A thick, smooth soup.
3. As a verb, to rub through a sieve so as to obtain a uniform, small-particled texture.

Puri (Ind.)

A type of bread made like a chapati of whole wheat flour, rolled into wafer-thin cakes, and baked on a griddle, or, traditionally, fried in deep fat. Also spelled *puree.*

Purslane

A weed whose thick, fleshy leaves and stalks are used in soup, in salad, or alone as greens. It is sometimes cultivated.

Put Down

A phrase used to designate the packing of beef or pork in salt, or of fruit in sugar, and the like, for the purpose of preserving.

Pyramid Sandwich

A sandwich consisting of five or more slices of bread of graduated sizes, filled with chicken, lettuce, chopped hard-boiled eggs, sliced tomatoes, olives, anchovies, etc., so arranged as to form a pyramid and usually eaten with a knife and fork.

Quahog

The Indian name for the hard, or little-necked clam, abundant south of Cape Cod. It is much favored, because of its distinct flavor, for use in New England clam chowder and also in the vegetable soup called Manhattan clam chowder. The quahog lives in deeper waters than the soft clam and is more often taken by raking than by digging.

Queen Elizabeth I Apples

Fine apples cooked whole in sugar without water until transparent, and then placed in jars filled with hot vinegar that has been boiled with honey, allspice, and rosemary. The jars are tightly sealed and put aside for the apples to ripen for a period of not less than two months.

Quenelle (Fr.)

A forcemeat ball, used for garnishing soups and other dishes.

Quesadilla (Mex.)

A tortilla folded around a mild cheese filling and then cooked lightly in an ungreased skillet.

Quetsch (Fr.)
A clear, colorless liqueur made with plums.

Quiche Lorraine (Fr.)
An open-faced custard cheese pie containing chopped bacon and served as a luncheon dish or as an hors d'oeuvre.

Quick Bread
A bread which uses baking soda, baking powder, air, or steam, rather than yeast, as the leavening agent, and thus expands in the baking without any preliminary period of rising before it is put into the oven.

Quiet Wine
Any wine which is not sparkling or effervescent.

Quill
The name given to a piece of the inner bark of cassia or cinnamon which while drying has curled into a stick-like cylinder. Quills may be either very short or several inches long.

Quince
A golden, somewhat pear-shaped fruit with a delicious, but acid pulp and a perfume-like aroma. It is best used in preserves or jelly, or as a flavoring in other dishes, and should be cooked until transparent to ensure digestibility.

Quoorma (Ind.)
See KORMA.

Qutaif (Arab.)
An exotic dish consisting of tissue-thin pancakes fried in virgin almond oil, sprinkled with rose water, and served with a thick syrup.

Raab
A type of broccoli, also called turnip-tops, used in the southwestern states.

Râble (Fr.)
The back or saddle of a hare.

Rack of Lamb
The rib section in front of the loin, which provides rib chops and, unsplit, such fine roasts as the crown.

Radicchio (It.)
A radish, especially of the long-rooted, white variety. The root is sliced and served as a salad with its young, green leaves; or, it may be boiled or steamed and served as a vegetable.

Raffinade (Eng.)
A term referring to the best quality of refined sugar.

Ragoût (Fr.)
A stew of meat and vegetables.

Rahat Lakoum (Turk.)
See TURKISH DELIGHT.

Raise
To make light by placing in a warm spot, thus activating the yeast into producing the gas which expands or raises the dough.

Ramekin
A small individual mould in which a food is baked; or the food itself. Also spelled *ramequin*.

Rampion
A European bellflower (i.e., a family

of plants, including some herbs, with bell-shaped flowers) with a long, thick, white root like that of a radish, used either raw in salads or cooked as a vegetable.

Rancid
An adjective usually applied to oil or fat describing a smell or taste that is stale, unpleasantly strong, or rank; also, when applied to other materials, refers to a smell or taste like stale fat.

Rangpar
A citrus fruit the size of a small lemon, globular in shape, with a reddish skin and orange-colored pulp.

Rape (Eur.)
A member of the cabbage family cultivated in Europe for the oil its seeds produce, and sometimes cooked as a substitute for spinach or other greens.

Rasher
A thin slice of bacon.

Raspings
Fine dry bread crumbs.

Rassolnick (Rus.)
A very salty soup made of cucumbers. Also spelled *rossolnik*.

Rastegai (Rus.)
An appetizer made with chopped salmon.

Ratafia
An after-dinner cordial or liqueur flavored with almonds, or the kernels of apricot, peach, or cherry, especially one made at home, notably in France and in Louisiana; or, a small cooky called a ratafia biscuit either flavored

with, or appropriately served with, such a cordial.

Ratatouille (Fr.)
A stew, which may either include meat or be made solely of vegetables.

Ravigote Butter (Fr.)
See CHIVRY BUTTER.

Ravigote Sauce (Fr.)
A sauce, which may be either hot or cold, containing vinegar, herbs, and various other seasonings. See also VINAIGRETTE SAUCE.

Ravioli (It.)
Small squares of an egg and flour dough, filled with a cheese or meat mixture, cooked in rapidly boiling water, and usually served with a tomato sauce and grated Parmesan cheese.

Raw Milk
Milk which has not undergone the partial sterilization of pasteurizing.

Razor Clam
One of the most common West Coast clams, which, like the New England soft clam, burrows down into tidal flats and must be dug for. Its shell is long and sharp, and its meat is good sautéed, in fritters, or in chowder.

Ready-to-Eat
Describing a food, such as meat, which has been given, before it is marketed, the preparation necessary to render it edible without further cooking on the part of the buyer. Also called ready-cooked.

Ream or Reamer

An orange or lemon squeezer having a ridged and pointed center, over which half the fruit is pressed, surrounded by a shallow trough into which the juice drips. Also, the act of removing juice from fruit with such a device. A ream is generally made of glass and is an effective juicer.

Red Chili Pepper

See RED PEPPER.

Redfish

A popular Southern food fish weighing from two to twenty-five pounds. Also called red drum.

Red Flannel Hash (U.S., New Eng.)

A baked corned beef hash containing chopped beets.

Red Pepper

Any of several seasonings made from capsicums. The mildest of these is paprika, derived from the bonnet pepper. After it, in ascending order of pungency, come cayenne, red chili, and tabasco. These are all hot, and while they may generally be used interchangeably, with some adjustment as to amounts, great care should always be taken with any recipes calling for them.

Red Snapper

A bass-like fish with excellent lean or dry meat, common in warm seas, especially the Gulf of Mexico. Specimens two or three feet in length are often used as display fish.

Reduce

To cook a liquid until a certain amount is cooked away, thus concentrating the flavor in, and thickening the consistency of, that which remains.

Red Wine Sauce (Fr.)

Any of various sauces containing red wine, especially those made with fish stock.

Refrigerator Cake

A chilled dessert composed of small cakes or wafers, whipped cream, nuts, fruits, etc., made several hours ahead of the time for its use and kept cold in the refrigerator.

Refrigerator Cooky

Any kind of cooky made with dough which must be chilled before it is shaped, sliced, or rolled out to be cut for baking.

Regence Sauce (Fr.)

A velouté sauce flavored with mushrooms and truffles to be served with poultry or fish.

Reggiano Cheese (It.)

A kind of Parmesan cheese.

Relevé (Fr.)

In formal usage, any of various dishes served immediately after the soup course, and thus often consisting of fish; but as commonly used, any main dish, generally one of meat and more substantial than an entrée.

Relever (Fr.)

To enhance, or to give a piquant flavor to a food by the use of seasonings.

Relish

1. Something appetizing but not es-

sential added to a meal, as olives, pickles, celery, etc.

2. To enjoy.

Rellenas (Sp.)
Stuffed.

Rémoulade Sauce (Fr.)
Mayonnaise seasoned with mustard, gherkins, capers, herbs, anchovies, etc., to be served with cold meat, poultry, lobster, or fried fish.

Render
To melt down or try out meat, especially pork, to separate the portions of lean or connective tissues from the clear fat.

Rennet
A curdling agent used in some milk puddings and cheeses. Rennet is the name given to the curdled milk found in the stomach of an unweaned calf, and also to any preparation from the stomach membranes of an animal or from various plants.

Rhine Wine
A white wine, usually rather delicate and light-bodied, produced in Germany; or one produced elsewhere and sold under this name. Either kind is served with fish or fowl and should be chilled before use.

Rhubarb
A garden plant, originally an Asiatic weed, cultivated for its long, fleshy, pink stalks which are cooked and sweetened to be used as a stewed fruit dessert or are used in pies, and tarts or in combination with other fruits in a variety of sweets.

Ribbon Cake
Variously colored layers of cake batter baked together to give a striped effect, or baked in separate layer pans and put together with fillings.

Ribier Grape
A very dark purple grape, grown for table use.

Rib Roast
The finest large roast in the entire beef, the first three ribs of which are the best. The meat tends to be quite rich, with a good deal of fat.

Rib Steak
Any steak, for example, club or minute, cut from the ribs of beef, preferably from the first few of these.

Rice
As a verb, to press a vegetable, especially the potato, through a heavy, sieve-like utensil which reduces it to rice-like pellets.

Ricotta Cheese (It.)
A fresh, moist, unsalted cottage cheese which is also used like cream cheese in sandwiches or salads, or sweetened and flavored and used in dessert dishes.

Riesling Grape
A white grape, light yellow in color, grown in Germany, and also in California; also, any of various white wines made from these grapes.

Rigatoni (It.)
Large curved and ribbed tubular pasta cut into three-inch lengths.

Rijsttafel (Indonesia)
Literally, "rice table," this meal com-

prises a large quantity of boiled rice and a wide assortment of hot and spicy dishes served with it.

Rind
The rather hard, generally inedible outer covering of fruit, cheese, bacon, and the like.

Ring Mould
A circular, ring-shaped mould used for gelatins, aspics, etc.

Rink Cake (Ir.)
A sweet cake made with chopped almonds and currants.

Rinktum Ditty
Another name for rum tum tiddy, which see.

Ripen
To allow a food, such as cheese or cake, to remain uneaten for anywhere from a few days to several months, often in a tightly closed container, in order to mellow and improve the flavor.

Ripieno (It.)
Stuffed.

Risi e Bisi (It.)
A dish made with rice and peas.

Risotto alla Milanese (It.)
Rice cooked in broth with saffron, and mixed with Parmesan cheese.

Rissole (Fr.)
A kind of turnover, or pastry-enclosed croquette, with a meat or fruit filling, which may be either baked or fried in deep fat and served as an hors d'oeuvre, main dish, or dessert.

Rissoler (Fr.)
To brown or sear.

Roast
To cook by exposure to dry heat; most often applied to meat or fowl.

Roaster
1. A large, heavy pan with a bottom rack on which the meat to be roasted is set, generally with a cover.
2. A chicken five to nine months old, from three and a half to six pounds in weight, and thus suitable for roasting.

Roasting Ear
An ear of corn, chosen while young, green, and tender, originally to be roasted in the husk, often in a bed of embers, now to be husked and boiled. The term, once applied to field corn, is now used almost interchangeably with "sweet corn," a more tender variety especially adapted for human consumption.

Roasting Jack (Eng.)
An old-fashioned mechanical device for turning the spit on which meat roasted before an open fire.

Robert Sauce (Fr.)
A brown sauce containing white wine, onion, and dry mustard, and usually served with pork.

Rocambole
A kind of leek, called the giant or Spanish garlic, with a milder flavor than garlic. A native of Asia Minor and southeast Europe, it has globular heads of purple flowers borne on stalks three feet high.

Rock

A drop cooky made with fruits, nuts, and spices.

Rock Candy

A kind of hard sugar candy made in large clear crystals which have formed around heavy threads placed in the cooking pan.

Rock Cornish Hen

A small fowl with small bones and all white meat, a favorite with gourmets, developed by cross-breeding the Cornish hen with other breeds of chicken. It may be roasted whole when not over a pound in weight.

Rocket

A Eurasian member of the mustard family, growing around two feet tall, which, in 1600, was a popular salad herb, and whose large, deeply cut leaves are still occasionally so used. They are pleasant in taste when young, though the flavor becomes rank as they mature.

Rockfish

Any of several bass-like fish; also, the striped bass.

Rock Lobster

A spiny lobster with the claws of the familiar American species. It is caught in Southern waters, and the tails imported from South Africa are the form in which it is best known in this country.

Rock Salt

Refined, though coarse, salt in blocks or chunks, which require drying and pounding for cooking or table use.

Roe

Fish eggs.

Rognon (Fr.)

Kidney or testicle (kernel).

Roll

A small, often rounded cake or miniature bread loaf made from dough which, as it is not usually kneaded, is softer than regular bread dough. Rolls may be either plain and baked in a variety of shapes, or sweet and flavored or decorated with fruit, nut meats, etc.

Rolled Cooky

Any cooky whose dough is rolled and cut into shapes rather than dropped from a spoon.

Rolled Roast

A roast with bone removed, rolled into a cylinder or chunk, and tied snugly.

Roll Mop

A small herring fillet rolled up around a gherkin slice, a caper, or the like, and marinated in spiced brine, to be served as an appetizer.

Roly-Poly Pudding

1. Shortcake biscuit rolled thin, spread with a fruit sauce, rolled up, steamed, and usually served with hard sauce.
2. (Eng.) A boiled pudding containing flour, suet, and jam.

Romaine Lettuce

A dark green lettuce with a crisp, broad, flat leaf, growing in a very loose, elongated bunch which hardly can be classified as a "head."

Romano Cheese (It.)

A sharp, hard cheese with a salty, smoky flavor. Like Parmesan, it is almost invariably grated for use.

Rome Beauty Apple

A good jelly apple from the West and Southwest, usually bright yellow with red streaks and of a medium size. It is also very attractive baked and is good in a variety of apple recipes. Its season is from November to May.

Root Beer

A non-alcoholic infusion of roots, bark, herbs, and yeast, in earlier days generally prepared at home.

Rope

In bread, a stringiness and sourness resulting from the use of flour made from green or sprouting wheat.

Roquefort Cheese (Fr.)

A white, blue-veined cheese, made from sheep's milk, creamy and crumbly in texture, and often used in salad dressings as well as with fruit or as an appetizer. See BLUE, GORGONZOLA, and STILTON CHEESE.

Rose

We seldom think of the rose as an herb, but for achieving exotic flavoring it is unsurpassed. Petals, usually a single one, are used in fruit cups and jellies; tea may be rose-flavored; honey can be flavored with several petals per pound, and a sweet herb and rose vinegar is exquisite with fruit salads. Any rose will do, though the requirements are fragrance and freshness, but three old-fashioned and extremely fine herb roses are Damask, Provence, and eglantine, also called sweetbrier.

Rosefish

A fish with an average weight of one and a half to two pounds and a rich, flavorful meat; also known as the ocean perch.

Rose Geranium Jelly

An apple jelly with a leaf or two of the very aromatic rose geranium in each glass.

Rose Hip

See HIP.

Roselle

A plant bearing brilliant red calyxes (leaves forming the outer case of the bud) from which jelly and certain drinks are made, and leaves which may be used to flavor soups, stews, or salad. Also called Indian sorrel and, in India, sour-sour and masha.

Rosemary

A shrubby, sweet-scented herb which may reach six feet in height. The slender, pale-green, needle-like leaves are sometimes an inch, though often less, in length. The name is derived from two Latin words meaning "dew of the sea," as it flourishes in the salt spray along the Mediterranean Sea. The leaves, fresh or dried, are excellent used with discretion to flavor sauces, soups, stews, and roasts.

Rosette (Ger.)

A type of waffle or fried cake which may be fried in a skillet, though preferably a special iron is dipped into the batter, then into hot fat, to be held there till the Rosette is golden and crisp.

Rosé Wine

A pink or rose-colored wine, often served with fish or fowl and also suitable with beef, veal, and cheese. It is properly chilled before serving.

Rossolnik (Rus.)

See RASSOLNICK.

Rotisserie

An oven-like device for cooking roasts of meat or whole fowl on a spit, which in a modern rotisserie is usually turned by electricity, thus ensuring even roasting and basting of the food.

Rouennaise Sauce (Fr.)

A bordelaise sauce in which puréed duck livers are poached, to be served with duckling.

Roughage

Bulk, which see.

Roulade (Fr.)

A preparation of meat or fish which is rolled up in the form of a scroll and then cooked.

Round Clam

Another name for the quahog.

Round Roast

A roast cut from the rear portion of the beef, just below the rump. It should be cooked long and slowly as a pot roast.

Round Steak

A reasonably good steak from the rear or round portion of the beef.

Roux (Fr.)

A cooked and blended mixture of fat, usually butter, and flour or some other starchy substance, used to thicken sauces and gravies. Brown roux is used for brown sauces; pale roux for veloutés, i.e., white sauces made with stock; and white roux for béchamel, a white sauce made with milk. The color of the roux depends upon the length of cooking time and degree of heat used.

Rowanberry (Eng.)

The bright red berry of the rowan tree or mountain ash; also called the ash berry. A jelly made from it is served with game.

Royal Anne Cherry

A sweet cherry having a yellow skin tinged with pink. When canned, the color becomes a pinkish yellow. Also called Napoleon cherry.

Royale (Fr.)

A kind of garnish for soups made of liquid such as cream or consommé, sometimes with a purée of chicken, fish, etc. added, thickened with egg yolks, strained into a mould, and poached. After cooling, the preparation is removed from the mould, sliced, and stamped with fancy cutters.

Rue

The bitterest of all herbs with the single exception of wormwood, and also one of the most beautiful. It is an evergreen shrub with thick, blue-green leaves and small, star-shaped golden flowers. Although bitter in taste and unpleasant, even nauseating, in odor, it imparts a musty flavor which is oddly pleasing when added in small amounts to chicken salad or soup, and Scandinavians sometimes put three or four crushed leaves between buttered slices of their rather bitter bread to form a unique variety of sandwich.

Rump Roast
A cut from the top and back of the beef which can be good and tender when it is from prime meat, but which otherwise should be cooked long and slowly.

Rump Steak
A boneless steak which to be good must be from the best beef and cut about three inches thick.

Rum Tum Tiddy
Tomato soup in which cheese is melted and to which mustard, egg, and onion are added before it is served over toast or crackers. Also called *rinktum ditty.*

Runner Bean
A long-podded green bean which grows on a climbing vine. The beans themselves, as the pods ripen, become large and red. Runner beans are often known as an old-fashioned or country bean which were grown in cornfields.

Rusk
Sweet or plain bread baked and then browned in an oven till very dry and crisp. A form of zwieback, literally, "twice baked."

Russet Apple
A fine dessert apple with a delicious flavor, the only possible objection to it being its dull, rough skin. It is especially popular in England.

Russian Brawn (Eng.)
A mixture of chopped cold meat, shallots, and semolina flavored with lemon, clove, etc., moulded, and served cold.

Russian Dressing
Mayonnaise mixed with chili sauce, a little powdered sugar, minced celery, pimento, and green pepper.

Rutabaga
A yellow turnip stronger in taste and usually larger in size than the white variety. Often the rutabaga is purplish around the stem and the skin feels slightly velvety. Also called swede and Swedish turnip.

Ruthven Cake (Scot.)
A sweet, lemon-flavored, yeast-raised cake which is prepared and baked like bread.

Rye Flour
A heavy, dark flour, made from grains of the cereal plant rye. It is usually combined with wheat flour, but Pumpernickel, for example, is a bread made of all-rye flour.

Sabayon Sauce (Fr.)
A dessert sauce made of sugar, egg yolks, stiffly beaten egg whites, and wine or orange and lemon juice and grated rind. A variation containing cream is also sometimes prepared. Sabayon is actually the French name for the Italian zabaglione, and in its simpler form is served by itself as a dessert.

Sablefish
A fish common along the Pacific coast, sometimes miscalled the Alaska black cod. Though excellent smoked, it is little used.

Sacher Torte (Aus.)
A rich chocolate-flavored cake with a chocolate icing and a filling of whipped cream and chocolate.

Sack
An old name for various kinds of white wine, very popular in sixteenth-century England, which were imported from Spain and the Canary Islands. The word supposedly derives from *sec,* French for "dry," and is still used as a name for certain kinds of sherry.

Saddle of Mutton or Saddle of Lamb
The loin and rack, i.e., the whole undersection in one intact piece.

Safflower
A thistle-like plant with orange flowers from which a fairly inexpensive substitute for saffron is obtained.

Saffron
The most expensive of all spices, and poisonous when taken in too large quantities, the rich, golden saffron consists of the powdered stigmas of a purple-flowered autumn crocus. As many as two hundred thousand blossoms are required to make one pound. The flavor is a little bitter, but unique and pleasing. Saffron is almost as much valued for the color it imparts, however, as for its flavor, and it is commonly used in French, Cornish, Italian, and Spanish cookery, especially in Cornish saffron cake and French bouillabaisse.

Sage
There are some five hundred varieties of this member of the mint family, all of which have small, rough leaves and purplish flowers, though they differ in taste, color, and odor. In color the leaves may be light or dark grey, grey-green, or green. The leaves of the best variety, Dalmatian sage, grown high in the mountains of Serbia and Yugoslavia, are green, warmly aromatic, and slightly bitter. Sage has a multitude of uses. It seasons Dutch cheese, is the best of all seasonings with pork, and in sage dressing accompanies many a holiday turkey to American tables. Over two million pounds are used each year in the United States. It also, unfortunately, has a tendency to cause indigestion.

Sage Cheese
Green cheese, which see.

Sage Tea
Tea made by an infusion of sage leaves.

Sago
A starch made from the pith of a kind of palm and used in puddings, etc., more often in England than in the United States.

Saguaro
A cactus whose fruit, one of the so-called prickly pears, can be eaten raw, used in jellies and jams, or as the source of a rich syrup.

St. Germain (Fr.)
Denotes a dish made or garnished with green peas, as St. Germain soup, a green pea soup.

St. John's Bread
See CAROB.

Sake (Jap.)

Rice wine, used almost as much in cooking sauces as it is alone. Also spelled *saki*.

Salad Bowl Lettuce

Another name for Boston or butter lettuce.

Salad Green

Any leafy green vegetable which may be used raw in a salad, for example, lettuce, endive, escarole, chicory, watercress, etc.

Salamander

A browning device consisting of an iron plate on the end of a rod which is heated, then held over a food preparation in order to brown or glaze it. Nowadays dishes are more often browned quickly under a broiler, and the old type iron is rarely found outside antique shops.

Salami

A dry sausage made of pork or beef, or both, and highly spiced. It is either smoked or air-dried. The best grades are made with red wine.

Salep

A starchy, gluey substance derived from an Oriental orchid and used mostly in an Oriental beverage.

Saleratus

An obsolete name for baking powder.

Salisbury Steak

Ground beef shaped into a fairly thick, oval or rectangular cake, and fried or broiled.

Sally Lunn (Eng. and U.S., South.)

A yeast-raised cake originated in Bath, England, and supposedly named for the woman who first sold them there in the early 1800's. The ingredients included flour, sugar, butter, milk, and eggs, and the finished cakes were sliced, toasted, buttered, and served with tea. In the South, individual Sally Lunns are baked in muffin tins.

Salmagundi

A term originating in France, apparently from salmigondis (or the shortened form, salmis), or hash, and once referring to an especially elaborate mixture of that sort, especially one of chopped meat, eggs, anchovies, and seasonings, while one old English recipe called for a mixture of diced fresh and salted meat, hard-boiled eggs, pickled vegetables, etc. on a bed of salad greens. Now, however, it is used to refer to any of various mixtures, a melon ball salad, for instance.

Salmis (Fr.)

A main dish containing game birds, roasted, minced, spiced, and then stewed in wine; also, a fancy hash, using left-over meat. Salmis sauce is one made of butter, vinegar, brown sugar, water, wine, herbs, and spices, and is served with roast duck or other wild fowl.

Salmon

A large ocean fish, highly prized for its rich pink or red meat which may be sliced into steaks, or used flaked in salads and other dishes.

Salmonberry

A wild member of the raspberry family common in the northeastern

United States and Canada, and usable for jams and jellies, but for little else.

Salpicon
1. (Fr.) Various diced foods combined with forcemeat and cooked as rissoles or croquettes.
2. (Costa Rica) A mixture of chopped beef, onions, and mustard greens, with a sauce of sour oranges or lemons, and hard-boiled eggs.

Salsa (Mex.)
A sauce, especially a hot relish made of green chilis, tomatoes, onions, and seasonings, used in preparing other dishes.

Salsiccia Secca (It.)
An extremely dry pork sausage served in wafer-thin slices as an antipasto. A kind made with a great deal of pepper is described as "con peperone."

Salsify
The longish white root of an herb belonging to the chicory family. It is rather parsnip-like but is darker in color, with a taste somewhat reminiscent of oysters. It is prepared in any way suitable for carrots, to which it is chemically similar, or parsnips. Also called oyster plant.

Saltpeter
Potassium nitrate, or niter, once used in preserving meats, but now replaced by sodium nitrate. It sometimes intensifies the red color of ham, salt beef, or sausage.

Salt Pork
The fatty portion of the pig's back, preserved in brine and used as a main dish, often called pickle meat, or as a seasoning in various dishes.

Salt-Rising Bread
An old-time bread which might have as its sole ingredients water, flour (usually coarse), and salt. The leaven was produced by leaving the batter to stand several hours in a bowl set in warm water. This was mixed with flour and water, or milk, and again left to rise for several hours. Such bread has a strong and rather objectionable odor, due to the fermentation. It requires less kneading than yeast-raised bread, and is dryer.

Salzstangen (Ger.)
Small rolls sprinkled with salt and, sometimes, caraway or poppy seed.

Sambal (East Indies)
A mixture of cooked foods such as hard-boiled eggs, chicken, fish, and vegetables in a very hot and spicy pepper sauce served as an accompaniment to curries, or, sometimes, with rice as a main dish.

Samovar (Rus.)
A metal tea-urn, usually made with an internal tube in which charcoal is burned to heat the water, and a spigot for drawing off the tea.

Samp
Coarse corn meal, very popular in the Northeast in the late nineteenth century, now more common in the South. It was boiled with milk either alone or with a combination of peas, beans, salt pork and the like, and used as a substitute for potatoes. In England the word is also applied to whole kernel corn, i.e., maize.

Samphire (Eur.)
A wild, aromatic herb with fleshy

leaves used in salads or pickles, which grows mostly on sea cliffs.

Samshu (Chin.)
Rice beer, similar to Japanese sake.

Sancocho (Pan.)
A meat stew, usually containing beef and pork, with tomatoes and other vegetables.

Sand Dab
A New England name for the flounder. See FLATFISH.

Sand Tart
A small, rolled cooky cut in rounds or fancy shapes, usually flavored with cinnamon and sprinkled with sugar before baking.

Sandwich
Two or more slices of bread with meat and/or some other filling, such as lettuce, cheese, mustard, etc., between. The name is supposed to have originated in England with the fourth Earl of Sandwich, who had bread with meat between brought to him at the gambling table. See also OPEN-FACED SANDWICH.

Santa Claus Melon
See CHRISTMAS MELON.

Sapodilla
A tropical American evergreen tree from whose sap the chicle used in chewing gum is obtained. Its edible fruit is shaped like a lemon and has an apricot-colored pulp. Also called sapote.

Sap Sago Cheese (Switz.)
A small, hard, green cheese flavored with a kind of clover and shaped like a cone with the pointed end cut off. It is almost invariably grated for cooking use.

Sapucaia Nut
See PARADISE NUT.

Saran
See PLIOFILM.

Saratoga Chips
Potato chips, served either hot or cold.

Sarawak Pepper
A name sometimes given a popular white pepper which comes from Sarawak.

Sardine
A collective name for any of several varieties of small, soft-boned fish caught and packed in a variety of ways in many parts of the world. Among the fish used as sardines are the pilchard, caught off Sardinia in the Mediterranean and the California coast, among other places; the brisling or sprat from Norwegian waters; and the alewife and herring from the Atlantic off New England, especially Maine. They are characteristically packed tightly in flat metal tins in an oil, mustard, or tomato sauce.

Sarma (Romania)
Cabbage leaves stuffed with a mixture of ground meat, minced onion, rice, and seasonings, and simmered in a covering liquid such as tomato juice.

Sarsaparilla
A tropical American plant whose roots are used in making the once

popular soft drink of the same name. The flavoring essence is dark brown and bitter-flavored, and is still used in carbonated beverages.

Sashimi (Jap.)
Raw fish sliced quite thin.

Sas-Phosphate Baking Powder
An alternate name for double acting baking powder. See BAKING POWDER.

Sassafras Tea
A tea made from the fragrant dried bark of the root of a slender tree of the same name belonging to the laurel family. A traditional folk medicine in the Middle West.

Sate
Roasted on a skewer, a method of cooking said to have originated in the Near or Middle East.

Saturated Fat
A natural food fat high in its number of hydrogen atoms per fat molecule. Among these fats, which promote the body's production of cholesterol, are those in meat and dairy products. See POLY-UNSATURATED FAT.

Saucepan
A pan with a longish side handle.

Sauerbraten (Ger.)
A pot roast of beef marinated several hours or days in vinegar, water, wine, onions, a variety of spices, etc., and then cooked as any other pot roast.

Sauté
To cook fully or partially in fat which is one-eighth to one-quarter of an inch deep, in an open pan over a burner. Also called pan-frying.

Sauternes
A delicate but sweet white wine made in the Bordeaux region of France and generally sold under the name of the estate producing it; also a somewhat drier white wine produced elsewhere, and in California spelled sauterne. The true Sauternes is generally served as a dessert wine, the namesakes with fish or fowl. Both should be slightly chilled.

Sautoir (Fr.)
A pan for sautéeing.

Savarin (Fr.)
1. A modified ring mould that looks like a small-crowned sombrero.
2. A bread made with almonds, orange peel, and citron baked in a Savarin mould.

Saveloy
A highly seasoned and smoked pork sausage, originally made from pigs' brains.

Savoiardi (It.)
Ladyfingers.

Savory
An herb, the two common varieties of which, summer and winter, are natives of the Mediterranean area. Both have a piquant, pleasant flavor and are fine mixers with other herbs, though the summer variety is milder. The leaves are dark green and slightly resinous in aroma, and of the two, winter savory is more attractive and huskier in appearance, summer savory being rather scraggly. Both are fine with vegetables, especially beans, but they may be used with almost any non-sweet food.

Savoury (Eng.)

A final tidbit to the meal, served just before coffee, for example, sautéed mushrooms, cheese, or a pâté on a small square of toast.

Savoury Pudding (Eng.)

A pudding from Derbyshire, served with pork or goose, just as Yorkshire pudding is with roast beef. It is made with oatmeal and bread crumbs, as well as flour, suet, eggs, milk, onions, and sage.

Savoy Cabbage

A mild-flavored, hardy, dark-green, curly-leaved winter cabbage, named for the Savoy region in France.

Savoy Cake (Eng.)

A light sponge cake, usually made in a tall, elaborate mould, often to be prepared as a tipsy cake.

Savoy Finger (Eng.)

A small, finger-shaped sponge cake.

Scald

To bring to a temperature just below the boiling point. In milk, tiny bubbles appear around the edge of the pan when the milk is scalded.

Scallion

A small, bulbless onion, rather like a leek, or any variety of onion used while very small and young.

Scallop

1. A salt-water mollusk with a double shell having ribs which ray out from a bottom muscle hinge. In America, this muscle is considered the edible portion and is prepared in many ways. The shell is often used as a baking dish and from this is derived the term "scalloped." Deep-sea scallops are larger and more plentiful than the tiny bay scallops, but not so tender and delicious.
2. To bake in a casserole with milk or a sauce, and often with crumbs, either as part of a mixture or arranged in alternate layers.
3. A small, thin slice of meat, often of veal.

Scaloppini (It.)

Small, thin slices of meat, generally of veal. However, popular usage of the term "veal scaloppini" refers to such slices in a sauce of wine or tomatoes and seasonings.

Scamozza Cheese (It.)

A smoked Mozzarella, smooth, white, and pear-shaped. It is usually eaten sliced, but is sometimes used in cooking.

Scampi (It.)

Large shrimps.

Schaum Torte (Aus.)

Meringue baked in a spring-form pan, or in layers, and served with fruit and whipped cream. This is an old and well-loved European dessert.

Schav (Jew.)

A cold soup containing sorrel (schav), onion, lemon juice, sugar, and eggs. After being chilled, it is served garnished with sour cream.

Schenkel (Fr.)

A finger-sized almond cooky fried in deep fat and sprinkled with powdered sugar.

Schlosserbuben (Aus.)
Prunes slowly cooked till plump, their seeds replaced with almonds, and each wrapped in a dough made of flour, eggs, sugar and white wine, baked till golden brown, and rolled in sugar and grated chocolate. The name means "locksmith's boys."

Schmierkäse (Ger.)
The German name for cottage cheese.

Schnecken (Hol.)
A rich cinnamon roll made of yeast-raised dough rolled out and spread with chopped nuts, brown sugar, and butter, and then rolled up like a pinwheel, sliced, and baked. In some cases the baking pan, as well, contains nut meats and brown sugar.

Schnitzel (Ger.)
A slice, cutlet, or fillet. See WIENER SCHNITZEL.

Schwarzbrot (Ger.)
Black bread made from dark rye flour. See PUMPERNICKEL.

Scolymus
A plant related to salsify, whose root is prepared in the same way. Spanish oyster plant is another name for it.

Scone (Eng.)
A plain or sweet biscuit, often cut in triangular or diamond shapes and eaten as tea cakes. They originated in Scotland, where they were made of oatmeal.

Score
To cut narrow gashes in a crossbar pattern, as, for example, across the outer surface of a roast or of a ham.

Scotch Barley
Hulled barley.

Scotch Broth
A thick vegetable soup, generally based on lamb or mutton and containing barley.

Scotch Currant Bun
A kind of bun or tart consisting of a mixture of flour, sugar, and milk with currants, raisins, almonds, spices, etc., baked in a pie pan lined with pastry and covered with a pastry crust.

Scotch Egg
A hard-boiled egg in a casing of sausage or minced meat, which is then fried; or, sometimes, an egg baked on a bed of grated cheese with a topping of parsley and crumbs.

Scotch Woodcock (Eng.)
1. A savoury made of butter, cream, egg yolk, and parsley poured on slices of toast spread with anchovy paste.
2. Scrambled eggs on anchovy toast.

Scramble
Referring to eggs, to mix thoroughly together so yolks and whites are well blended, and to cook in an open pan, stirring and mixing all the while.

Scrapple (U.S., Pa. Dutch)
A boiled mixture of ground pork, corn meal, flour, and onion packed into small loaf pans and chilled. It is then sliced and fried golden brown.

Scripture Cake
An old-fashioned fruit cake whose ingredients are given by reference to book, chapter, and verse of the Old

Testament where the particular ingredient is mentioned.

Scrod
A young cod or haddock.

Scullery
The old-time area off the kitchen where the dish-washing and such tasks were performed, usually having a stone floor which could be washed down easily.

Scup
See PORGY.

Scuppernong Grape
A uniquely musky-flavored grape of large size and great sweetness, cultivated in the South. The name is also given to a white wine made from it.

Sea Cucumber
Also called the trepang, this slug-like sea animal has the shape of a cucumber, though it is rough-skinned and has an enlarged "head" with short tentacles. In the Orient it is regarded as a delicacy and is used in a soup.

Sea Grape
The grape-like berry of a tropical American tree, whose roots often reach into the sea, near which the trees always grow. The fruit is not good eaten raw, but is used in jams and jellies.

Sea Kale (Eng.)
A perennial belonging to the mustard family, whose root may be served boiled or baked, while the young shoots are used as a vegetable.

Sear
To brown the surface, usually of meat, by a brief exposure to high heat, usually in a skillet or heavy-bottomed pan to which a little fat has been added.

Sea Salt
A coarse, unrefined salt obtained by the evaporation of sea water. It is used occasionally in cooking, as it has more a flavor of its own than rock, or culinary, salt. Also called grey salt.

Season
1. To enhance flavor by the addition of salt, or other ingredients. See SEASONING.
2. To mature; to bring to a proper condition by aging or special preparation; usually applied to beef. See AGE.

Seasoned Salt
Salt to which a flavoring, such as garlic, onion, or herbs, has been added.

Seasoning
Anything which is used to heighten flavor, or to throw it into relief. Seasonings may be primarily salty, acid, hot or pungent, or sweet. See CONDIMENTS.

Sea Squab
See BLOWFISH.

Sec (Fr.)
See DRY.

Seckel Pear
A small, plump, oval pear, bronze in color, with a sweet, firm, pleasingly flavored meat. Long a favorite in this country, it is widely grown non-commercially. Also called Sickel pear.

Seed Cake
A sugar cooky to which caraway, sesame, or some other sort of seed has been added.

Sekihan (Jap.)
A dish containing rice and red beans.

Selianka (Rus.)
A casserole made with layers of sauerkraut alternating with slices of fish, meat, or game.

Sembei (Jap.)
See O-SEMBEI.

Semillon Grape
A sweet grape, native to Europe, but now cultivated in California for wine-making.

Semmelkloss (pl. *Semmelklösse;* Ger.)
A small, rich dumpling made of stale bread and a great deal of butter, to which sugar and chopped peel are often added, and which is served with fruit compote.

Semmelknodel (Aus.)
A dumpling made of fried white bread softened with eggs and milk.

Semmeln (Ger.)
Sweet, yeast-raised rolls.

Semolina
The hard grains which remain after wheat flour is sifted thoroughly, used in the making of macaroni and similar products, in puddings, etc.

Serviceberry
The small berry-like fruit of any of several species of North American trees, related to the apple and pear. It may be fairly sweet but is sometimes puckery, and is best used in jams and jellies. Other names are shad plum, shadberry, and June berry.

Sesame Seed
The small dried seed of an Asiatic herb, white or ivory in color, shaped in a pointed oval, and with a flavor resembling that of toasted almonds. Sesame seeds are used whole in cookies and bread, or toasted in butter and spread over cheese, noodles, etc., as well as in certain candies, especially the rich "halva."

Seven-Minute Icing
A white frosting which derives its name from the fact that sugar, egg whites, and water are beaten together for approximately seven minutes over boiling water in the top of a double boiler. Thereafter vanilla is added and the icing is beaten until cool and thick enough to spread.

Seville Orange
Another name for the bitter orange.

Sfinge di San Giuseppe (It.)
A tiny cream puff made of pastry containing grated lemon and orange peel, with a filling of ricotta cheese, chocolate, and crème de cacao, traditionally served as dessert on March 19, the feast of Saint Joseph, hence the name. *Sfinge* is the Italian word for sphinx.

Shad
A herring-like, but full-bodied, fish whose rich flesh is considered a great delicacy. It is native to the Atlantic and, since 1870 when it was transplanted, has also been found along

the Pacific coast. Shad roe is particularly relished.

Shadberry
See SERVICEBERRY.

Shaddock
A fruit similar to the grapefruit named after the man who introduced it into the West Indies from the Far East.

Shad Plum
See SERVICEBERRY.

Shallot
A plant related to the onion but with a smaller, milder, more aromatic bulb, separated into cloves like those of garlic. The papery outer skin is reddish or grey, and the inside generally has a purplish tinge. It may be used wherever fresh onions are suitable.

Shank End of Ham
The lower, narrower portion of the ham, extending toward the foot.

Shashlik (Rus.)
Cubes of mutton or lamb marinated in vinegar, water, and spices, and then grilled or, ideally, roasted on a spit. Sometimes cubes of eggplant, ham, and cucumber are roasted on the same spit in the same manner as a kebab.

Shchi (Rus.)
A national soup, made of sauerkraut or fresh cabbage. Also spelled *stechi* and *stehy*.

Sheepshead
1. A salt-water relative of the porgy, common in warm seas. It is sold whole or filleted.
2. A fish belonging to the same family as the drum or croaker, and not related to the above, usually weighing from one to twelve pounds with a white, lean, tender, well-flavored flesh. It is available whole and filleted in Southern and Midwestern markets.

Shepherd's Pie
Cooked beef or lamb, minced or cubed, seasoned, moistened with gravy or water, and baked in a casserole with a covering layer, or surrounding border, of mashed potatoes.

Sherbet
A frozen dessert containing fruit juice, sugar, milk, and, often, egg whites.

Sherry
A white wine varying in color from pale to quite dark, and from dry to sweet, made in southern Spain at Xeres (now Jerez) de la Frontera, near Cadiz, from which it derives its name; or a wine made elsewhere by a similar process and sold under this name. Though mainly an after-dinner wine, sherry is preferred by many people to the cocktail, and a light sherry may also be served at a luncheon or brunch.

Ship's Bread
Another name for hardtack.

Shirataki (Jap.)
Very thin and threadlike noodles resembling vermicelli.

Shirr
To cook by baking in individual moulds or ramekins; applied only to eggs.

Shish Kebab (Turk.)
Kebabs, i.e., meat cubes, skewered and roasted over an open fire, often with mushrooms, tomatoes, onions, etc.

Shoo-Fly Pie (U.S., Pa. Dutch)
A pie with a molasses filling topped by a crumb crust of flour, shortening, and sugar.

Short
A term applied to pastry, meaning very tender, flaky, and rich; usually a desirable quality, it is obtained by the use of a good quantity of butter or other shortening, though a pastry may be too tender and thus fall apart.

Shortbread (Scot.)
A kneaded dough made only of flour, sugar, and butter, which is rolled out to a thickness of about one-half to one inch, cut into rounds or squares, and baked.

Short Broth
See COURT-BOUILLON.

Shortcake
A fruit dessert consisting usually of a biscuit split horizontally, with sliced raw fruit, often strawberries, placed between the two halves and on top, served with plain or whipped cream. In the finest shortbreads, the dough used is much richer and shorter than ordinary biscuit dough. A thin layer of this is patted into a shallow round pan, such as a layer cake pan, brushed with melted butter, and topped with a second similar layer; the art of separating the two layers when they are baked is one which must be practiced before it can be done perfectly.

Short Crust
A pastry for pie crust with either lard or butter to make it very tender and flaky.

Shortening
Any fat, liquid or solid, used in pastry, dough, or batter. The most commonly used include hydrogenated vegetable fats (the white, creamy solids sold under various brand names); liquid vegetable fats such as corn oil; lard; butter; and margarine.

Shot Pepper
An alternate name for fine mignonnette pepper, also called paradise pepper or grains of paradise.

Shoulder Roast
A cut taken from low in the chuck, or front section of the beef. It should be cooked long and slowly in the manner of a pot roast.

Shoyu (Jap.)
Soy sauce.

Shred
To tear or cut into small fragments or strips.

Shrewsbury Cake (Eng.)
A small, rich, lemon-flavored, yeast-raised cake cut out, often in star shape, and baked like a cooky. An old recipe, dating back to 1765, calls for richer ingredients including eggs and rosewater. Shrewsbury in Shropshire is the place of origin.

Shrimp
A small, salt-water crustacean with a slender, elongated body and a soft, translucent shell, which, when raw,

may be greenish-grey, pale pink, or brown. At one time any pink shrimps sold raw were believed to be spoiled, and it is still advisable to inquire of the origin, and better still to investigate the freshness by smelling them. Shrimps are used in a variety of ways, from the plainly boiled shrimp served with a hot sauce as a cocktail, or first course, to those elaborately prepared for the main dish of a meal, and are popular in almost all parts of the world.

Shrub

A kind of drink, usually one containing liquor combined with a sweetened fruit syrup.

Shuck

The outer covering, for example, the shell of an oyster or clam or the husk of an ear of corn; or, to remove any of these.

Sickel Pear

See SECKEL PEAR.

Sids (Scot.)

The inner husk of the oat grain, used in the preparation of sowens, or flummery.

Sieve

A device for separating coarser particles from finer by letting the latter pass through holes too small for the larger bits. Usually woven wire or a sheet of finely perforated metal forms the separating surface, and a handle allows for the utensil to be held and shaken to facilitate the process.

Sift

To put through a sieve.

Sikbaj (Arab.)

A stew made with a sheep's head, which, though a favorite in the Near East, may be sickening to unaccustomed Western palates as it is extremely gelatinous.

Sild (Scan.)

A herring; also, a sardine resembling the brisling but with a somewhat firmer texture.

Silver Cake

A delicate, rich, white cake.

Silver Dragee

A tiny, round, silver-colored candy.

Silver Leaf

A name for sorrel sometimes used in seed catalogs.

Silverskin Onion

A small onion rarely over one and a half inches in diameter, having a nearly transparent white or silver skin. These little onions are cooked whole and creamed or buttered.

Simmer

To cook slowly in a liquid over very low heat, usually in a covered pan.

Simnel Cake (Eng.)

A cake containing currants and candied peel and traditionally eaten on the fourth Sunday in Lent, known as Mothering Sunday, when scattered families once customarily met to worship at the parish church, and when mothers were honored. Spices were sometimes included, and there was generally also a center layer of almond paste and a border of almond paste around the top. Legend has it that the cake's name is derived from a husband and wife named Simon and Nellie who could not decide whether to have an almond cake or a plum cake or a baked cake or a boiled cake, and so combined the two ingredients in a cake which was first boiled and then finished off by baking. More prosaically, "simnel" is derived from a Latin word for very fine flour.

Simple Syrup
Sugar and water boiled together for use where sugar alone might be hard to dissolve, for example, in cold drinks.

Singe
To remove the remaining down, feathers, or pin feathers from a plucked fowl, or the bristles from a pig, by exposing them to a flame, or to a hot iron, often one especially made for the purpose.

Singing Hinnie (Eng.)
A griddle cake popular in the North Country and usually made only of flour and butter, though sugar, currants, and baking powder may be added.

Sippet
A small piece of bread fried in hot fat, or one soaked in milk, broth, or some other liquid.

Sirloin
The upper, or front part of the loin of beef including the meat both above and below the bone.

Sirloin Roast
A very fine cut of beef from the section behind the ribs and in front of the round. It is the classic English roast, and is regarded by some as better than a rib roast. While the price is higher than that of a rib roast, it is probably more economical in the end, as there is less waste.

Sirloin Steak
A well-flavored and only moderately expensive steak cut from the high part of the loin.

Sirniki (Rus.)
Sweet cheese cakes shaped into small, flat pats and fried in butter.

Sirup
See SYRUP.

Skate
A fish with flat, winglike side fins, often seen lying dead on beaches after a storm, generally regarded as inedible, probably because of its odd appearance. Actually, the "wings" are excellent cooked, having a delicate, gelatinous texture and a distinctive flavor.

Skewer
1. A metal rod which is run through cubes of meat and, often, whole vegetables which are to be cooked in a broiler or over the coals of a barbecue pit; or, to run the rod through the food.
2. A metal pin used to lace up fowl, or to keep meat in shape during roasting; or, to so lace up or fasten.

Skilligalee
An impromptu stew made up from whatever game the hunter may have bagged.

Skilly (Eng.)
A nineteenth century term for a very thin porridge or gruel.

Skim Milk
Milk from which the cream has been removed. Colloquially, blue john.

Skinklada (Swed.)
A ham omelet.

Skirt Steak
A novelty steak cut from the skirt, or edge, of the forequarter of beef and frequently rolled into a pinwheel for broiling or frying.

Skunk Cabbage
An early-blooming plant, the white leaf stalks of which are good eating if the water in which they are cooked is changed several times during the process. These are served creamed or used cold in a salad.

Skyscraper Sandwich
A sweet sandwich consisting of five slices of bread in graduated sizes, spread with cream cheese, marmalade, ground nuts, shredded pineapple, ham, etc. It is usually eaten with knife and fork.

Slab Cake
Generally a large, flat, bakery cake sold in cuts according to the size and price desired by each customer.

Slapjack
A flapjack or pancake.

Slaw
See COLESLAW.

Slip
A popular dessert in the nineteenth century, consisting of rennet-soured milk chilled and served with sugar and nutmeg. It lacked the acidity of bonny-clabber, naturally soured milk served in the same way, but had to be prepared shortly before serving, or it would become tough and watery.

Slipcoat Grape
A name given the Concord grape, which see.

Slipcote Cheese (Eng.)
A soft, mild, unripened cheese made from cow's milk and rennet, popular around 1750.

Slivovitz (Hung.)
A plum brandy resembling Quetsch, and also distilled in Yugoslavia and other central European countries.

Sloe
A small, blue-black, wild plum, the fruit of the European black thorn tree. Sloes are steeped in gin to produce "sloe gin," and are also used combined with apples in jelly and in a cake.

Sloke
An edible seaweed, or alga, like Irish moss or laver. Also spelled slouk.

Slumgullion
A soup, stew, or meat sauce, depending upon how it is served and also upon its ingredients, which vary greatly, but which often include ground beef, onions, tomatoes, and seasonings.

Slump (U.S., New Eng.)
A dessert made of apples, sugar, cin-

namon, and water, topped with biscuit dough, covered tightly, and cooked over a low flame.

Small Sauce
Any sauce based on one of the "mother" sauces, i.e., brown, velouté, and béchamel. Also called compound sauce.

Smearcase
See SCHMIERKÄSE.

Smelt
A small, trout-like food fish of European and North American coasts and the Columbia River, sometimes called the "king" of the small fish because of its distinctive flavor and pleasing texture. Sometimes river smelt are too oily or full of river odor to be palatable, but those taken off the coast rarely have these defects.

Smetane (Rus.)
Sour cream.

Smetanick (Rus.)
A pie with a filling of sour cream, ground almonds, jam, and cinnamon; or, sometimes, a pie containing sour cream and ham.

Smithfield Ham
See VIRGINIA HAM.

Smorgasbord (Swed.)
In Sweden, a table or "bord" laid with appetizers such as pickled fish, salads, cheeses, etc. In the United States, the name is also given to a whole meal offering several hot dishes and desserts, all set out on a large table from which the diners help themselves.

Smørrebrød (Den.)
Literally, "bread and butter," but used to designate an elaborate assortment of open-faced sandwiches, made of buttered rye bread topped with an attractive arrangement of hot or cold sliced meat, fish, salads, hard-boiled eggs, and various mixed spreads, which often serve as a whole meal.

Smother
1. To cover completely, as with a sauce or gravy.
2. To cook in a covered dish.

Smyrna Raisin
A raisin originally shipped from Smyrna, in Turkey, in contrast to that shipped from Corinth, Greece, called a currant. Now called sultana.

Snap Bean
Any young, crisp, string or wax bean, such as makes a sharp snapping sound when broken.

Snow Apple
Another name for the Fameuse, which see.

Snow Eggs
Egg whites beaten stiff with sugar and poached in milk.

Snow Pea
A very small, bright green, flat-podded pea so tender and crisp that the pods are used whole, especially in Chinese cookery. Also called Chinese pea.

Soba (Jap.)
Noodles made with buckwheat flour and served hot or cold with various dishes.

Soda

See BAKING SODA and BENZOATE OF SODA.

Soda Cracker

A plain, white cracker, usually square and characteristically salted on top, made chiefly of flour, water, shortening, and the leavening agent. Recipes for these crackers are not generally available as they have for so long been a commercial product.

Soda Farl

An Irish soda bread baked on a griddle rather than in an oven.

Soft Ball

The stage in cooking at which candy syrup forms a soft ball when a drop is placed in very cold water and flattens out when removed from the water.

Soft Clam

A mollusk common north of Cape Cod, where it burrows into tidal flats, and much relished by New Englanders. Also called the long-neck clam.

Soft Crack

The stage in cooking at which candy syrup spins into hard but not brittle threads when a drop is placed in very cold water.

Soft Roe

Another name for milt, which see.

Soft-Shelled Crab

The common blue, or hard-shell, crab of the Atlantic coast, when caught just after shedding its shell and before growing a new and larger one, as it does several times before reaching maturity. The smaller the soft-shelled crab is, and the sooner it is caught after shedding its shell, the tenderer the meat and the better the flavor. It cooks quite rapidly, and is often fried in butter or deep fat.

Soft Wheat

Wheat with a rather soft grain, which yields a smooth, soft, white flour, suitable for cakes. Bread flour and macaroni are made from hard wheat.

Sole

A flatfish having a small mouth, small gill openings, and small eyes placed quite close together, usually flounder in the United States; the true sole, in England called Dover sole, is one of the most highly esteemed of food fish, and fillets of sole, sole meunière, and a variety of other preparations are much relished.

Sorb

A European name for the service tree, or for the mountain ash (or rowan) and their fruit.

Sorbet

1. (Fr.) Sherbet.
2. (U.S.) A dessert resembling a frappé, which is frozen to a mush.

Sorghum

A tropical, cornlike cereal grain; also, a thick, sweet dark-amber syrup derived from its juice.

Sorrel

An acid-leaved plant, also called sour grass, having large, pale-green leaves used when very young and fresh as a cooked green, or with others such as spinach, cabbage, lettuce, etc., in salads. Its most common use, however, is in soups, for example, *schav*.

Soubise Sauce (Fr.)
A sauce containing onions, made in any of several ways.

Souchong Tea
A black tea having a very small leaf, which may be from India, Ceylon, or Java.

Soufflé (Fr.)
A baked dish having a light and fluffy consistency, made of beaten egg whites combined with various other ingredients and served hot as an entrée, a main dish, or, sweetened, as a dessert.

Soul Cake (Eng.)
A sweet, yeast-raised bun, originally baked in the shape of a human figure, either male or female. An ancient custom was for girls to go from door to door, singing for these cakes on All Souls' eve (November 1), which is the evening of All Saints' day. These two days are the occasion of numerous and varied local customs the world over.

Sound (Eng.)
The swimming bladder of a fish. The sounds of the cod, dried, pickled or salted, soaked, and then cooked are considered a delicacy. They are also sometimes eaten fresh.

Soupçon (Fr.)
A very small amount, used especially in reference to seasonings.

Sour Cream
Cream which has been acted upon naturally by lactic acid bacteria or artificially by the addition of an acid.

Generally speaking, recipes for cakes, cookies, pancakes, etc. which call for sour milk or sour cream require the naturally soured variety, while the smooth, thick, rich, commercially soured cream is used more in combination with meat, vegetables, etc. in main dishes.

Sour Grass
See SORREL.

Sour Gum
A native American tree, large and handsome in appearance, bearing a small, black, berry-like fruit which, though acid, may be used in preserves.

Sour Milk
Milk which has been acted upon by an acid, thus causing it to ferment and thicken. At a certain stage in the souring process, milk separates into curds and pale, watery whey.

Soursop
See GUANABANA.

Sour-Sour
See ROSELLE.

Souse (U.S., Pa. Dutch)
The meat from a pig's head, feet, and hocks, boiled with onions, peppercorns, and herbs. All these are then placed in a crock, thoroughly chilled, and sliced to be fried or eaten cold.

Sowens (Scot.)
Flummery, usually prepared with sids and water.

Soy
In the last century, this term referred not necessarily to the soy bean or

sauce (see following entries) but to a sauce or ketchup, as in recipes for "green tomato soy" and "ripe tomato soy"; both call for making a highly spiced sauce containing tomatoes and vinegar. In England, a popular commercial ketchup or sauce in Victorian times was called Soy; black and sweet, it was evidently made with soy beans, though a cheaper version was said to be merely molasses saturated with salt.

Soy Bean
An Asiatic bean, now widely cultivated in North America as a source of oil, meal, and other products. Also spelled *soya*.

Soy Flour
A flour made of ground soy beans, very rich in protein and used to enrich other flour, though seldom used alone.

Soy Sauce
A dark sauce originating in China and Japan and made from fermented wheat or barley, soy beans, salt, and water. It is so popular that probably a majority of Oriental main dishes either include, or are served with, soy sauce. In Japanese, *shoyu*.

Spaghetti (It.)
A food paste made from semolina and shaped in long slender cords.

Spaghettini (It.)
A very thin spaghetti, but not quite as thin as vermicelli.

Spanish Cream
A custard containing milk, egg yolks, and sugar, combined with gelatin and beaten egg whites in such a way that it separates into two layers as it cools, the top one foamy, the bottom one smooth.

Spanish Juice
A dark extract from the root of the licorice plant. Also called black sugar.

Spanish Mackerel
A fish appearing off the Atlantic coast around July, prized as a game fish and excellent for food, usually sold whole at a weight of about two pounds.

Spanish Onion
Usually a medium large, round, yellow-skinned onion, though the term may refer generally to any imported onion.

Spanish Oyster Plant
See SCOLYMUS.

Spanish Paprika
See PIMENTO.

Sparerib
A cut from the lower rib section of pork, below the loin. Spareribs are flat, thin, and slightly curved, and their meat is rich and delicious in flavor, though somewhat limited in quantity. Barbecuing is a popular way of preparing them.

Sparkling Wine
Any wine which is effervescent or bubbly. See CHAMPAGNE.

Sparrowgrass (Eng.)
A rural name for asparagus.

Spatchcock (Eng.)

1. A chicken or other bird cooked hurriedly; the term possibly comes from "dispatch cock."
2. Spread out flat to be broiled or baked, in the manner known in French as "crapaudine."

Spatula

A broad, flat-bladed knife with a cutting edge, used to spread icing, etc.; also generally used to refer to a pancake turner.

Spelt

A cereal grain, actually a variety of wheat called German wheat, which yields a very fine flour.

Spencer Roast

A rib roast of beef with the bones removed.

Spencer Steak

A steak cut from the rib section of beef, but with the bone removed.

Spice Cake

As the name implies, a cake containing spices, usually cinnamon, cloves, and nutmeg. Sour cream and brown sugar are generally also used.

Spider

A cast-iron skillet, or frying pan, which originally had three long legs that allowed it to be set directly over the fire.

Spiedino (pl. *spiedini*; It.)

A meat roll cooked on a skewer; also, a loaf of bread sliced not quite through, with slices of Mozzarella cheese alternated with bread slices, the whole buttered, topped with anchovy fillets and oregano, and placed in a hot oven till the cheese melts.

Spiny Lobster

See ROCK LOBSTER.

Spitzbuben (Aus.)

Very thin rolled almond cookies made in two layers with jelly or jam between.

Spitzenburg Apple

A red apple marked with darker red stripes, crisp and excellent for eating raw or for use in most apple recipes. It is in season from October to February.

Split (Eng.)

A kind of yeast-raised sweet biscuit which is split open like shortcake and served with fruit, butter, or clotted cream.

Sponge

1. A light batter or dough to which yeast has been added; one of the first steps in making yeast bread.
2. A dessert made of gelatin and egg white or whipped cream.

Sponge Cake

A light, fluffy cake containing beaten egg whites, egg yolks, lemon juice, and grated lemon rind, with no shortening or leavening. It may be baked like an angel food cake, a type of sponge cake, in a high, round pan with a center tube, or in any cake tin.

Sponge Method

A method of bread making in which about half of the flour is added after the dough has risen once.

Spoon Bread (U.S., South.)

An exceedingly soft, moist bread made with corn meal, rice, or hominy, and served in place of mashed potatoes.

Spot

A fish, one of the croakers, taken along the Atlantic coast and used like the butterfish or sea trout, though relatively little known.

Spot Bass

A West coast name for the redfish.

Spotted Dick or Spotted Dog (Eng.)

A plain suet pudding containing currants as the "spots," whence the name.

Sprat

A small European food fish much like a herring; also used as another name for the young herring.

Springerle (Ger.)

A traditional Christmas cooky, anise-flavored and sprinkled with anise seed. It is either shaped in a mould which leaves a raised impression in the dough, or imprinted with a raised design from a special kind of rolling pin.

Spring-Form Pan

A cake pan having a removable bottom or removable sides held in place by a clamp which facilitates removal of the cake after baking.

Sprinkle

To distribute lightly and evenly over a surface; often used interchangeably with dust, though the former generally refers to a liquid and the latter to a dry, powdered ingredient.

Spritz (Scan.)

A creamy, almond-flavored cooky made in various shapes, and even in initials, by the use of a cooky press.

Spumone (It.)

Italian moulded ice cream consisting of an outer layer of custard containing chopped almonds, and an inner filling made from heavy cream, sugar, maraschino cherries, and candied orange peel. There are special spumoni moulds, but a jello mould also serves the purpose.

Spun Sugar

Sugar syrup boiled till it will form a long thread, and then drawn out into such threads, which are often colored.

Spy Apple

See NORTHERN SPY.

Squab

A young pigeon, usually commercially raised, four or five weeks old and weighing from twelve to fourteen ounces. Young chickens are sometimes called squab chickens.

Squid

An elongated, ten-armed relative of the octopus, usually quite small when taken for food. Italians and Spaniards like it cooked in its own ink, but other cooks prefer to cut up the tentacles, dip them in batter, and fry them in deep fat. Squid may also be stuffed and baked. It is generally served with a highly seasoned sauce.

Stachys

See ARTICHOKE, JAPANESE.

Stag

The name sometimes given a stewing chicken, usually weighing between five and nine pounds, whose flesh has begun to darken and toughen.

Standing Rib Roast

See RIB ROAST.

Star Apple

An apple-sized tropical American fruit, of almost cloying richness and sweetness, which shows the distinct outline of a star when cut across.

Starch

Chemically, a complex carbohydrate; in practical usage, a white, odorless, tasteless, granular or powdery substance found in many food plants, but especially in corn and potatoes.

Starchy

An adjective which may be applied to a meal containing a high proportion of foods containing starch; or to a food preparation which contains, or, because of a dry, granular, and unpleasant texture, feels as if it contains, a too-high proportion of starch, either in the form of potatoes, flour, cornstarch, or a similar product.

Stark Apple

A cooking apple in season from December to May.

Stayman Apple

A red and yellow apple recommended for baking, as well as for eating raw and for use in general cooking. In season from November to April in the West and Southwest.

Steam

As a verb, to cook by steaming (rather than, for instance, by exposure to a direct flame as in broiling, or by immersion in a hot liquid, as in boiling), either in the top of a double boiler, on a rack inside a deep covered kettle containing a small amount of water, or in a steamer, i.e., a perforated kettle set over a saucepan containing boiling water.

Steam-Bake

To cook in an oven over a container of hot water.

Steam-Blanch

To blanch in a pressure saucepan containing a small amount of water, and with the vent open. The time required is about one and one half that for blanching in boiling water.

Stechi (Rus.)

Another spelling of *shchi*.

Steep

To allow to stand in a liquid just below the boiling point.

Steeped Coffee

Coffee made by adding boiling water to ground coffee and allowing it to stand in a tightly covered pot for about five minutes, after which the infusion is strained before serving.

Stehy (Rus.)

Another spelling of *shchi*.

Stelk (Ir.)

A dish consisting of mashed potatoes into which pre-cooked spring onions have been pounded, usually served with a lump of butter placed in a depression in the center of each portion. See COLCANNON.

Sterilize

To destroy bacteria and other micro-organisms, usually by immersing in boiling water or by subjecting to the action of steam or dry heat.

Stew

1. To cook long and slowly in liquid, generally in a covered pot.
2. Any dish so prepared, usually one containing meat and one or more vegetables.

Sticky Bun (U.S., East.)

A varient of Pennsylvania Dutch Schnecken, a pinwheel-shaped cinnamon roll, to which currants, raisins, and citron are added, and which is topped with a quantity of brown sugar and butter.

Stiff

When referring to egg whites, beaten to stand in peaks which hold their shape, but which are still glossy, moist-looking, and not too fine-grained.

Stifle (U.S., New Eng.)

A casserole consisting of eels, potatoes, and onions arranged in layers and covered with bits of salt pork.

Still Wine

Any wine which is not effervescent.

Stilton Cheese (Eng.)

A cheese resembling Roquefort, creamy white in color, blue-veined, crumbly, and pungent, originating in the town of Stilton, Huntingdonshire, and considered one of the aristocrats among English cheeses.

Stir

To mix with a circular motion.

Stirabout (Ir.)

A porridge made of oatmeal or corn meal and stirred while cooking.

Stock

An extract of meat, poultry, or fish obtained by boiling with vegetables, seasonings, and liquid, and used as the basis of sauces or soups. Brown stock is made from beef and other meats, which are browned at the beginning of the process, while white stock is made from veal and chicken. Fish stock, made from fish, usually contains wine, as well.

Stock Pot

A large pot in which stock is prepared; usually standard equipment in French kitchens.

Stollen (Eur.)

A rich yeast bread, usually filled with raisins.

Stone Crab

A delicate-meated crab native to Cuba and Florida, now available elsewhere in the United States, especially in the East. The larger claws are served whole and the rest of the meat as in any crabmeat recipe.

Store Cheese

A domestic Cheddar.

Stout (Eng.)
The strongest kind of porter, i.e., a dark bitter beer brewed from charred or browned malt.

Strachino Cheese (It.)
A very sharp, light yellow cheese made from goats' milk, which is eaten sliced.

Straight Dough Method
A method of bread making in which all the flour is added at one time and the dough is allowed to rise only once. See SPONGE METHOD.

Strain
To clear of solid materials by putting through a sieve, a finely woven cloth, or some other filtering device.

Strawberries Romanoff
A dessert consisting of strawberries marinated in a liqueur, for example, Cointreau or Curaçao, and then combined or topped with whipped cream, which is often flavored with lemon or orange.

Strawberry Pear
The pear-shaped fruit of a cactus found in Mexico and the West Indies, with a bright red skin and white, slightly acid meat.

Strawberry Tomato
See GROUND CHERRY.

Straw Wine
A wine obtained from grapes which have been dried in the sun, often on straw mats.

Strega (It.)
A sweet, highly perfumed, golden-yellow liqueur which resembles Chartreuse and is widely exported.

Streusel (Aus.)
A crumblike cake topping consisting of sugar, cinnamon, flour, butter, and chopped nut meats creamed together.

String Bean
Any of several varieties of bean whose green pods are used when young and tender.

Strip Steak
A fine cut of beef, consisting of a porterhouse steak with the fillet and bone removed; in the West called a New York cut.

Stroganoff (Rus.)
A dish containing strips of meat, often beef, cooked with sour cream and seasonings.

Strudel (Ger.)
A cake made of dough rolled thin, covered with any of various fillings, rolled up, and baked. Apple strudel is probably the best known variety, but other fruits, poppy seed, and meat and vegetable mixtures are also used.

Stud
As a verb, to attach or inject into a surface at regular intervals, as, for example, cloves into a ham, or (as in certain French dishes), small pieces of fat into incisions made in lean meat.

Stuff
To pack or fill, often to the point of distension.

Stuffed Derma (Jew.)
See KISHKE.

Sturgeon

A large, tough-skinned fish with lean or dry flesh, whose roe is used as caviar.

Sub Gum (Chin.)

A mixed vegetable stew, using a variety of Chinese vegetables.

Submarine Sandwich

A sandwich originally sold along the Atlantic seaboard, but now spreading westward, consisting of a large roll made of French or Italian bread, containing cheese, salami, lettuce, onions, olive oil, red pepper flakes, and any of various other ingredients.

Subric

A puffed preparation, containing egg yolks and often fried by the spoonful in butter. Spinach is sometimes an ingredient; other subrics are sweetened and served as a dessert. Also spelled *soubric*.

Succotash

Corn and beans, usually limas, combined after cooking and served together. The name is said to be derived from an Indian word meaning "an ear of corn."

Sucker

A fish which James Beard has called "a sort of underwater vacuum cleaner," from the fact that it has a sucking mouth and acts as a scavenger along the bottom of ponds and lakes. However, some people like its lean flesh, which may be broiled or pan-fried, though, understandably, it needs a good sauce.

Suet

The hard, white fat around the loins, heart, and kidney of any food animal, especially beef or mutton.

Suet Pudding

Any steamed or boiled pudding which has chopped beef suet as an ingredient.

Suffolk Bun (Eng.)

A small sweet bun containing currants and caraway seed, for which the dough, made without yeast, is rolled to a thickness of one inch and cut in rounds to be baked.

Sugaring

See CRYSTALLIZATION.

Sugar Pea

A pea whose pod lacks the parchment-like lining characteristic of most peas, and which is thus edible pod and all when young and tender.

Sugar-Plum

Originally, a piece of fruit dipped in sugar or cooked in syrup just long enough to form a coating on it, and then drained. However, the term has come to refer to any sweetmeat or candy, but especially one made with boiled sugar.

Sugar Sand

A turn-of-the-century name for red-colored sugar.

Suimono (Jap.)

A clear soup made of meat or fish and vegetables, flavored with salt, soy sauce, and dashi.

Sukiyaki (Jap.)

A mixture of vegetables such as mushrooms, leeks, and celery, cut up and cooked briefly with thin slices of beef, soy sauce, and dashi. The word is said by some to mean "cooked on a plough," but by others to mean "sliced thin and fried."

Sultana
A small, seedless, usually purplish raisin, i.e., a sun-dried grape, originally called a Smyrna raisin.

Sulze (Ger.)
Calf's foot jelly, or anything served in aspic.

Sumatra Tea
Any of various black teas, generally named after the estate in Sumatra on which it is grown, but ordinarily one of medium strength and flavor.

Summer Squash
Any of several varieties of squash, for example, crookneck, zucchini, marrow, and patty-pan, which are cooked immediately rather than stored, and which may usually be creamed, fried, sautéed, stewed, or steamed without being peeled.

Sundae
An American dessert consisting of ice cream topped with a heavy syrup, fruit, whipped cream, nut meats, or any of a variety of combinations of these.

Sunfish
A small, flat, nearly oval, fresh-water pan fish with brilliant metallic coloration.

Sunomono (Jap.)
Any of various pickled vegetable, meat, or fish dishes.

Sunshine Cake
A yellow sponge cake.

Supper
A light meal taken during the evening hours.

Suprême (Fr.)
Originally, breast of poultry; but now sometimes referring to a choice part of some other food animal.

Suprême Sauce (Fr.)
A sauce made from poultry stock, velouté, mushroom liquor, and cream, distinguished for its delicacy and whiteness.

Surinam Cherry
A soft, small, aromatic, juicy fruit native to Brazil and now cultivated in the United States, having a ribbed skin which is red in color and a rather acid pulp. It is eaten fresh or preserved, for example, in jelly.

Sushi (Jap.)
Cooked rice with fried tofu (soy bean curd), egg, fish cake or smoked eel, and a variety of vegetables. This combination may be shaped into balls, rolled thin with seaweed, or placed in cornucopias.

Sussex Heavy (Eng.)
A small pastry cooky made with lard, raisins or currants, and lemon-soured milk.

Sussex Pudding (Eng.)
A boiled suet and flour pudding which is sliced and laid in the pan in which meat is roasting, where it absorbs the drippings and is browned. Like Yorkshire pudding, it is some-

times served as a course by itself, but usually comes on with the meat.

Suwannee Chicken
A terrapin from the salty coastal waters or clear streams of the Southern states.

Swats (Scot.)
The liquid in which sids have been soaked in the preparation of sowens.

Swede (Eng.)
A yellow turnip, originally a kind that grew in Sweden, but now sometimes applied to any turnip. Also called rutabaga or Swedish turnip.

Swedish Meat Balls
Small, well-seasoned meat balls served in a sauce or gravy, often as a hot appetizer or supper dish.

Swedish Turnip (Eng.)
See SWEDE.

Sweet Autumn Swar Apple
A fall apple which should be baked.

Sweet Basil
An herb commonly cultivated in the United States. See BASIL.

Sweet Bough Apple
A late summer apple, good for baking.

Sweetbreads
The pancreas and thymus glands, especially those of the calf, when used as food.

Sweetbrier
Another name, commonly used in America, for the eglantine.

Sweet Cicely
An herb belonging to the parsley family, used to flavor various foods and drinks, including the liqueur Chartreuse. The oil of the seeds is thought to act as a preservative of flavor. Because of its myrrh-like odor, it sometimes goes by that name, though it is not related to the gum-producing tree of that name.

Sweet Corn
A variety of corn developed for human consumption, and especially distinguished by its tenderness and sweetness. See ROASTING EAR.

Sweet Flag
A marsh plant with long, grass-like leaves and aromatic roots, which have some culinary use in creams and custard desserts.

Sweet Herb
A term used to refer to any herb used in cookery, for example, parsley, thyme, bay, marjoram, mint, sage, etc.

Sweet Marjoram
Another name for marjoram, as distinguished from oregano, or wild marjoram.

Sweetmeat (Eng.)
Any shaped piece of confectionery, whether made primarily of sugar, or chocolate, or of fruit.

Sweet-Sour (Chin. and Poly.)
Containing sugar and vinegar; used to describe a sauce or a method of preparing meat, vegetables, etc.

Sweet Wine

A wine having a higher proportion of unfermented sugar than that described as "dry," and commonly served after a meal or with dessert. Certain sweet white wines, however, are suitable with fish or shellfish.

Sweet Woodruff

See WOODRUFF.

Swiss Chard

A variety of the common beet grown for its top and stems, the leaves being cooked as greens, while the stalks are cooked like celery.

Swiss Cheese

A hard, nut-flavored cheese of pale creamy color, easily recognized by its rather large, shiny-sided holes which form naturally. Genuine "Swiss" originates in Switzerland, but similar varieties are commonly made in the United States.

Swiss Fondue

Melted cheese combined with wine in a chafing dish and usually served with French bread, which is dipped into it.

Swiss Steak

A cut of about an inch and a half in thickness from the rear portion of beef, the rump, round, or chuck, pounded to increase its tenderness, and pan-cooked with a seasoned sauce.

Swordfish

A large fish of warm seas, so named from the long, swordlike beak formed by the bones of its upper jaw. The meat is lean but rich, and is excellent cut into steaks.

Syllabub (Eng.)

Traditionally a drink made of cream whipped up with brandy or wine, sugar, and lemon juice. As made nowadays, syllabub is frothy but less rich, resembling a milk punch. When combined with gelatin, the above becomes a chilled dessert. Also spelled *sillabub*.

Sylte (U.S., Scand.)

An aspic of veal, pork, herbs, and seasonings cooked together, combined with gelatin, and poured into a mould to set.

Syrup

Any thick, sweet, sticky liquid; often, the light-colored, uncrystallized residue from the refining of cane sugar, i.e., a pale molasses. Also spelled sirup.

Tabasco Pepper

A very small, very pungent, finger-shaped red pepper, used as a flavoring in Tabasco sauce.

Tabasco Sauce

A trade name for an extremely fiery liquid condiment used by the drop as a seasoning.

Table d'Hôte (Fr.)

A complete meal consisting of specific courses at a set price. The literal meaning is "table of the host."

Table Salt

Sodium chloride mixed with a certain quantity of magnesium carbonate to prevent its caking in damp weather.

Taco (Mex.)

A sandwich consisting of a tortilla folded around a filling of cheese, ground meat, shredded lettuce, and hot sauce. The tortilla is generally fried in hot fat just beforehand, and is thus somewhat crisp.

Taffy

A chewy candy made of molasses or brown sugar boiled till very thick and then pulled to give it body and gloss. Also sometimes called toffee.

Tagliarini (It.)

Very narrow egg noodles, about one-eighth of an inch in diameter.

Taiglach (Jew.)

A dessert candy made of dough rolled into pencil-thin strips, cut into half-inch pieces, and baked. The pieces are then cooked briefly in a hot mixture of honey, brown sugar, and spices, to which nuts are added, and the whole, when done, is poured out onto a board, allowed to cool until it can be handled, and, finally, rolled into balls. Also spelled teiglach.

Takuanzuke (Jap.)

The pickled radish, or daikon, a popular salad-type dish.

Talmouse (Fr.)

A small, individual, pastry-like soufflé or cheesecake served at the end of a meal.

Tamale (Mex.)

Masa, or Mexican corn meal, spread on a corn husk or a parchment square, covered with a chili-seasoned filling of chicken, beef, or cheese, and then rolled up, tied, and steamed.

Tamarind

A tropical fruit whose pulp is enclosed in a long pod which has an acid-sweet taste, and which is used in chutneys and preserves. The juice is used in pickling fish, and a syrup made from it is used, much diluted, in a cool drink.

Tamis (Fr.)

A fine cloth or sieve through which soups and sauces are strained.

Tammy-Cloth (Eng.)

A fine linen cloth used for straining soups and sauces; derived from the French tamis.

Tangelo

A fruit produced by crossing the tangerine and the grapefruit and pleasantly combining certain qualities of each. Also called ugli.

Tangerine

A small, loose-skinned, flattened orange of a deep orange color, which is easily peeled and separated into sections.

Tangle (Scot.)

A seaweed similar to laver.

Tansy

Once an important herb in New England and Europe, where it was used in herb teas, egg dishes, cakes, and puddings, now cultivated in the Mid west for its oil, used in drugs and liqueurs. Its attractive dark green foliage is sometimes used as a garnish for meats or salads, and tansy pudding is still occasionally made.

Tapioca

A white, granular, starchy substance obtained by heating the root of the cassava, or manioc, plant which grows in the West Indies, and used as a thickening agent, especially in puddings.

Tarata (Gr.)
A soup consisting of green peppers and eggplant cooked in olive oil and yogurt, seasoned with pepper, cayenne, mint, and garlic, and served ice-cold.

Taro
A plant of the Pacific islands, and also of parts of the Orient, whose potato-like root forms a staple food of the tropics, that is, poi. The nearly-round root generally weighs around five pounds. An alternate Hawaiian name is *luau*.

Tarragon
An herb related to wormwood, much valued for the aromatic flavor it gives to vinegar, as well as to meat, poultry, fish, salads, sauces, and certain vegetables. A native of the temperate zone, tarragon grows about eighteen inches high, with widely spaced, dark green, pointed leaves and small clusters of greenish-yellow flowers.

Tarragon Vinegar
Wine vinegar to which crushed fresh tarragon leaves, or a sprig of tarragon, and, sometimes, certain spices have been added.

Tart
1. A small, individual-sized pie containing fruit, meat, etc.; or, a piece of pastry spread with jam.
2. Sharp or biting in taste.

Tartar
1. Lean raw beef ground fine and mixed with onion, seasonings, and, often, raw egg, and used as a sandwich spread or appetizer.
2. An acid substance deposited during fermentation of grape juice, used in making cream of tartar.

Tartar Sauce
A sauce consisting of mayonnaise combined with chopped onions, pickles, capers, olives, etc., which is served with fish. Also spelled *tartare*.

Tartaric Acid
A mild acid derived from, or resembling that derived from, tartar.

Tartine
A slice of bread spread with butter, jam, preserves, fish paste, or the like.

Tartlet
A very small tart.

Tartrate Baking Powder
See BAKING POWDER.

T-Bone Steak
A porterhouse steak cut from the small end of the loin, and thus relatively small in size, but also quite expensive as it should be cut fairly thick. The distinctive "T" shape of the bone gives the steak its name.

Tea
1. The leaves of a shrub of the camellia family grown in various parts of the Orient, which are dried and prepared by various processes for brewing; the brew, or infusion, of these leaves, or of other leaves; or, sometimes, a broth, as beef tea, used as a beverage.

2. In England, a light meal taken in the late afternoon or early evening, consisting of tea with cakes and bread and butter; or an entire meal, often called "high tea."

Teiglach (Jew.)
See TAIGLACH.

Tellicherry Pepper
A mild-flavored black pepper from the Malabar coast of southern India.

Temple Orange
A large, loose-skinned orange, apparently a hybrid between the mandarin and the sweet orange.

Tempura (Jap.)
Any dish prepared by dipping in batter and frying in deep fat. In the West, the term is most often used to refer to shrimp cooked in this style.

Tender
Having a consistency such as can be easily pierced with a fork, or about that of butter which has been out of the refrigerator for an hour.

Tenderloin
The fillet of the loin, the tenderest, though not necessarily the tastiest, portion. Filet mignon, Châteaubriand, and tournedos are all cuts from the tenderloin of beef.

Ten Thousand Arrows Piercing Through the Clouds
The fanciful name for shark's fins and eggs, said to be a second course in a typical Chinese meal.

Tequila (Mex.)
A strong liquor made from the agave.

Teriyaki (Jap.)
Cubes of pork, chicken, beef, shrimp, etc., marinated in a spiced soy sauce, then broiled, preferably on skewers over live coals.

Terrapin
A river and swamp turtle, whose meat has a unique odor which many people find offensive and others can't resist. It is eaten more in the South than elsewhere, most often in stews, though diamondback terrapin has some fanciers in the eastern part of the country.

Terrine (Fr.)
An earthenware dish, or a pâté or similar preparation made and served, or sold, in it.

Tetrazzini (It.)
A combination of cooked chicken, turkey, veal, or lobster with spaghetti and mushrooms, covered with a velouté sauce seasoned with nutmeg and sherry, and baked.

Texture
The structural arrangement or disposition of particles in a resultant whole; or the effect of these upon the sense of touch, for example, smooth, rough, fine, coarse, slimy, etc.

Thermidor
A manner of cooking first applied to lobster, but since extended to other seafood as well. The meat is first boiled in the shell, removed, creamed, returned to the shell, sprinkled with cheese, and browned. This recipe was created in Paris by Tony Girod of the Café de Paris.

Thickening Agent
Any ingredient used primarily for thickening. See ARROWROOT, CORNSTARCH, FECULA, FLOUR, GELATIN, LIAISON, and ROUX.

Thimbleberry
Any of several wild raspberries common in New England, ranging in color from pink or red to black, and sometimes rather insipid in flavor. Also called wood mulberry and black raspberry.

Thompkins King Apple
An apple to be eaten raw or to be used in general cookery, in season from November to February.

Thompson Seedless Grape
A small, pale-green, seedless grape, very tasty and popular for eating raw and in salads and fruit cocktails when in season during late summer and early fall. Out of season it is very expensive.

Thousand Heads (Eng.)
An unusual plant mentioned by Alexis Soyer in *Soyer's Cookery Book*, published in England in 1854, consisting of many small heads springing from a single root and sometimes covering a square yard. These were cooked like greens or Brussels sprouts, but apparently gained no popularity.

Thousand Island Dressing
A Russian dressing, i.e., a mixture of mayonnaise, chili sauce, and other seasonings such as minced celery, pimento, and green pepper, to which whipped cream has been added.

Threaded Eggs
Eggs beaten and strained into boiling consommé, where they coagulate into threads which are then used to garnish clear soups.

Thread Stage
The stage in the cooking of candy syrup at which a bit dropped from a fork spins a short thread.

Thuringer Sausage (Ger.)
A fresh, i.e., unsmoked sausage similar to cervelat.

Thyme
A commonly used herb of the mint family, having grey-green leaves and tiny lavender flowers, with a warm aroma somewhat resembling that of sage. A native of the Mediterranean area, it is now cultivated all over Europe and North America for a multitude of uses, especially in stuffings and mixed herb seasonings for use with meats, and in sauces. The sixty varieties include lemon scented thyme, wild thyme, and a mountain plant called mother of thyme.

Tiffin (Anglo-Ind.)
Luncheon or a light midday meal; sometimes also used to refer to "elevenses," or mid-morning coffee.

Tilefish
A fish abundant along the coast of Maine, often weighing from fifteen to thirty pounds, which is cut and sold in steaks. It is in season all year round, has a well-flavored, rich meat, and is reasonably priced.

Tile Tea
Tea packed in brick form.

Timbale

A drum-shaped mould; also, a preparation of meat, fish, or cheese cooked and served in, or a pastry shell baked in, such a mould.

Tin

Any pan in which cake, bread, or pie is baked; a usage dating back to a time when such utensils were invariably made of tin.

Tinware

Cooking utensils made of tin, not common nowadays.

Tipsy Cake (Eng.)

A sponge cake baked in a tall mould, soaked with wine, and frequently filled and garnished with nuts and whipped cream.

Tipsy Pudding (Eng.)

A kind of trifle consisting of a sherry-flavored custard cooled and poured over slices of sponge cake, or some other plain cake, and garnished with whipped cream.

Tisane

A nourishing drink, frequently barley-water or an herb tea, especially camomile.

Toad-in-the-Hole (Eng.)

1. Originally, a dish of chops baked in a simple batter; now used to refer to any kind of meat so prepared.
2. An egg fried and served in a piece of bread with the center cut out.

Toast

As a verb, to brown by direct heat, as a flame or electric coil.

Tocana (Romania)

Any meat and vegetable stew, of which there are many varieties. Also, *tokany*.

Tocinos del Cielo (Sp.)

A candy made of sugar, water, and egg yolks, cooked, poured out, cooled, and topped with a chocolate sauce. Literally, "little pigs of heaven."

Toe

A name sometimes given to a clove of garlic.

Toffee (Eng.)

A kind of chewy candy made of sugar, butter, and, usually, nuts; in the United States, however, another name for taffy.

Tofu (Jap.)

Soy bean curd, usually solid or semi-solid in form, and having a cheese-like consistency.

Tokany (Hung.)

An alternate spelling of *tocana*.

Tokay Grape

The name of a very large, purple-red, sweet grape cultivated in California; and also of a sweet white wine made in Hungary, as well as a dessert wine made in California, although neither is made from Tokay grapes.

Tolman Sweet Apple

A good jelly apple, which may also be eaten raw or baked, in season from October to March.

Tomalley

A soft, greenish material, often called the liver, in a lobster; used as a sauce for certain dishes.

Tomato Sauce
A sauce containing tomatoes, prepared and seasoned in any of a number of ways.

Tonka Bean
The seed of a tropical tree, used in making imitation vanilla extract. Its flavor, while resembling vanilla, is inferior to it.

Top
To place on, or spread over, the upper surface.

Topepo
A tomato-like vegetable, said to be a hybrid between a tomato and red pepper.

Top Milk
Milk from the top of the bottle after cream has risen there.

Torinabe (Jap.)
A dish made like sukiyaki, but using chicken rather than beef.

Torta de Carne (Mex.)
A meat loaf.

Torte (Aus.)
A rich, rather heavy cake, usually with beaten eggs as the only leavening and often served with whipped cream.

Tortilla (Mex.)
The national bread, consisting of a very thin, flat, round corn meal pancake cooked till done, but not brown, on a special griddle.

Tortoise
A land turtle; one species is also known in parts of the South as a gopher.

Tossed Salad
A salad made up of one or more greens, tomatoes, onion slices, etc., with a dressing, and mixed, or tossed, with a large-sized spoon and fork.

Tostada (Mex.)
A tortilla fried golden and crisp and piled with refried beans, cheese, chorizo, shredded lettuce, and sauce.

Tournedos (Fr.)
A fillet steak cut from the tenderloin of beef.

Tourtière (Fr. Can.)
A ground pork, veal, and onion pie, ordinarily topped with a thin layer of gelatin just under the top crust and most often, though not always, served cold.

Transparent Apple
A yellow variety, in season during July and August, excellent for eating raw or for cooking purposes.

Trappist Cheese
See PORT DU SALUT.

Treacle (Eng.)
Molasses.

Trepang
One of several names for the sea cucumber.

Trifle (Eng.)
A dessert consisting of sponge cake, or a similar plain cake, sliced, spread with jam, soaked with wine, and combined with fruits, nut meats, custard, or whipped cream.

Tripe

The white, rubbery, inner lining of the stomach of a beef animal. The best grade, from the second stomach, has a honeycombed texture. It is thoroughly cleaned and boiled, and, as rather tasteless itself, is generally served in a sauce or stew.

Triple-Sec (Fr.)

An orange-flavored liqueur, usually colorless, sold in squarish bottles.

Trivet

A short-legged metal plate on which hot dishes are placed at the table, or for use in a skillet or Dutch oven, in which foods are braised or simmered.

Tronçon (Fr.)

A section or slice, for example, of a fish.

Trotters

The feet of an animal, such as a pig, calf, or lamb, when used as food.

Trout

Any of several food and game fish, mostly fresh-water, whose excellent meat is greatly prized in both Europe and America. Pacific, brook, and rainbow trout are especially popular in the United States.

Truffle

A plump, edible fungus, very delicate in aroma, used to decorate and flavor various dishes. It grows underground and is located by trained truffle hounds, or by pigs. The truffles available in the United States are imported, mainly from France, and are very expensive. There are both black and white varieties.

Truss

To tie, or fasten tightly, by sewing or with metal pins or skewers; used in referring to a stuffed fowl.

Try Out

See RENDER.

Tsukemono (Jap.)

Pickled vegetable.

Tubettini (It.)

Pasta cut into one-eighth-inch lengths and used in soups. Literally, "little tubes."

Tuna

A valuable game and food fish, one species of which is found in the Pacific and another along the Florida coast. The meat, sometimes called the chicken of the sea, is tender and flaky and varies in color from nearly white to a rosy pink-orange.

Tunbridge Wells Cake (Eng.)

A thin, rolled cooky containing caraway seeds, originated in the town of Tunbridge Wells, in the county of Kent.

Tunny

Any of a group of large, coarse-fleshed, oily-meated food fish, often called horse mackerel on the Atlantic coast. Zoologically speaking, the tunas belong to this group.

Turban

An ornamental dish of fish, poultry, or meat, made in the shape of a turban, with a central cavity in which a garnish of some appropriate mixture is placed.

Turbot
A large flatfish, common in European waters.

Tureen
A covered vessel, usually of porcelain or earthenware, in which soup, gravy, or sauce is served at the table.

Turkish Delight
A candy made of gelatin and sweetened fruit juice, cut into cubes or rectangles, and dusted with sugar. The Turkish name is *rahat lakoum*.

Turk's Head Pan
A tall, round cake pan with a central tube and a spiraling indentation of the outer walls.

Turmeric
A spice from the ground aromatic root of a tropical member of the ginger family. It gives curry powder its golden color and has a mild, clean, rich, but peculiarly bitter-sweet flavor. It is also used to color cakes and cookies, as well as in pickles and relishes. While it is probably most popular in East Indian cookery, the plant is also cultivated in China, Haiti, and elsewhere.

Turnip Cabbage
See KOHLRABI.

Turnover
A small pie made from a circle or square of dough which is topped with a spoonful of meat, fruit, or jam filling, and then folded over on itself, sealed, and baked or fried.

Turtle
Any of various shelled reptiles, including the land turtle, the tortoise, and the swamp and river turtle, the terrapin; but most often referring to the large, seagoing species. Of these, the edible green turtle is noted for the excellent thick soup, usually flavored with Madeira or sherry, which is made from it. Key West is the center for turtle fishing, and in that area turtle steaks are a specialty. Turtle fins are also eaten, usually browned and then simmered in a wine sauce, and turtle eggs, considered a delicacy, and generally eaten hard-boiled (though only the yolks solidify) are also available.

Turtle Sauce
A spicy sauce containing veal stock, half-glaze, tomatoes, and seasonings.

Tutti-Frutti (It.)
Containing a mixture of candied, dried, or fresh fruits.

Twankay Tea
A kind of green tea deriving its name from the *Tun-ki*, a river in China.

Twelfth-Day Cake (Eng.)
A white fruit cake, i.e., one without molasses, traditionally made several months beforehand and served on Epiphany, the twelfth day after Christmas. It is covered with almond paste and a thin white icing, and is often accompanied by lamb's wool, an apple drink.

Twenty-Ounce Apple
One of the few good varieties for making jelly, also used in applesauce; in season from September to November.

Tzimmes (Jew.)
Any of various combinations of meat,

vegetables, and/or fruits, either baked a long time or cooked slowly over very low heat.

Uccelli Scappati (It.)
The name for veal birds in a dialect of northern Italy.

Udo
An Oriental plant, now grown in California, the young shoots of which are used like asparagus.

Udon (Jap.)
A wheat-flour noodle.

Ugli (Eng.)
See TANGELO.

Umbles (Eng.)
An obsolete name for the edible entrails of any animal, but especially applied to those of a deer, which, several hundred years ago, were used in umbles, or "humble," pie.

Unpolished Rice
See BROWN RICE.

Upside-Down Cake
A cake baked with a layer of fruit, brown sugar, and nut meats at the bottom of the pan, and then turned out with the bottom uppermost.

Usquebaugh (Ir.)
The Gaelic word meaning "water of life," from which "whiskey" is said to be derived.

Vacuum Coffee
Coffee made in a two-vessel device in which water passes, after heating, from a lower bowl into an upper one which contains the ground coffee, is cooked briefly, removed from the heat, and allowed to drain back into the lower bowl.

Vadai (Ind.)
A fried patty of boiled lentils mixed with onions, chilis, and spices.

Valencia Almond
An almond from Spain, next in favor to the Jordan almond.

Valencia Orange
A summer variety of orange, cultivated in California and Florida, paler in color than the navel orange, and not entirely seedless.

Valois Sauce
A béarnaise sauce with meat glaze added, to be served with meat. Also called Foyot sauce.

Van der Hum (Un. of S. Af.)
A fine liqueur flavored with herbs and fruits, among which the nartje, or South African tangerine, is predominant.

Vanilla Sugar
Sugar into which a pod of the vanilla bean has been placed, thus imparting that flavor. The French use this sugar in desserts.

Vareniki (Rus.)
An appetizer consisting of cheese-filled noodle paste, poached in boiling water; also, sometimes, cherry dumplings.

Variety Meats
Liver, tongue, kidneys, heart, sweet breads, feet, oxtails, and the like, as well as such sandwich meats as "pickle loaf" and minced ham.

Vatroushki (Rus.)
Puff pastry tartlets filled with cream cheese, eaten as a *zakouska*, or appetizer, or with borsch.

Veal
The flesh of a calf, generally one from six to eight weeks old and weighing not over two hundred pounds, and, ideally, though not usually, milk-fed. It is generally tender and very lean.

Vegetable Ice Cream
See CHERIMOYA.

Vegetable Oil
Any oil obtained from a plant, for example, corn, olives, sunflower seed, soy beans, cottonseed, peanuts, and the like, especially when refined for use in cooking. Vegetable oils are often solidified by hydrogenation, i.e., charging with hydrogen, and are sold as shortenings under various brand names.

Velouté Sauce (Fr.)
A basic, or mother, sauce made with pale roux and a white stock; distinguished from béchamel in that it contains no milk or cream. *Velouté* means, literally, "velvet," and the sauce is sometimes so called in English.

Venitienne, à la (Fr.)
In the Venetian style; for example, fish served with a rich cream sauce.

Verbena
A plant of the vervain family, one variety of which is called lemon verbena because of its aroma. The long, narrow, yellow-green leaves are used as a garnish in fruit cups, salads, jellies, and fruit and wine drinks, and are also steeped to make a tea.

Verjuice
The acid juice of unripe fruit, usually of grapes or apples.

Vermicelli (It.)
A very thin, thread-like pasta. Literally, "little worms."

Vermouth
A white wine, more or less sweet, highly flavored with aromatic herbs and spices, notably wormwood. Italian vermouth is darker in color and has a higher sugar content than the French.

Véronique (Fr.)
Having a garnish of seedless white grapes.

Vert-Pré (Fr.)
Containing, or garnished with, bright green herbs.

Vichy (Fr.)
A method of preparing carrots, using butter and very little water.

Vichysoisse
A rich cream soup made from leeks and potatoes, which is characteristically served chilled. Literally, the name means "in the manner of Vichy," a French city, and though the soup did not originate there, it is said to have been first made by a chef from Vichy.

Vienna Sausage
A very small, pink, mildly seasoned, cylindrical sausage in a soft casing.

Viennese Coffee
Strong coffee served with sweetened whipped cream.

Villeroy Sauce (Fr.)
A thickened velouté sauce flavored with truffles and ham.

Vinaigrette Sauce (Fr.)
A French dressing, especially one to which chopped onions and green herbs have been added.

Vincent Sauce (Fr.)
Mayonnaise containing hard-boiled egg yolks, Worcestershire sauce, and various herbs which have been parboiled.

Vindaloo (Ind.)
A meat dish prepared by marinating in a paste of vinegar, garlic, onions, and spices, often referred to as vindaloo paste.

Vinegar
A liquid containing acetic acid obtained by the fermentation of cider, wine, malt, or, sometimes, the juice of such fruits as pears and pineapples. It is sour and clear, and anywhere from almost entirely colorless to a very dark shade of amber, and is used in pickling, the making of salad dressings, and the like.

Vinegar Pie
A one or two crust pie with a filling made of butter, sugar, flour, egg, vinegar, water, and spices cooked in the top of a double boiler till thick. The crust is sometimes partially baked beforehand.

Virginia Ham
A ham which, if it is of the finest quality, has been cured for over a year and then smoked and aged, sometimes for several years. It should also, correctly, be from the sort of half-wild hog known as a razorback that has been partially fed on acorns and peanuts, a diet which is said to account, at least to a degree, for the special delicacy of the ham's flavor. These hams must be well soaked and simmered prior to baking. Smithfield ham, though a trade name, is sometimes used as a synonym for Virginia ham.

Virgin Olive Oil
Oil obtained from the first pressing of ripe olives, or skimmed from the top of the vat. It is superior in flavor and appearance to that from the later pressings.

Visitandine (Fr.)
A small, light, almond cake baked in a muffin pan and often spread with apricot jam and a Kirsch-flavored icing. The name is said to derive from the nuns of the order of the Visitation, who first baked it.

Vitamin
Any of a group of food substances contained to a greater or lesser degree in most foods in their natural state, and necessary in varying quantities to maintain life and health, though they do not supply energy.

Vol-au-Vent (Fr.)
A puff paste shell with a separately baked cover, which is served filled with some hot creamed mixture.

Wafer

A very thin, crisp cooky or biscuit.

Waffle

A cake made by baking a light batter in a special mould, or iron, with hinged top and bottom characterized by a checkerboard pattern of indentations. Waffle irons are now heated electrically both top and bottom so that baking is quick and accurate, but they were once heated on the top of a stove and turned by hand. Waffles are usually served with butter and syrup, though fruit, ice cream, chicken à la king, etc. are occasional accompaniments.

Wagener Apple

An apple for eating raw or for use in general cooking, in season from November to January.

Waldmeister (Ger.)

Another name for woodruff.

Waldorf Salad

Cubes of apple combined with celery, chopped nut meats, and, often raisins, and mayonnaise dressing.

Walnut

A rounded or oval nut; either the strong, distinctively flavored black walnut, or the pale tan, mild-flavored English (or California) walnut. Recipes calling for walnuts refer to the latter, unless specifying the former.

Wasabi (Jap.)

The Oriental horseradish.

Washed Butter

Butter from which salt and excess fluid have been removed by squeezing under cold running water.

Washington (Fr.)

Containing or garnished with corn.

Washington Pie

A sponge cake filled with jam or custard and sprinkled with sugar.

Wassail (Eng.)

A medieval drink made of spiced and sweetened ale or wine, and drunk on festive occasions, such as New Year's day.

Water

In cooking, this term is frequently used to refer to the liquid in which a vegetable has been cooked, as, for example, potato water; or, as a verb, it often means to dilute.

Water Chestnut

The fruit kernel of a water plant with floating leaves and small white flowers, resembling a true chestnut, or marron, in shape and color, but crunchy in texture. It is widely used, generally diced or sliced, in Oriental cookery.

Water Cress

A water plant whose small, smooth, pungent, dark-green leaves are often used in salads.

Watermelon

The large, rounded or oval fruit of a vine belonging to the gourd family, having a rind which may be either a plain dark or light green color, or green striped, and a sweet, reddish-pink, watery meat. The meat is always eaten fresh and chilled, while the rind is sometimes pickled or made into a preserve.

Watermelon Rind Pickle

A condiment made from watermelon rind with all outer green skin and inner pink meat removed, cut in squares or other shapes, cooked and rested over-night, and then simmered till clear in a syrup of vinegar, sugar, cloves, and cinnamon.

Wax Bean

A bean whose immature pods are pale yellow in color.

Weakfish

A spiny-finned food fish with lean or dry flesh, found along sandy shores on the Atlantic coast.

Wealthy Apple

An excellent apple for eating raw or for general cooking, in season from August to December. It is red streaked with yellow and is grown throughout the United States.

Wedding Cake

A white cake, often with spices and candied peel added, and flavored with almond extract, traditionally baked in tiered layers, covered with white icing, and decorated. The first piece is supposed to be cut by the bride and groom together. See also BRIDE'S CAKE and GROOM'S CAKE.

Welsh Cawl (Eng.)

A boiled dinner of lamb or mutton, leeks, carrots, and potatoes.

Welsh Rabbit

Melted cheese combined with ale or beer and seasonings, and served on toast. Milk is sometimes substituted for the traditional ale or beer. Though "rabbit" is the correct name in that it was the original one used, "rarebit" is also frequently heard.

Western Sandwich

Another name for a Denver sandwich.

Westphalian Ham

A specially cured, hard ham originating in Germany.

Wheat Germ

The nutritionally rich embryo of a grain of wheat, having a granular texture and a pleasantly nutty flavor. It may be sprinkled on cereal, ice cream, etc., or added to such foods as pancakes, muffins, and meat loaf.

Whetstone Cake (Eng.)

A small, thin, rolled cooky containing caraway seed and rose water. One old Leicestershire recipe dates from 1741.

Whey

The part of milk which remains as a thin liquid when the rest forms curds in the process of souring or of cheese-making.

Whip

1. To beat (usually a liquid) rapidly with a fork, beater, or electric mixer so that air is introduced, thus lightening the mixture and increasing its volume.
2. A dessert made light by the addition of beaten egg whites, whipped cream, or gelatin.

Whipping Cream

Heavy cream which may be changed from a liquid to a semi-solid state and expanded in volume by whipping.

Whiskey Cake
A Christmas holiday cake containing nuts, raisins, and bourbon whiskey.

Whitebait
Any of several fish so tiny and delicate of texture that they can only be cooked by frying, and that for only one or two minutes. The young fry of herrings and sprats are called by this name, also.

White Cake
A basic cake leavened with baking powder and containing the whites, but not the yolks, of eggs.

Whitefish
Any of several fish, but especially a small-mouth fresh-water species having fat or oily flesh, which is sold smoked in the Midwest and along the East coast, and is available fresh, either whole or in fillets, usually from specimens weighing two to six pounds.

White Peach
A pale-skinned, white-meated peach tinted with pink, delicate in flavor, and exceedingly sweet and juicy.

White Pearmain Apple
An apple to be eaten raw or used in general cooking, in season from December to March.

White Sauce
A basic sauce made with white roux, i.e., butter and flour which are not browned, as distinguished from brown roux used in brown sauce. In most United States recipes, white sauce is identical with béchamel in that it is made with milk rather than stock, but this is not invariably so.

White Vinegar
A clear, colorless, rather strong vinegar distilled from malt rather than from cider or wine.

White Wine Sauce (Fr.)
Any of various sauces containing white wine.

Whiting
A tender, delicate fish of the Atlantic coastal waters, having lean white flesh and a bland flavor.

Whole Milk
Milk from which no cream or butterfat has been removed.

Whole-Wheat Flour
A flour, either finely or coarsely ground, containing the bran and the germ of wheat. Graham flour is a kind of whole-wheat flour.

Whortleberry
Another name for the huckleberry, or, in Europe, the bilberry.

Wiener Schnitzel (Aus.)
A veal cutlet, especially one prepared by dipping in egg, flour, and bread crumbs, and frying to a golden brown. Often a poached egg accompanies it. Literally, the name means "a cutlet in the manner of Vienna."

Wig (Eng.)
An old-fashioned yeast-raised cake, shaped in the form of a wig, or wedge.

Wiggle
Shrimp, salmon, or some other seafood served in a white sauce with peas.

Wild Ginger

An herb native to the New World, whose root was used by the Indians to flavor maize or hominy. The plant grows in cool, moist, shady places and has rather large leaves. The flavor of the root is similar to, but not identical with, that of true ginger.

Wild Marjoram

See OREGANO.

Wild Rice

The seed of a native North American swamp grass found east of the Rocky Mountains under various local names. The rather large grains are whitish-brown in color, and are prepared in the same way as ordinary rice, though a more thorough cleaning and a longer cooking are needed.

Williams Apple

An apple to be eaten raw or used in general cooking, in season during August and September.

Windfalls

Any fruit blown down by the wind, usually after the best has been picked. Old recipes often refer to such apples as being suitable for use in pies.

Windsor Bean (Eng.)

An old name for the broad bean.

Windsor Cherry

A dark-colored, sweet cherry, widely grown commercially as it ships well; it is in season during the summer.

Wine Jelly

A moulded gelatin dessert containing orange and lemon juice and flavored with wine, for example, sherry, Madeira, or sauterne.

Winesap Apple

An excellent, medium-sized, deep red winter apple used for pies or applesauce and for eating raw, in season from January to May.

Wine Vinegar

Vinegar made by fermenting red or white wine, so that the alcohol is converted into acetic acid. A fine vinegar, often recommended for use in French dressing.

Winkle (Eng.)

Short for periwinkle, which see.

Winter Banana Apple

A variety almost invariably eaten raw, in season from October through December.

Winter Cherry

See GROUND CHERRY.

Wintergreen

A low-growing evergreen shrub whose aromatic leaves and red berries yield an oil used in flavoring candies, chewing gum, and medicines. Also called checkerberry, boxberry, spiceberry, and mountain tea.

Winter Nelis Pear

A fine-flavored, greenish-yellow or russet colored pear which, though very tender and juicy, keeps very well in cold storage. It is grown primarily in the West.

Winter Squash

Any of several varieties of squash having a hard rind which, unlike that of summer squash, is never eaten. Acorn, Hubbard, and butternut are leading winter varieties.

Wirre Gedanken (Aus.)

A kind of thin cake which is fried in deep fat. The dough is rolled into three-inch rounds which are placed one at a time on a wooden spoon or similar implement and dipped quickly into hot fat, after which they are dipped in powdered sugar and eaten piping hot. The name means "jumbled thoughts."

Wishbone

A forked bone in front of the breast bone in most fowl, deriving its name from the old superstition that the person left holding the longer fork, or prong, when a wishbone is pulled in two, will have his wish come true. In England, sometimes called merry thought.

Witloof Chicory

See ENDIVE.

Wolf River Apple

A variety used for baking or other cooking purposes, in season from September to December. In color it is yellow broadly striped with red.

Won Ton (Chin.)

A preparation resembling kreplach or ravioli, consisting of small squares of dough filled with a fried mixture of ground pork, onion, and fresh ginger, folded in thirds and pinched together into a shape resembling that of a Dutch cap, and either cooked and served in a clear soup or separately fried in oil. Also spelled *wun tun*.

Wood Mulberry

See THIMBLEBERRY.

Woodruff

A sweet, perennial herb, often called sweet woodruff, which grows in wooded places in Europe and is used to flavor May wine (a German product), lemonade and other fruit drinks, punches, and fruit cups.

Worcestershire Sauce

A thin, dark, pungent seasoning sauce, primarily to be used with meat, containing garlic, soy, vinegar, onions, and spices, and originally made in Worcester, England.

Wormwood

The bitterest of all herbs, surpassing even rue, an extract of which is used in making absinthe and in small and diluted quantities in flavoring wines (notably vermouth), spirits (notably bitters), and certain liqueurs. The quantity used in absinthe was such that overindulgence could cause convulsions and even death, and for that reason its manufacture is prohibited in many countries. The wormwood plant grows two to three feet high, and has silky grey leaves, and yellow flowers. As a medicinal herb it is very ancient, and stomach remedies employing it were known to the Greeks and Romans and were still in use during the Middle Ages. The plant is often called absinthe, and is related to mugwort and tarragon.

Wort

1. An infusion of unfermented malt; also, an infusion of malt or any other liquid just beginning to ferment.
2. An herb plant, generally used medicinally, but of which the member called chickweed is edible, though not especially good.

Wurst (Ger.)
A sausage.

XXX
The notation often placed on the label of powdered sugar to distinguish it from the still finer confectioner's sugar.

XXXX
The notation placed on confectioner's sugar, which see.

Yablouchni (Pol.)
A sweetened cold soup containing sieved apple pulp and, sometimes, red wine.

Yakitori (Jap.)
Chicken roasted on a spit and basted with sake and soy sauce.

Yam
The yellow or orange underground tuber of a tropical vine, similar to the sweet potato but rather sweeter and juicier, as well as deeper in color. Yams are generally boiled or baked, and are either seasoned with salt and pepper or sweetened with brown sugar.

Yankee Pot Roast
A cut of beef cooked by braising, often with vegetables, and served in its own thickened gravy.

Yarrow
An herb whose strongly aromatic leaves may, when finely chopped, replace chervil in salads.

Yeast
A substance consisting of the cells of certain kinds of fungi, producing the chemical change known as fermentation, necessary in making wine, beer, and raised breads; or, a commercial product consisting of some material, such as meal, impregnated with these cells. See COMPRESSED and DRY YEAST.

Yeast Bread
Any bread in which yeast is the leavening agent.

Yellow Cake
Any cake which is yellow in color, generally one containing egg yolks.

Yellow Newton Apple
A red-striped, yellow apple to be eaten raw or used in general cooking, in season in the West and Southwest from January to May. Also called the Albemarle pippin.

Yellow Perch
A greenish-gold, rather small freshwater fish very common in the Great Lakes region, highly prized for food and as a game fish. It is also taken commercially in large quantities.

Yellowtail
A Pacific coast fish, good as game and plentiful in spring and early summer. The flesh is juicy and rather heavy in texture, but pleasing in flavor.

Yerba Maté (S. Am.)
See MATÉ.

Yogurt
A preparation of fermented, concentrated milk similar to kumiss and kefir. It may be either semi-solid or fluid, but is usually about the consistency of heavy cream. It is eaten by itself or as a spread, or is used plain

or flavored as a drink, and is a common ingredient in Middle Eastern and Indian cookery. It is sometimes spelled *yaghoust, yogart, yoghurt,* and *yohourt.*

York Biscuit (Eng.)
A thin, round, rolled cooky made from plain dough and undecorated.

York Imperial Apple
A variety to be eaten raw or used in general cooking, in season from October to February.

Zabaglione (It.)
A mixture of egg yolks, sugar, Marsala, and cinnamon beaten till thick over boiling water in the top of a double boiler, and served as a dessert, either hot in a liquid state or chilled to a semi-solid. Also spelled *zabaione.*

Zakouski (Rus.)
A general term for hors d'oeurves.

Zampino (It.)
A dish containing boiled salt pork, often served with French beans; or, a stuffed fresh ham served either hot, with sauce and vegetables, or cold as an appetizer.

Zéphire (Fr.)
Small forcemeat balls simmered and served in their own sauce.

Zest
The colored, glossy outermost layer of an orange or lemon rind, which has a pleasant taste and is grated for culinary use.

Ziti (It.)
A tubular pasta about half an inch in diameter.

Zoolak
A preparation of fermented milk, closely resembling yogurt.

Zouave Sauce
A brown sauce containing chili, vinegar, tomato purée, garlic, and mustard.

Zrazy (Rus., Pol.)
Various stuffed meat dishes, for example, fillets of haddock or thin slices of beef stuffed with a mixture of chopped onion and bread, and then breaded, fried in butter, and, often, poached.

Zucchini (It.)
A dark-green summer squash, somewhat resembling a cucumber in shape and size, which is cooked without peeling unless very old and rough. Sautéeing, creaming, and stewing are among the methods of preparation. Also called Italian squash.

Zuppe Inglese (It.)
Although the name is literally translated "English soup," this is actually a dessert consisting of sponge cake split into three layers, which are sprinkled with vermouth and rum and spread with orange marmalade, after which the whole cake is covered with custard, zabaglione, or whipped cream.

Zwieback (Ger.)
A hard, dry, sweet, toasted slice of bread. Literally, the name means "twice baked." Also called rusk or Brussels biscuit.

Also available from Hippocrene Books . . .

DICTIONARY OF GASTRONOMIC TERMS, FRENCH/ENGLISH
Bernard Luce
Here is the reference book cooks and gourmands have been waiting for! Now you can discuss the delicious dishes you have been savoring for years with gusto and precision!
500 pages · 5 ½ x 8 ½ · 20,000 entries · 0-7818-0555-4 · $24.95pb · (655)

International Cookbooks from Hippocrene . . .

WORLD'S BEST RECIPES
From Hippocrene's best-selling international cookbooks, comes this unique collection of culinary specialties from many lands. With over 150 recipes, this wonderful anthology includes both exotic delicacies and classic favorites from nearly 100 regions and countries. Sample such delights as Zambian Chicken Stew, Polish Apple Cake, Colombian Corn Tamales, and Persian Pomegranate Khoreshe.
256 pages · 5 1/2 x 8 ½ · 0-7818-0599-6 · W · $9.95pb · (685)

ART OF SOUTH AMERICAN COOKERY
Myra Waldo
This cookbook offers delicious recipes for the various courses of a typical South American meal. Dishes show the expected influence of Spanish and Portuguese cuisines, but are enhanced by the use of locally available ingredients.
266 pages • 5 x 8 1/2 • b/w line drawings • 0-7818-0485-X • W · $11.95pb · (423)

THE ART OF BRAZILIAN COOKERY
Dolores Botafogo
Over three hundred savory and varied recipes fill this cookbook of authentic Brazilian cuisine, ranging from Churasco (barbecued steak) and Vatapa (Afro-Brazilian fish porridge from the Amazon) to sweets, and aromatic Brazilian coffees.
240 pages • 51/2 x 81/2 • 0-7818-0130-3 • W • $11.95pb • (250)

A SPANISH FAMILY COOKBOOK, REVISED EDITION
Juan and Susan Serrano
Over 250 recipes covering all aspects of the Spanish meal, from tapas (appetizers) through pasteles (cakes and pastries). Features a new wine section, including information on classic Spanish sherries and riojas.
244 pages • 5 x 81/2 • 0-7818-0546-5 • W • $11.95pb • (642)

BEST OF GREEK CUISINE: COOKING WITH GEORGIA
Georgia Sarianides
Chef Georgia Sarianides offers a health-conscious approach to authentic Greek cookery with over 100 tempting low-fat, low-calorie recipes. Also includes helpful sections on Greek wines, using herbs and spices, and general food preparation tips.
176 pages • 51/2 x 81/2 • b/w line drawings • 0-7818-0545-7 • W • $19.95hc • (634)

GOOD FOOD FROM AUSTRALIA
Graeme and Betsy Newman
A generous sampling of over 150 Australian culinary favorites. "Steak, Chops, and Snags," "Casseroles and Curries," and "Outback Cooking" are among the intriguing sections included. In time for the 2000 Olympics in Sydney!
284 pages • 51/2 x 81/2 • b/w line illustrations • 0-7818-0491-4 • W · $24.95hc • (440)

BEST OF REGIONAL AFRICAN COOKING
Harva Hachten
Here is a gourmet's tour of Africa, from North African specialties like Chicken Tajin with Olives and Lemon to Zambian Groundnut Soup and Senegalese Couscous. With over 240 recipes that deliver the unique and dramatic flavors of each region: North, East, West, Central and South Africa, this is a comprehensive treasury of African cuisine.
274 pages • 5 1/2 x 8 1/2 • 0-7818-0598-8 • W • $11.95pb • (684)

TRADITIONAL SOUTH AFRICAN COOKERY
Hildegonda Duckitt
A collection of recipes culled from two previous books by the author, this volume provides ideas for tasty, British- and Dutch-inspired meals and insight into daily life of colonial Africa.
178 pages • 5 x 8 1/2 • 0-7818-0490-6 • W • $10.95pb • (352)

THE JOY OF CHINESE COOKING
Doreen Yen Hung Feng
Includes over two hundred kitchen-tested recipes and a thorough index.
226 pages • 5 1/2 x 7 1/2 • illustrations • 0-7818-0097-8 • W • $8.95pb • (288)

EGYPTIAN COOKING
Samia Abdennour
Almost 400 recipes, all adapted for the North American kitchen, represent the best of authentic Egyptian family cooking.
199 pages • 5 1/2 x 8 1/2 • 0-7818-0643-7 • NA • $11.95pb • (727)

ART OF SOUTH INDIAN COOKING
Alamelu Vairavan and Patricia Marquardt
Over 100 recipes for tempting appetizers, chutneys, rice dishes, vegetables and stews—flavored with onions, tomatoes, garlic, and delicate spices in varying combinations—have been adapted for the Western kitchen.
202 pages • 5 1/2 x 8 1/2 • 0-7818-0525-2 • W • $22.50 • (635)

BEST OF GOAN COOKING
Gilda Mendonsa

This book is a rare and authentic collection of over 130 of the finest Goan recipes and 12 pages of full color illustrations. From Goa—a region in Western India once colonized by the Portuguese—comes a cuisine in which the hot, sour and spicy flavors mingle in delicate perfection, a reflection of the combination of Arabian, Portuguese and Indian cultures that have inhabited the region.

106 pages • 7 x 9¼ •12 pages color illustrations • 0-7818-0584-8•NA•$8.95pb • (682)

THE BEST OF KASHMIRI COOKING
Neerja Mattoo

With nearly 90 recipes and 12 pages of color photographs, this cookbook is a wonderful introduction to Kashmiri dishes, considered the height of gourmet Indian cuisine.

131 pages • 5½ x8½ • 12 pages color photographs • 0-7818-0612-7 • NA • $9.95pb • (724)

THE ART OF PERSIAN COOKING
Forough Hekmat

This collection of 200 recipes features such traditional Persian dishes as Abgushte Adas • (Lentil soup), Mosamme Khoreshe • (Eggplant Stew), Lamb Kebab, Cucumber Borani • (Special Cucumber Salad), Sugar Halva and Gol Moraba • (Flower Preserves).

190 pages • 5½ x 8½ • 0-7818-0241-5 • W • $9.95pb • (125)

THE ART OF ISRAELI COOKING
Chef Aldo Nahoum

All of the 250 recipes are kosher.

"[Includes] a host of new indigenous Israeli recipes with dishes that reflect the eclectic and colorful nature of Israeli cuisine."

—Jewish Week

125 pages • 5½ x 8½ • 0-7818-0096-X • W • $9.95pb • (252)

THE ART OF TURKISH COOKING
Nesret Eren

"Her recipes are utterly mouthwatering, and I cannot remember a time when a book so inspired me to take pot in hand."
—Nika Hazelton, *The New York Times Book Review*
308 pages • 5 1/2 X 8 1/2 • 0-7818-0201-6 • W • $12.95pb • (162)

COOKING THE CARIBBEAN WAY
Mary Slater

Here are 450 authentic Caribbean recipes adapted for the North American kitchen, including Bermuda Steamed Mussels, Port Royal Lamb Stew, and Mango Ice-cream.
256 pages • 51/2 x 81/2 • 0-7818-0638-0 • W • $11.95pb • (725)

BAVARIAN COOKING
Olli Leeb

With over 300 recipes, this lovely collector's item cookbook covers every aspect of Bavarian cuisine from drinks, salads and breads to main courses and desserts. Includes a large fold-out map and cultural calendar along with 10 pages of color photographs.

"*Bavarian Cooking* is what a good regional cookbook should be—a guide for those who wish to know the heart and soul of a region's cooking, a book that anchors its recipes in the culture that produced them, and a cookbook that brings delight to the casual reader as well as to the serious cook."   —*German Life*

171 pages • 6 1/2 X 8 1/4 • line illustrations and 10 pages color photographs • 0-7818-0561-9 • NA • $25.00 • (659)

A BELGIAN COOKBOOK
Juliette Elkon

A celebration of the regional variations found in Belgian cuisine.
224 pages • 5 1/2 X 8 1/2 • 0-7818-0461-2 • W • $12.95pb • (535)

CELTIC COOKBOOK: Traditional Recipes from the Six Celtic Lands Brittany, Cornwall, Ireland, Isle of Man, Scotland and Wales
Helen Smith-Twiddy
This collection of over 160 recipes from the Celtic world includes traditional, yet still popular dishes like *Rabbit Hoggan* and *Gwydd y Dolig* (Stuffed Goose in Red Wine).
200 pages • 51/2 x 81/2 • 0-7818-0579-1 • NA • $22.50hc • (679)

ENGLISH ROYAL COOKBOOK: FAVORITE COURT RECIPES
Elizabeth Craig
Dine like a King or Queen with this unique collection of over 350 favorite recipes of the English royals, spanning 500 years of feasts! Try recipes like Duke of York Consommé and Crown Jewel Cake, or even a Princess Mary Cocktail. Charmingly illustrated throughout.
187 pages • 51/2 x 81/2 • illustrations • 0-7818-0583-X • W • $11.95pb • (723)

TRADITIONAL RECIPES FROM OLD ENGLAND
Arranged by country, this charming classic features the favorite dishes and mealtime customs from across England, Scotland, Wales and Ireland.
110 pages • 5 x 81/2 • illustrated · 0-7818-0489-2 •W · $9.95pb • (157)

THE ART OF IRISH COOKING
Monica Sheridan
Nearly 200 recipes for traditional Irish fare.
166 pages • 51/2 x 81/2 • illustrated • 0-7818-0454-X • W • $12.95pb • (335)

ART OF DUTCH COOKING
C. Countess van Limburg Stirum
This attractive volume of 200 recipes offers a complete cross section of Dutch home cooking, adapted to American kitchens. A whole chapter is devoted to the Dutch Christmas, with recipes for unique cookies and candies that are a traditional part of the festivities.
192 pages•51/2 x 81/2 •illustrations •0-7818-0582-1•W•$11.95pb (683)

TASTE OF MALTA
Claudia Caruana
Includes over 100 Maltese favorites like *timpana* (macaroni baked with tomatoes and ground meat enclosed in pastry), *ross fil-forn* (rice baked in meat sauce), and *aljotta* (fish soup with potatoes and garlic.)
250 pages • 5 1/2 x 8 1/2 • 0-7818-0524-4 • W • $24.95hc • (636)

MAYAN COOKING: RECIPES FROM THE SUN KINGDOMS OF MEXICO
Cherry Hamman
This unique cookbook contains not only 200 colorful and exotic recipes from the Mexican Yucatan, but also the author's fascinating observations on a vanishing way of life.
250 pages • 51/2 x 81/2 • 0-7818-0580-5 • W • $24.95hc • (680)

All prices subject to change. To purchase Hippocrene Books contact your local bookstore, call (718) 454-2366, or write to: HIPPOCRENE BOOKS, 171 Madison Avenue, New York, NY 10016. Please enclose check or money order, adding $5.00 shipping (UPS) for the first book and $.50 for each additional book.